FINANCING SCHOOLS FOR HIGH PERFORMANCE

FINANCING SCHOOLS FOR HIGH PERFORMANCE

Strategies for Improving the Use of Educational Resources

Allan Odden and Carolyn Busch

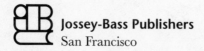
Jossey-Bass Publishers
San Francisco

Substantial discounts on bulk quantities of Jossey-Bass books are available to corporations, professional associations, and other organizations. For details and discount information, contact the special sales department at Jossey-Bass Inc., Publishers (415) 433–1740; Fax (800) 605–2665.

For sales outside the United States, please contact your local Simon & Schuster International Office.

Jossey-Bass Web address: http://www.josseybass.com

 Manufactured in the United States of America on Lyons Falls Turin Book. This paper is acid-free and 100 percent totally chlorine-free.

Library of Congress Cataloging-in-Publication Data

Odden, Allan.
    Financing schools for high performance : strategies for improving
the use of educational resources / Allan Odden and Carolyn Busch.—
1st ed.
        p.   cm.—(The Jossey-Bass education series)
    Includes bibliographical references (p.   ) and index.
    ISBN 0-7879-4060-7 (hardcover : alk. paper)
    1. Education—United States—Finance.   2. Education—England—
Finance—Case studies.   3. Education—Australia—Victoria—Finance—
Case studies.   4. School-based management—United States.
5. School-based management—England—Case studies.   6. School-based
management—Australia—Victoria—Case studies.   7. Educational
change—United States.   I. Busch, Carolyn.   II. Title.
III. Series.
LB2342.023   1998
379.1′1′0973—dc21   97-44062

FIRST EDITION
HB Printing   10 9 8 7 6 5 4 3 2 1

THE JOSSEY-BASS EDUCATION SERIES

CONTENTS

PART THREE: RECOMMENDATIONS   129

LIST OF TABLES, FIGURES, AND APPENDIXES

Tables

Figures

Appendixes

PREFACE

"Show me the money!"—the catchphrase from the 1997 movie *Jerry Maguire*—is a line often articulated by principals who are said to be involved in "school-based management" programs or in accountability systems that hold schools responsible for results. The refrain does not necessarily mean, as in the film, that the principals want more money; it means that if the district or state wants to hold sites accountable for student achievement results, it should also give them substantial control over their money.

This book is about "showing the money" for the purpose of boosting education results at the district and school levels. It is also, more broadly, about the education dollar—how the dollar could be distributed more fairly to districts and schools and, even more important, how the dollar could be used more productively, in ways to dramatically improve student performance.

The goal of current education reform in the United States is to teach students to high standards. Seeing that even by optimistic analysis, only about 25 percent of students achieve at reasonable levels today (National Center for Education Statistics, 1996c), teaching students to high standards means increasing that percentage to at least 50 percent and ideally to 75 percent. The education reform goal, then, is to double or triple results. Indeed, the reformers' slogan "Teach *all* students to high standards" suggests even greater improvement results.

Considering that education revenues are unlikely to come close to doubling or tripling during the same time period, the only way the education reform goal can be accomplished is by improving the productivity of the education system. Thus the financial challenge for the public schools is not to ferret out "fat" in the system and cut it out—the challenge thrown down by the simplistic critics of the public schools—but to determine a new vision for the education system, a vision so powerful that it can dramatically improve what students learn at no additional cost to the system or with only modest increases in new money that might flow into the system during the next five, ten, or fifteen years. This book addresses several of the financial aspects of this challenge.

Chapter One sets the context by telling the current story of the education dollar. Basically, public school funding has been increasing throughout the twentieth century so that today we have substantial resources supporting the public schools; however, these dollars are, and have always been, distributed very unequally across states and districts, and within districts and school sites they have been used in standard and predictable but quite ineffective ways.

Chapter One first quantifies the degree of overall financial inequality using figures for all districts in the country. The chapter then argues that the nature of school finance disparities has changed dramatically since the modern era of school finance reform began in 1970 and because of the change suggests that financial equity goals—distributing base funds more equally—could now be more focused on the districts and schools in just the bottom half of the distribution. The chapter next reveals that producing financial equity for this 50 percent of the distribution is quite affordable. Later, Chapter Seven demonstrates how this approach to financial equity can be linked to educational adequacy, that is, how the school finance system can provide a level of funding to permit teaching students to higher standards and hence support high-performance schools.

Finally, Chapter One shows how the education dollar is currently spent, analyzes why education dollars are used in ineffective ways in schools, and suggests how different and more high-performance notions of school organization are potential routes to improving the productivity of the education dollar and thus improving student achievement results with current educational resources.

Chapter Two discusses the management strategy that school systems can use to dramatically improve results. Both public and private sector organizations around the world are under enormous pressure to improve productivity; the general strategy to accomplish improved results and enhanced productivity is to set clear goals and directions at the top, flatten the organization structure through a reengineering process, provide decentralized work teams and groups with the authority to produce results, and hold them accountable for performance. This high-involvement, decentralized strategy has great potential in education and has been embodied in the standards- and school-based reform agendas. Based largely on research in education but drawing on relevant experiences in noneducation settings as well, Chapter Two identifies the key elements of this new organizational and management strategy to significantly enhance results, thereby increasing organizational productivity. A key element of this strategy is to give the service units (schools, in education) substantial control over their budget. The remainder of the book then addresses issues related to providing this budgetary authority.

Chapter Three discusses the current primary approach to school-based budgeting in the United States, the financing of charter schools. The chapter surveys the key characteristics of how the states structure charter school financing. Such financing schemes have been evolving rapidly, but few, if any, states have created a strong, fair, and systematic approach. The conclusion is that this country needs better ideas about how to provide school sites with budgets.

Chapters Four and Five move outside the United States to examine the policies and practices used by two other advanced English-speaking democracies that have adopted a standards- and school-based reform program and linked it with dramatic school autonomy that includes school control over the budget. Chapter Five describes the structures created in England to provide schools with a budget under the auspices of local education authorities (LEAs). The chapter details both the centrally defined budgetary framework that structures each LEA's specific school financing systems and the precise formulas that several LEAs created. In 1997, the 109 local education authorities budgeted about 90 percent of the potential school budget to each school site in a lump sum, through an age- and need-related per-pupil funding formula.

England implemented a policy of site-based financing within a structure that included local school districts, much as would likely be implemented in most states in the United States. The chapter suggests that the existence of a district structure was actually an advantage (as compared to a direct state-to-site funding system), as the various districts could decide which roles and functions should remain with the central office and which should devolve to the site. Given the diversity of districts in England and in most American states, the ability of districts to tailor the details of a school financing structure to the unique context and culture of different localities was clearly beneficial.

By contrast, Victoria, Australia, implemented a direct state-to-site financing system when it turned nearly all its eighteen hundred schools into charter schools over a three-year period beginning in 1993. The information on Victoria in Chapter Four is useful, however, both because it describes another large effort to decentralize education funding and because it shows several of the details that need to be addressed by any district in designing a school-based financing formula, such as weightings for different grade levels and for different student needs and the need to address the special circumstances of all schools, including small and geographically isolated ones.

Chapters Four and Five show that implementing a site-based financing policy ultimately

- Initiates heated debate over the equity of school financing, raising issues concerning differential funding across school districts (deemed unacceptable in England when the funding unit becomes the school rather than the district) and between elementary and secondary schools (differentials that become much more public—and hard to defend—when the policies on school-based financing are made public)
- Can be implemented in a relatively few number of years
- Should be accompanied by computerization of the financial system, or schools will use some of their new money to hire administrative staff to "manage the books"

Chapter Six takes the best ideas from both England and Victoria and incorporates them into a proposal for structuring a school-based financing system for a state in the United States. The essence of the ideas discussed in the chapter are threefold:

- That the state should structure the overall system, providing a statewide framework within which all districts would create a specific site-based financing policy
- That the core of the district task is to identify which roles and functions should remain centrally provided and which roles and functions should be decentralized to school sites, with these substantive decisions driving what percentage of the budget is retained at the district and what percentage is devolved to school sites
- That districts need to create a comprehensive but still parsimonious and largely pupil-weighted formula to budget the bulk of the revenues in a fair way to each school building

The chapter makes clear that one important district function is to design and administer an accountability system and that this function should be adequately funded. The chapter also argues that the instructional, support (for instruction and pupils), and site administration functions should be the minimum of those functions devolved to sites; these functions comprise about 75 percent of the average district's operating budget.

Chapter Seven addresses the important issue of how schools could use resources more effectively and more productively than they currently do. Using national data from the Schools and Staffing Survey, the chapter first describes the staffing of the typical elementary, middle, and high school in the United States. It then discusses the staffing, cost structure, and total costs of several high-performance school designs, focusing on the seven designs offered by New American Schools (Stringfield, Ross, and Smith, 1996) and the Edison Project. The chapter explores how American elementary, middle, and high schools of a given size could afford all of these designs with currently available resources. It also shows that many of the schools implementing New American School designs already have the resources to finance design requirements if they implement a resource reallocation strategy in which current resources are reconfigured.

Echoing a theme developed at the end of Chapter One, this chapter demonstrates that for the most part, resource reallocation pertains to resources currently available to schools but spent for "specialist" services outside the regular classroom. This analysis again suggests that criticisms of the public schools' "bloated central offices" are somewhat off the mark in that the more substantive resource reallocation potential involves resources already in the budget but currently used for outside services.

Chapter Eight completes the argument by identifying the key new roles and responsibilities of the district when it adopts a true site-based decentralization strategy for the purpose of improving results. A typical misunderstanding among many public school people is that decentralization throws all responsibility on the shoulders of the site and none on the district. Chapter Eight argues that the district needs to lead a large-scale change effort, converting from a bureaucratic, top-down management system to a high-performance, site-based management system; identifies the new structures—including a comprehensive accountability system—that the district must design; and discusses the new behaviors of superintendents, central office staff, and the school board in a decentralized structure.

Chapter Nine, the final chapter, summarizes the major points made in each of the preceding chapters. Although this chapter could be read as a précis of the book, it is no substitute for reading the book. The devil is in the details, and the book is about the details of site-based financing: why it is needed, how and why current U.S. efforts fall short, how states and districts should think about designing such a system, what schools then need to do differently to make the effort worthwhile, and how all of this changes the roles, responsibilities, and behaviors of central office staff.

The country is moving forward to implement an education agenda never before imagined: improving the productivity of the public schools. This is the right agenda; indeed, it is an agenda that must be addressed if we are to accomplish the education reform goal of teaching all students to high standards. As this book shows, creating a school-based financing system is crucial to implementing this agenda. Or as the beginning of this preface suggested, the *Jerry Maguire* mantra "show me the money" is the refrain for a system that demands school-level involvement for improving student academic achievement by giving schools increased responsibility over their funding.

Acknowledgments

First, we would like to thank system leaders, principals, and teachers in both Victoria, Australia, and England for helping us understand how their versions of school-based financing work; Allan Odden would especially like to acknowledge the advice, insights, and colleagueship provided by Professors Brian Caldwell and Peter Hill at the University of Melbourne.

Second, we extend our thanks to Bill Fowler at the National Center for Education Statistics for providing us access to the numerous NCES databases and to Anita Tychsen, a Ph.D. student in the educational administration program at the University of Wisconsin–Madison, for her tireless efforts in helping us analyze these data to determine the degree of financial equity within and across states and the costs of various strategies to improve equity.

Third, Allan Odden would like to thank the New American Schools, and especially John Anderson and Cheryl Kane, for asking him to become involved in the financing dimension of that exciting education effort; much was learned both about how current resources are used in schools today and how they could be used in different and better ways, not only in the New American School designs but also in several other whole-school high-performance designs.

Fourth, we would like to thank Adam Gamoran, a professor, and Eric Grodsky, a research assistant, at the Wisconsin Center for Educational Research, for helping us in analyzing the Schools and Staffing Survey data.

Fifth, we also would like to thank our secretarial team, particularly Lisa Armstrong, who once again tracked down missing references and made sure the entire book was completed in a high-quality way, and Lynn Lunde, who helped put the manuscript in its final polished form.

Sixth, we appreciate the proofreading, editorial suggestions, and index work provided by two doctoral students in the educational administration program at the University of Wisconsin–Madison: Anita Tychsen and David Wakelyn.

Seventh, portions of the research in this book were supported directly or indirectly by the Consortium for Policy Research in Education (CPRE), Grant No. OERI-R3086A60003 from the National Institute on Educational Governance, Finance, Policy-Making and Management, U.S. Department of Education, Office of Educational Research and Improvement and by the Wisconsin Center for Education Research, School of Education, University of Wisconsin–Madison.

Finally, Allan Odden also would like to thank the Hoover Institution at Stanford University, where he spent the summer of 1997 in a quiet office, thinking through some final arguments and completing the manuscript.

The opinions expressed in this book are those of the authors. We acknowledge all the help and assistance we have received for the research we have conducted and for the writing of this book. As usual, any shortcomings are surely ours.

January 1998
Madison, Wisconsin   Allan Odden
Madison, Wisconsin   Carolyn Busch

To Dick and Billy Ruth Rubottom, my father-in-law and mother-in-law, who taught me that to influence public policy one needs knowledge, diplomatic skill, and persistence, and that to do so is a noble pursuit.

—A. O.

To my grandmother, Louise Benton Oliver, who continues to teach me the skill of diplomacy and the virtues of honesty and compassion. An accomplished musician and a caring person, she is an inspiration to me in my pursuit to live a full life personally and professionally.

—C. B.

THE AUTHORS

Allan Odden is professor of educational administration at the University of Wisconsin–Madison. He also is codirector of the Consortium for Policy Research in Education (CPRE), a consortium of the University of Wisconsin–Madison, the University of Pennsylvania, Harvard University, the University of Michigan, and Stanford University that is funded by the U.S. Department of Education. He is the director of the CPRE Education Finance Research Program and principal investigator for the CPRE Teacher Compensation project, sponsored by the Pew Charitable Trusts and the Carnegie Corporation. Earlier in his career, Odden was professor of education policy and administration at the University of Southern California and director of Policy Analysis for California Education (PACE), an educational policy studies consortium of USC, Stanford University, and the University of California, Berkeley. He is an international expert on education finance, school-based financing, resource allocation and use, educational policy, school-based management, teacher compensation, district and school decentralization, and educational policy implementation. He worked with the Education Commission of the States for a decade, serving as assistant executive director, director of policy analysis and research, and director of its educational finance center. He was president of the American Educational Finance Association in 1979–80 and served as research director for special state educational finance projects in numerous states. He is currently directing research projects on school-based finance, school-based management, and teacher compensation. In 1997 he was selected as a consultant by the judge who was asked by the New Jersey Supreme Court to monitor implementation of its 1997 decision that found the state's school finance system unconstitutional.

Odden has written widely, publishing over 170 journal articles, book chapters, and research reports and 20 books and monographs. His books include *Paying Teachers for What They Know and Do: New and Smarter Compensation Strategies to Improve Schools* (1997) with Carolyn Kelley, *Educational Leadership for America's Schools* (1995) with Eleanor Odden, *Rethinking School Finance: An Agenda for the 1990s* (1992), *School Finance: A Policy Perspective* (1992) with Lawrence Picus, *Education Policy Implementation* (1991), and *School Finance and School Improvement: Linkages for the 1980s* (1983).

He received his Ph.D. and M.A. degrees from Columbia University, a Master of Divinity degree from the Union Theological Seminary, and a B.S. from Brown University.

Carolyn Busch became an education advisor to Washington's governor Gary Locke in 1997. Prior to that, she was an associate researcher with the Consortium for Policy Research in Education (CPRE) at the University of Wisconsin–Madison. Her research emphasizes state-level educational policies as they affect districts and schools. In the past three years at CPRE, she has been tracking and analyzing charter school legislation in the United States and conducting international research to better understand the implications and implementation issues associated with site-based school financing. Complementary to that work, she calls on her extensive quantitative background when examining school district and state financing for equity and adequacy. Her writing has been published in numerous scholarly publications.

FINANCING SCHOOLS
FOR HIGH
PERFORMANCE

PART ONE

INTRODUCTION

CHAPTER ONE

HOW THE EDUCATION DOLLAR IS SPENT

Student achievement in American schools needs to improve dramatically if all students are to have equal access to the labor market and society of the future (Murnane and Levy, 1996). Indeed, the goal of current standards-based education reform is ambitious. It is to raise current levels of achievement in which only about 20 to 25 percent of students perform proficiently (National Center for Education Statistics, 1996c) to much higher levels so that 75 percent or more of all students master the complex subjects of mathematics, reading, writing, science, and history.

This goal represents significant, not just marginal, improvements in performance and will be difficult to accomplish. Reaching this goal will require major change. Schools will need to upgrade the curriculum and instructional program and restructure around a higher-performing whole-school design. They will also have to use current and any new resources in substantially more productive ways. This poses a serious challenge for the education system.

The good news is that there is plenty of money in the education system. Contrary to popular perceptions, education funding for public elementary and secondary schools in this country has experienced relentless growth. Though the

---

This chapter is based in part on Odden, Monk, Nakib, and Picus (1995).

precise magnitude is hard to pin down, education revenues per pupil, even after adjusting for inflation as measured by the consumer price index, grew between 25 and 75 percent each decade during the first ninety years of the twentieth century (Hanushek and Associates, 1994). As a result, it is estimated that for the 1995–96 school year, the country spent $260 billion in local, state, and federal dollars for current and capital purposes on public elementary and secondary schools, or about $6,993 per student (National Center for Education Statistics, 1996a). Compared to all other countries in the world, this represents one of the highest levels of per-pupil dollars spent (in terms of purchasing power) on a country's K–12 public education system (Organization for Economic Cooperation and Development, 1995).

But the bad news concerns the unique ways in which the United States raises, distributes, and spends education dollars (Barro, 1996; National Commission on Teaching and America's Future, 1996). Rather than one national education system, there are fifty state systems that raise revenues from local, state, and federal sources. Dollars are distributed quite unequally across states, districts, and schools. And only a small fraction of the education dollar supports regular classroom instruction—significant proportions are spent in schools, but outside of the classroom.

These key characteristics of the education dollar will have to change if the education system is to boost student achievement to the level needed for the workforce of tomorrow—to triple current levels of achievement so that at least three-quarters of American students master the academic subjects of mathematics, reading, writing, science, and history. The quandary is that educational funding is unlikely to increase by the same amount. Although education dollars per pupil increased substantially during each of the previous nine decades of this century, inflation-adjusted education dollars per pupil have been relatively flat during the 1990s (National Center for Education Statistics, 1996a). While the National Center for Education Statistics (NCES) (1996b) predicts that inflation-adjusted per-pupil spending will rise by approximately 24 percent over the ten years from 1996 to 2006, those projections are based largely on historical trends and current economic growth but ignore many larger political realities constraining school funding (Gold, 1995).

Yet comparing even the optimistic NCES projections of the rate of revenue increase (24 percent) to the desired rate of results increase (200 percent) suggests a productivity challenge. The only way to boost results with the level of current and possibly new dollars (even an optimistic 24 percent more) is to improve the productivity of the educational system, that is, to use current and any future dollars much more effectively.

This is a daunting task. It poses a new type of education reform question. Rather than asking how much more money the system needs to dramatically improve results, the question is how much more achievement can be produced with current and any new resources.

Some analysts might take issue with this question and argue that more money is needed to improve student achievement, that educational results will improve only if political leaders at the federal, state, and local levels provide more money to the schools. They might argue that class sizes need to be reduced, that special-needs programs must be fully funded, and that teacher salaries should be hiked to allow the system to recruit and retain the most able individuals in the teaching profession (Bracey, 1996; Molnar, 1995). They might also argue that conditions of children outside of schools must be improved in order to boost school results—that too many students live in poverty, receive inadequate health services, and suffer from neglect and abuse.

There is some truth to these arguments. Indeed, the only large-scale randomized experiment of class size reduction shows that it does improve performance, and by substantial amounts (Achilles, 1996; Achilles, Nye, and Zaharias, 1995; Achilles, Nye, Zaharias, and Fulton, 1993; Mosteller, Light, and Sachs, 1996). Most special-needs programs are underfunded and so do not serve all students. In addition, higher teacher salaries will be needed to raise teaching standards and upgrade teacher quality (National Commission on Teaching and America's Future, 1996). Further, less poverty, better health conditions, and more personal attention would help boost student performance in schools.

However, using current resources better might be required before much additional money is provided. As we will argue in Chapter Two, one strategy for accomplishing this goal is to create a high-performance management system for public education that would include decentralizing education management to schools, having schools determine how to use education dollars better, and holding them accountable for results. Before turning to how schools could use current and any new resources better, it is necessary first to understand how current education dollars are raised, distributed, and spent and the factors that account for these resource use patterns. The remainder of this chapter discusses these issues. The remainder of the book discusses how to redesign the education system for higher performance, with a focus on how to design a school-based financing system.

Sources of Education Revenues and Changes over Time

Table 1.1 identifies the sources of education revenues since 1960. Most education dollars are provided by local and state governments, but there have been changes in the shares provided by the different levels of government. Three periods of trends are reflected by the numbers in Table 1.1, the first from 1960 to 1980, the second from 1980 to 1990, and the third from 1990 to 1997. In the 1960–1980 period, the trend was a rising federal and state share and a declining local share. The federal share peaked at 9.8 percent in 1980; the state share peaked just below 50 percent in the mid-1980s.

Since 1980, however, the trends in sources of education revenues have become more complex. First, the federal role dropped in the 1980s to 6.1 percent and then grew modestly to 7.0 percent. Few predict any significant increase in the federal fiscal role, though as we argue later, federal money to offset large financial differences in education funding across the states can be justified. Second, the state role has slipped from its nearly 50 percent level in the mid-1980s to the mid-40 percent range. Third, during this time period, the local role has been rising, from the low 40 percent range to the mid-40 percent range.

Although the federal role is expected to remain fairly constant, state and local financial roles are less clear. On the one hand, the state had the lead role in funding schools during the 1970s and 1980s, but the state and local roles have been about equal in the 1990s. However, there was a modest trend of a declining state and rising local role. Whether this trend will continue is uncertain. But if it should, local school districts would become the leading source of school funding again by the end of this century, which likely would increase the disparities in educational revenues across school districts within any state.

On the other hand, recent movements to cut property taxes in Colorado, Michigan, Oregon, and Wisconsin, for example, suggest that there is rising resistance to the growth of local revenues for education or other local government ac-

TABLE 1.1. SOURCES OF PUBLIC SCHOOL REVENUES, 1959–1996.

	Sources of Total Revenue (percent)		
Year	Federal Sources	State Sources	Local Sources
1959–60	4.4%	39.1%	56.5%
1969–70	8.0	39.9	52.1
1979–80	9.8	46.8	43.4
1989–90	6.1	47.1	46.8
1990–91	6.2	47.2	46.7
1991–92	6.6	46.4	47.0
1992–93	7.0	45.8	47.2
1993–94	7.0	45.2	47.8
1994–95	7.0	47.8	45.2
1995–96 (est.)	7.0	47.7	45.3

Sources: National Center for Education Statistics, 1996a; National Education Association, 1996.

tivities. While there is similar resistance to state tax increases, state revenue coffers have been overflowing both because of tax hikes enacted in the 1980s and early 1990s and a healthy national economy (Gold, 1995), which gives states the flexibility to continue their lead role in funding education. In short, although the federal role is unlikely to increase much beyond 7 percent of school revenues and there is uncertainty over the state role, the odds are that the states will retain their current funding position.

Table 1.2 shows the levels of and changes in educational expenditures per pupil since 1960 (using inflation-adjusted dollars). Again, contrary to the opinion of many observers, the numbers show that education has been a financial growth industry over this thirty-five-year period. In the three decades from 1960 to 1990, real educational expenditures per pupil increased by over 200 percent. Put a different way, spending per pupil doubled in the two decades between 1960 and 1980 and then increased another 50 percent in the 1980s so that by 1990, expenditures per pupil were more than three times what they were in 1960—certainly not representative of an industry in financial decline. These increases occurred in times of enrollment growth (the 1960s), enrollment decline (the 1970s), and enrollment stability (the 1980s).

Moreover, rising educational expenditures occurred through periods of both economic decline and economic growth. The experience of the 1980s is illustrative. In the early 1980s, when the country was beset by an acute recession, real education spending per pupil dropped; but after 1982, when the country rebounded

TABLE 1.2. EDUCATIONAL EXPENDITURES PER PUPIL, 1959–1997 (CONSTANT 1995–96 DOLLARS).

Year	Expenditures per Pupil in Average Daily Attendance ($)	Change (percent)	Cumulative Change (percent)
1959–60	$1,976		
1969–70	3,343	69.0%	69%
1979–80	4,529	35.0	129
1989–90	6,060	34.0	206
1990–91	6,076	0.3	207
1991–92	6,071	0.0	207
1992–93	6,063	0.0	207
1993–94	6,104	0.7	209
1994–95	6,159	0.9	212
1995–96 (est.)	6,213	0.9	214
1996–97 (proj.)	6,315	1.6	220

Sources: National Center for Education Statistics 1996a, 1996b.

from that recessionary period, educational spending rose so that over the entire decade, real spending per pupil grew by nearly 50 percent, a growth predicted by few at the beginning of the decade. Such consistent growth in per-pupil dollars is characteristic of education from 1900 to 1990 (Hanushek, 1994; National Center for Education Statistics, 1996a).

However, in the 1990s, education spending has not continued to grow as rapidly. Inflation-adjusted expenditures per pupil were generally flat in the first four years of the 1990s and have since grown only modestly, a seven-year phenomenon very different from any other similar period in the twentieth century. The growth of inflation-adjusted education spending from 1990 to 1997 was just 4.2 percent. Experts in state-local fiscal relations do not seem confident that the remainder of the 1990s will improve this financial state of education (Gold, 1995).

Yet the National Center for Education Statistics (1996b) predicts that real education revenues and expenditures per pupil will increase by 41 and 24 percent, respectively, in the next ten years; the latter figure accounts for increases in student enrollment. Only time will tell whether this scenario of fiscal abundance will prevail. Such a prediction is consistent with trends during the first nine decades in this century. But rising resistance to local revenue increases, more stringent limits on state spending, and squeezes on federal domestic discretionary spending could cloud the fiscal future for education. Nonetheless, the numbers show that the country has provided a substantial investment in its public schools over the past thirty-seven years, and despite the flat trends of the past few years, this consistent growth in revenues provided to public education does show a commitment to the country's youth and gives cause for optimism.

Nationwide Disparities in School Funding

The substantial growth in the overall level of education dollars masks the fact that for historical and political reasons, the country has distributed educational revenues unequally across states and school districts. In fact, the distributional characteristics of education dollars in the United States is one of the most inequitable of any country in the world (Barro, 1996). Clearly, wide disparities in educational revenues that have little relationship to pupil needs or education prices are at odds with the national goal of teaching students in all districts in all states to high academic standards.

Across the fifty states, we see wide variations in both the levels of education dollars and changes over time. For example, the National Education Association (NEA) publishes an annual listing of state-level school finance characteristics; in 1996, the NEA showed that the *national* average expenditure per pupil was about

$6,098, but it exceeded $8,000 in Alaska ($10,156), Connecticut ($8,705), New Jersey ($9,967), and New York ($9,877) and fell below $4,500 in Alabama ($4,479), Arizona ($4,332), Arkansas ($4,370), Idaho ($4,449), Mississippi ($4,190), Oklahoma ($4,458), and Utah ($3,908). Even when adjusted for the purchasing power of the education dollar, dollars per pupil may be as much as two and a half times more in one state than in another (Chambers, 1995).

There were also large differences in the change in education revenues across states and the District of Columbia. While the national average increase in education funding from 1960 to 1990 was 206 percent, it was over 300 percent in New Jersey (377 percent), Connecticut (303 percent), Maine (340 percent), North Carolina (316 percent), South Carolina (330 percent), Vermont (319 percent), and the District of Columbia (378 percent) but under 140 percent in Arizona (133 percent), Nevada (121 percent), New Mexico (125 percent), and Utah (96 percent). In short, there are large differences from state to state in both the level of funding per pupil and in the changes in education resources from 1960 to 1990 (National Education Association, 1996).

Within states, researchers have measured disparities in education dollars per pupil that exceed those between the states (General Accounting Office, 1997; Hertert, Busch, and Odden, 1994; Schwartz and Moskowitz, 1988; Wyckoff, 1992). These studies have demonstrated that equity has improved very little over the past two decades, despite state efforts to remedy the problem.

Using a slightly different research slant, we conducted our own equity analysis. Like the General Accounting Office (GAO) report (1997), we used the most recent year of finance data for all school districts across the United States, 1991–92 (U.S. Bureau of the Census, 1992). However, we targeted our efforts on horizontal equity—the equal treatment of equals or, in school finance terms, equal spending per "regular" pupil (pupils not requiring additional educational services, such as special, bilingual, or compensatory education). The selection of the appropriate revenue categories is crucial here. We focused on two revenue sources to construct what we term "basic education revenues": (1) total local revenues, which are revenues raised exclusively from local sources (mostly property taxes), and (2) state general revenues, revenues usually received through the state school finance equalization formula—in other words, all state revenues for general, noncategorical state assistance (for a more detailed description of the data employed, see Appendix 1.1). Concentrating only on state general and local revenues (hereafter called basic education revenues) allowed us to evaluate more accurately the horizontal equity of regular basic education programs across the country without the confounding factor of other revenues for categorical programs, which may disproportionately increase per-pupil revenue figures for districts with relatively large numbers of students with additional education needs.

In addition, most previous analyses of state fiscal equity (General Accounting Office, 1997; Hertert, Busch, and Odden, 1994) did not separate districts by type. But districts typically spend more funds for high schools and less funds for elementary schools, so separate analyses should be conducted by district type. All of the revenue figures have also been adjusted by a cost-of-education index, developed by Chambers (1995), which adjusts for the varying purchasing power of the education dollar within states; the index is normed to a weighted average (weighted by the district's number of students) of 1.0 for each state.

We standardized district revenues further by dividing the total basic education revenues by the district's number of students. The status of financial equity within each state and the District of Columbia for 1991–92 is shown in Table 1.3. Similar equity data for high school and elementary districts are provided in Appendixes 1.2 and 1.3. (Statistics for *total* revenues per pupil, including federal and state categorical, as well as capital and debt service, are provided in Appendixes 1.4, 1.5, and 1.6.)

The coefficient of variation (CV) is one of the most often used measurements of variation. The CV is the percent variation about the average—in this case measuring the spread in per-pupil basic education revenues for two-thirds of each state's school districts compared to the average per-pupil basic education revenues within the state. The CV ranged from a high of 28 percent in Alaska and Missouri to a low of 8 percent in West Virginia and Kentucky. In other words, in these states, two-thirds of the state's students are in districts with basic education revenues 28 percent more or less than the state average per-pupil revenues—thus representing a hefty difference in basic education revenues for education within these states. Only three states (Delaware, Kentucky, and West Virginia) had a CV of 10 percent or less, which is a standard norm for expenditure equity (Odden and Picus, 1992). The smaller the CV, the more similar basic education revenues are across the state. In nineteen states the coefficient of variation equaled or exceeded 20 percent.

The federal range ratio is the difference between the per-pupil revenues of the district at the 95th percentile and the per-pupil revenues of the district at the 5th percentile divided by the value for the 5th percentile. If the district at the 5th percentile is funded at $4,000 per child, a federal range ratio of 0.75 would mean that the district at the 95th percentile is funded 75 percent ($3,000) more, for a total of $7,000 per pupil. The federal range ratio was over 1.0 in three states, indicating that basic education revenues per pupil at the 95th percentile were double those at the 5th percentile; in fifteen states the federal range ratio was greater than 0.75 though less than 1.0, and in fourteen states the ratio was less than or equal to 0.50.

The McLoone Index measures the equity of the bottom half of a distribution. A McLoone Index of 1.0 should be a minimum equity standard; it would

TABLE 1.3.   DISPARITIES IN STATE GENERAL PLUS LOCAL REVENUES PER PUPIL FOR K–12 DISTRICTS, 1991–92, BY STATE.

State	Mean ($)	Median ($)	Coefficient of Variation (CV)	Federal Range Ratio	McLoone Index	Verstegen Index
Alabama	$2,003	$1,923	0.22	0.95	0.882	1.201
Alaska	6,618	6,043	0.28	0.96	0.902	1.283
Arizona	4,407	4,307	0.12	0.50	0.961	1.084
Arkansas	3,221	3,148	0.13	0.31	0.958	1.081
California	3,545	3,491	0.14	0.38	0.950	1.081
Colorado	4,858	4,760	0.19	0.42	0.926	1.109
Connecticut	6,885	6,627	0.16	0.77	0.920	1.154
Delaware	4,820	4,921	0.09	0.47	0.925	1.048
District of Columbia	8,801	n/a	n/a	n/a	n/a	n/a
Florida	4,009	3,855	0.14	0.56	0.942	1.129
Georgia	3,946	3,838	0.16	0.66	0.912	1.145
Hawaii	5,704	n/a	n/a	n/a	n/a	n/a
Idaho	2,763	2,628	0.16	0.54	0.927	1.172
Illinois	3,920	3,947	0.16	0.51	0.944	1.066
Indiana	4,570	4,472	0.15	0.55	0.915	1.125
Iowa	4,551	4,429	0.12	0.43	0.944	1.111
Kansas	4,523	4,347	0.22	0.82	0.906	1.192
Kentucky	3,406	3,361	0.08	0.27	0.945	1.082
Louisiana	3,675	3,632	0.13	0.44	0.923	1.099
Maine	4,799	4,732	0.14	0.50	0.906	1.124
Maryland	4,786	4,642	0.20	0.88	0.886	1.167
Massachusetts	5,141	5,084	0.22	1.09	0.846	1.181
Michigan	5,178	4,897	0.20	0.90	0.909	1.205
Minnesota	4,847	4,776	0.14	0.39	0.917	1.113
Mississippi	2,658	2,557	0.15	0.51	0.919	1.160
Missouri	3,140	2,955	0.28	1.44	0.851	1.278
Montana	3,915	3,891	0.23	1.32	0.879	1.142

TABLE 1.3. (continued)

State	Mean ($)	Median ($)	Coefficient of Variation (CV)	Federal Range Ratio	McLoone Index	Verstegen Index
Nebraska	4,694	4,376	0.22	0.83	0.936	1.204
Nevada	3,446	3,344	0.24	0.72	0.954	1.083
New Hampshire	5,291	5,054	0.18	0.71	0.916	1.178
New Jersey	6,848	6,681	0.17	0.64	0.888	1.160
New Mexico	3,527	3,513	0.15	0.57	0.946	1.066
New York	7,088	6,585	0.25	0.90	0.884	1.269
North Carolina	3,633	3,550	0.15	0.55	0.923	1.134
North Dakota	3,748	3,560	0.22	0.85	0.898	1.190
Ohio	4,375	4,210	0.24	0.88	0.878	1.200
Oklahoma	3,379	3,266	0.17	0.58	0.936	1.132
Oregon	4,788	4,719	0.15	0.60	0.903	1.127
Pennsylvania	5,405	5,336	0.16	0.68	0.895	1.131
Rhode Island	5,750	5,737	0.13	0.59	0.921	1.093
South Carolina	2,799	2,740	0.18	0.78	0.882	1.161
South Dakota	3,583	3,473	0.24	0.87	0.871	1.189
Tennessee	2,691	2,679	0.22	0.78	0.832	1.182
Texas	3,560	3,402	0.25	0.86	0.884	1.209
Utah	2,249	2,155	0.22	0.39	0.937	1.132
Vermont	5,650	5,557	0.17	0.74	0.899	1.128
Virginia	4,181	3,877	0.23	0.88	0.888	1.269
Washington	4,451	4,442	0.14	0.42	0.918	1.084
West Virginia	3,755	3,664	0.08	0.30	0.963	1.086
Wisconsin	5,060	4,920	0.12	0.41	0.936	1.120
Wyoming	5,775	5,310	0.23	0.72	0.929	1.248

Note: All statistics are weighted by pupils. n/a = not available.

Source: Analysis of data from U.S. Bureau of the Census, 1992.

mean that 50 percent of low-revenue districts all spent at the median. Producing this modest level of equity simply requires raising all districts to the median in some set year. Such an approach to equalization would eliminate the lowest-revenue districts in each state. No state had a McLoone Index of 1.0, but five states had a McLoone equal to or above 0.95 (Arizona, Arkansas, California, Nevada, and West Virginia).

The Verstegen Index, a new school finance equity statistic (Verstegen, 1996), indicates the dispersion of revenues per pupil in the top half of the distribution; it is the ratio of all revenues above the median to revenues if all districts were spending at the median. The data show that the Verstegen Index is farther above 1.0 than the McLoone Index is below 1.0, indicating that dispersion in basic education revenues per pupil for districts above the median is greater than for those below the median. In fact, the Verstegen Index is above 1.25 for four states (Alaska, Missouri, New York, and Virginia), but there is no McLoone below 0.75. Indeed, there is no McLoone Index below 0.80; the lowest McLoone Index is 0.83 in Tennessee.

Table 1.4 shows the equity statistics for all districts without regard to state boundaries, for all districts combined, as well as for K–12, elementary, and high school districts separately. These revenue figures have also been adjusted by the Chambers cost index but normed to a weighted *national* average of 1.0, so the actual dollar figures cannot be compared to those in Table 1.3. For K–12 districts, the federal range ratio indicates that basic education revenues across the United States were 1.52 times greater at the high end than at the low end. Therefore, if the low-revenue district were at $3,000 per child, this would mean the district at the 95th percentile had basic education revenues of 152 percent more, or $7,560. The coefficient of variation was large at 30 percent and higher than in all but two states; at a national average of $5,000 per child, a CV of 30 percent means that two-thirds of students were in districts with basic education revenues between $3,500 and $6,500. The McLoone Index was 0.81, showing that basic education revenues per pupil for the bottom half of the districts in the country were less equal than within any one state and equaled just 81 percent of the median, or about $3,375 per child.

Reducing Fiscal Disparities

The figures on resource inequity pose a real dilemma for the country. If the national goal is to teach all, or at least all but severely disabled, students to high achievement standards, the historical practice of leaving education funding to the fifty states and fourteen thousand local districts, which has produced the widely

TABLE 1.4. NATIONWIDE DISPARITIES IN STATE GENERAL PLUS LOCAL REVENUES PER PUPIL, 1991–92.

Statistic	K–12 Districts	High School Districts	Elementary Districts
Mean	$4,323	$5,633	$4,263
Median	$4,166	$5,077	$3,573
Federal range ratio	1.52	1.95	2.24
Coefficient of variation	0.30	0.39	0.46
McLoone Index	0.81	0.77	0.83
Verstegen Index	1.27	1.45	1.56
Total students	38,312,021	856,747	2,432,240

Source: Analysis of data from U.S. Bureau of the Census, 1992.

unequal distribution of resources just described, is probably no longer appropriate. Remedying this situation, though, is challenging. It is unlikely that the country would adopt a national funding system, as most other advanced English-speaking democracies have (Barro, 1996).

Barro (1994) shows how complicated and difficult it would be to reduce fiscal disparities in education by changing the requirement of *current* fund allocation formulas for federal education programs. A reasonable conclusion from his analysis is that the only viable way to reduce the most dramatic financial differences in the country is for some national program to focus on precisely that problem.

Although there would be numerous strategies for providing this common fiscal base, each of which needs to be analyzed carefully, Hertert, Busch, and Odden (1994) took a modest perspective and analyzed alternative costs for raising the fiscal base in all school districts to the median level of spending. With more recent data, we assessed two strategies for raising basic education revenues to a median figure. From recent research into two midwestern states' spending, the median was a reasonable approximation of the funding level needed to teach the average student to desired standards on state assessments (Alexander and others, 1995; Hinrichs and Laine, 1996). Chapter Seven explores in more detail the concept of uniting equity and adequacy objectives in education finance.

The first strategy is from the state perspective. As such, it recognizes the constitutional responsibility of the state for educational services and seeks to raise the bottom half in each state to the spending level of the median district. Under this scenario, districts with basic education revenues per pupil below the median are raised to the median basic education revenues per pupil for each state. Table 1.5

TABLE 1.5. COSTS OF RAISING DISTRICTS TO THE STATE MEDIAN OF STATE GENERAL PLUS LOCAL REVENUES PER PUPIL, 1991–92 (BILLIONS OF DOLLARS).

	K–12 Districts	High School Districts	Elementary Districts	All Districts Combined
Total revenues	$173.804	$5.445	$11.663	$190.912
Additional revenues needed to raise to median	$7.634	$0.306	$0.610	$8.550
Revenue increase	4.39%	5.62%	5.07%	4.48%
Total number of districts	10,634	559	3,518	14,711
Number of districts with revenues raised	4,104	196	1,173	5,473
Percentage of districts with revenues raised	38.59%	35.06%	33.34%	37.20%

Source: Analysis of data from U.S. Bureau of the Census, 1992.

indicates the costs and other effects of this alternative; Appendixes 1.7, 1.8, and 1.9 provide the state data for K–12, high school, and elementary school districts, respectively. The estimated cost was $8.5 billion, which represents a 4.48 percent increase in basic education revenues. Using the same percentage increase, this would represent $10.9 billion in 1996–97 dollars. Revenues would have been raised in 5,473 of the total number of school districts, or 37.2 percent of the nation's school districts.

The second strategy is from a federal viewpoint. This proposal raises all district basic education revenues per pupil to the *national* median of basic education revenues per pupil; this would hike funding in most districts in several low-revenue states but would raise funding for very few districts in some high-revenue states. Nevertheless, it would raise basic education revenues per pupil across the nation for students now attending schools in districts spending below the national median; hence this finance reform would affect half of all students in the country. Table 1.6 presents the costs and impacts of this alternative. Appendixes 1.10 through 1.12 and 1.13 through 1.15 provide the state data for basic education and total revenues per pupil, respectively.

The estimated cost was $16.56 billion, or just 9.2 percent of estimated state plus local revenues per pupil. Using the same percentage increase, this would represent $22.3 billion in 1996–97 dollars, or 108 percent of 1996–97 federal education revenues. Revenues would have been raised in 4,845 of the total number of school districts, or 32.9 percent of the school districts in the nation. The impact of such a program would vary quite dramatically across states. Several states, including Alabama, Arkansas, Idaho, Illinois, Kentucky, Mississippi, Nevada, Oklahoma, Tennessee, and Utah, would have revenues increased for more than 90 percent of their students; conversely, Alaska, Hawaii, Maryland, New Jersey, New York, and Wyoming would have revenues hiked for none of their students, and several other states would receive additional revenues for fewer than 10 percent of their students.

Both strategies show that fiscal equity can be provided for the bottom half of all students in the country at a modest national cost. Put another way, all "savage fiscal disparities" in the country can be reduced, both within and across states, with a modest number of dollars, at least compared to current spending for public schools. To be sure, the increase in funding for a new federal role would represent a large increase in federal education spending. But given the national goal of teaching all students to high achievement standards, the time may have come for such a federal fiscal role in public school funding, though admittedly the politics would be challenging.

TABLE 1.6. COSTS OF RAISING DISTRICTS TO THE NATIONAL MEDIAN OF STATE GENERAL PLUS LOCAL REVENUES PER PUPIL, 1991–92 (BILLIONS OF DOLLARS).

	K–12 Districts	High School Districts	Elementary Districts	All Districts Combined
Total revenues	$165.642	$4.826	$10.368	$180.836
Additional revenues needed to raise to median	$15.300	$0.509	$0.751	$16.560
Revenue increase	9.24%	10.55%	7.24%	9.16%
Total number of districts	10,634	559	3,518	14,711
Number of districts with revenues raised	3,953	136	754	4,843
Percentage of districts with revenues raised	37.17%	24.33%	21.43%	32.92%

Source: Analysis of data from U.S. Bureau of the Census, 1992.

Uses of the Educational Dollar: Expenditure Patterns

Whatever the amount and however distributed, districts and schools must use education dollars to produce student achievement. Research shows, disappointingly, that most districts follow relatively standard practices in using education resources, producing a system characterized by good values but unimpressive results, at least in terms of student achievement. Although the major resource use is for instruction, districts provide many education-related services outside the classroom as well as run buses, heat and clean schools, serve meals, and administer a complex system. The result is that large portions of the education budget are used for purposes other than teaching.

Table 1.7 identifies how the education budget is allocated by function. The table draws from several studies of resource allocation and use in districts and schools (including Monk, Roellke, and Brent, 1996; Nakib, 1995; Picus, Tetreault, and Murphy, 1996). The data show that districts spend about 60 percent of the education budget on instructional services, which includes regular instruction in the classroom in mathematics, language arts, writing, science, history, social science, and other content areas, as well as instruction for special-needs students such as the physically and mentally disabled, those with limited English proficiency, and low-achieving students.

TABLE 1.7. CURRENT ALLOCATION OF EXPENDITURES BY FUNCTION, NATIONALLY AND IN SELECTED STATES (PERCENT).

Expenditure Function	Nation	California[a]	Florida	New York
Instruction	61.2%	60.8%	58.4%	61.8%
Instructional support and student services	8.7	7.9	9.9	8.6
Total administration	8.4	11.4	8.1	10.2
District administration	2.6	3.2	1.2	5.7
School administration	5.8	8.2	6.9	4.5
Operations and maintenance	10.3	13.4	10.7	9.3
Transportation	4.2	1.5	4.2	6.3
Short-term capital		0.4	0.3	1.1
Food services	4.2	4.6	5.2	2.7

[a]Large unified districts.

Sources: Monk, Roellke, and Brent, 1996; Nakib, 1995; Picus, Tetreault, and Murphy, 1996; National Center for Education Statistics, 1996a, tab. 160.

The proportion of 60 percent for instruction is surprisingly consistent across districts and states. Researchers have analyzed these numbers across states and districts in rural and urban areas of all sizes, with various percentages of minority students and various concentrations of poverty. The results, somewhat surprisingly, show that districts tend to spend their resources similarly, in about the same proportions. The coefficient of variation for instruction was about 10 percent, suggesting that two-thirds of all districts spent between 54 and 66 percent of their budget on instructional services, which supports the results in Table 1.7. The 60 percent spent on instruction was also found for Pennsylvania (Hartman, 1994) and other studies at the district level (Cooper, 1993; Speakman and others, 1995). In addition, the National Center for Education Statistics (1996a) shows that this pattern has not changed that much over the past thirty-five years.

When instructional expenditures are combined with time spent on teaching academic subjects, links between spending and results become complicated. A recent national study showed that elementary teachers tend to spend about two-thirds of the school day teaching academic subjects—reading, mathematics, science, and social studies (National Center for Education Statistics, 1997b). They spend about one-third of the day teaching reading; half that, or one-sixth of the day, teaching mathematics; and half that, or one-twelfth of the day, teaching science and teaching social studies. Combining these fractions with the 60 percent spent on instruction, 20 cents of the education dollar (one-third of 60) is spent on reading, 10 cents on mathematics, and 5 cents on each of science and social studies at the elementary school level. But only small portions of students achieve proficiency in any of these subjects (National Center for Education Statistics, 1996c), and in international assessments of student achievement, the country performs above average in reading (Elley, 1992) but second in the world in science and just above the average in mathematics (National Center for Education Statistics, 1997a).

Administration's Share

Does administration account for large chunks of spending, particularly in big urban districts? Basically, no. Administrative expenditures in education generally do not make up a large portion of expenditures. Indeed, Tables 1.7 and 1.8 show that administrative expenditures are usually less than 10 percent of the budget. In most districts, moreover, the larger portion of administrative expenditures occurs at the school level, the place where educational services are actually delivered. Relatively modest expenditures on administration have been confirmed by other research as well (Cooper, 1993; Hartman, 1994; Raimondo, 1994; Speakman and others, 1995).

It should be noted that although administrative expenditures per se, especially in the central office, are not large as a percentage of the budget, several functional activities, including transportation, operation and maintenance, and most professional and curriculum development, are conducted largely from the central office. This means that central office activities are much greater than indicated by the expenditure category of central office administration. Moreover, several central office administration functions need to be performed such as financial and accounting services, personnel administration, and some amount of district management. It could be argued, though, that many of these functions could be more productively conducted on site, at the school level.

Even more surprising, research shows that administrative expenditures in the largest urban districts are less in percentage terms than the average in their respective states (Table 1.8). The data show that in California, Florida, and New York, the percentage spent on administration in each state's largest district was less than the statewide average! Further, the percentages spent on administration in these districts are so low that if the added value provided by central office services were deemed not worthwhile and the central office were eliminated, there would not be large amounts of money to disperse to school sites. Moreover, since many central office functions—financial services, transportation coordination, personnel administration, and so on—need to be performed at some level, even eliminating central offices would not allow a district to use all central office administrative dollars for other purposes.

Thus there is little empirical support for the alleged "administrative blob" in education. Expenditures on administration tend to be less than 10 percent of the budget, a modest level compared to benchmarks in other organizations.

TABLE 1.8. SHARE OF BUDGET SPENT ON ADMINISTRATION IN BIG CITY DISTRICTS.

District	Spending on Administration (percent)		
	Central Office	**Site**	**Total**
Dade County (Miami)	3.0%	6.3%	9.3%
Los Angeles	4.5	5.3	9.8
New York	2.7	3.6	6.3
San Francisco	4.5	5.4	9.9

Sources: Monk, Roellke, and Brent, 1996; Nakib, 1995; Picus, Tetreault, and Murphy, 1996.

Resource Use Patterns

Do resource use patterns vary between high-spending and low-spending districts? Interestingly, higher-spending districts tend to spend their resources in the same proportion as the average district, a behavior that is also typical of lower-spending districts. Although there is some variation both within and across states, higher-spending districts also tend to spend approximately 60 percent of their budget for instruction. But similar percentages of budgets produce much different dollar amounts spent on direct instructional services between high- and low-expenditure districts. Sixty percent of a $7,500 per-pupil budget provides $4,500 per pupil for instruction, compared to $3,000 for the average district spending $5,000 and only $2,100 per pupil for the district spending at the $3,500 level.

Further, Picus (1993a, 1993b) and Picus and Bhimani (1993), analyzing data from a large, nationally representative sample of districts, found that higher-spending districts tend to spend the bulk of their extra funds on more staff and only a small amount on higher salaries. Their research found that higher-spending districts spent about 50 percent of each additional dollar on more teachers and the other 50 percent on noninstructional services. Of the amount spent on teachers, 80 percent was used to hire more teachers and only 20 percent to provide higher salaries. Barro (1992) found similar results with state-level data; the bulk of extra revenues was used to hire more staff rather than for higher salaries.

But the schools tend not to use the additional staff for the regular instructional program. In a fascinating analysis of teacher resources by core subject areas (English, mathematics, science, social studies, and foreign language) in New York secondary schools, Monk, Roellke, and Brent (1996) showed that staffing in core subjects changed very little across district spending levels. Table 1.9 shows the remarkable stability of the number of teachers per thousand students in five subject areas. Yes, teacher resources spiked a bit in the highest-spending quintiles, but only modestly. The average spending between the highest and lowest deciles differed by almost 100 percent, but teacher resources differed by only 20 percent. Teacher resources varied by negligible amounts across the four lowest-spending quintiles, though spending varied by thousands of dollars.

Uses of New Money

These cross-sectional findings fit with longitudinal trends, which have shown that rising real dollars per pupil have been accompanied by declines in the pupil-staff ratio; the average pupil-staff ratio fell from a high of 25 in 1960 to about 14 in 1990 (National Center for Education Statistics, 1993, tab. 41). But these small pupil-staff ratios are at odds with the large actual class sizes of thirty or more stu-

TABLE 1.9. INSTRUCTIONAL STAFF PER THOUSAND PUPILS BY SUBJECT AREA IN NEW YORK SECONDARY SCHOOLS (GRADES 7–12), 1991–92.

Subject	Quintile 1	Quintile 2	Quintile 3	Quintile 4	Quintile 5
English	5.20	5.25	5.43	5.31	6.10
Mathematics	4.46	4.51	4.67	4.54	5.00
Science	3.86	3.98	4.01	4.18	4.95
Social studies	4.04	4.05	4.06	4.09	4.65
Foreign language	2.18	2.36	2.35	2.46	3.23

Note: Quintiles refer to spending levels, with quintile 1 the lowest and quintile 5 the highest.
Source: Monk, Roellke, and Brent, 1996, tab. 7a.

dents in many districts. The resolution of this dilemma illuminates how dollars and teacher resources typically are used in schools.

Historically and today, schools have had a bureaucratic form of organization. Jobs are defined narrowly: principals manage schools and teachers teach students, often with a fairly set curriculum and assumed teaching strategies. As schools face new issues (such as desegregation; disabled, low-achieving, and English-language learner students; and students with more emotional and psychological problems) programs are created that provide money to enable schools to hire "specialist" staff to deal with varying student needs. Teachers remain in the regular classroom, and "specialists" are hired to teach disabled, low-achieving, and English-language learner students in settings outside of the regular classrooms or to counsel and help students with emotional or psychological needs. Earlier examples of this phenomenon were the specialists added to school staffs to teach vocational education, physical education, and even art and music. Growth by addition and specialization has characterized the education system for several decades (Odden and Massy, 1993).

Indeed, recent studies have shown that the vast bulk of new dollars provided to schools over the past thirty years was not spent on staff for the core instructional program but on specialist teachers and other resources to provide services to special-needs students, usually outside of the regular classroom (Lankford and Wyckoff, 1995; Rothstein and Miles, 1995). Studies have shown that these programs and services have produced only modest, if any, long-lasting effects on student achievement (Allington and Johnston, 1989; Odden, 1991). These dollars are spent in support of laudable values: low-income, disabled, and English-language learner students need extra services. The values behind the extra dollars for these services should be retained, but the productivity resulting from the expenditure of these dollars needs to rise.

As a result of the increase of specialist staff and programs, regular classroom teachers—the primary service providers—comprise a declining portion of professional staff in schools. The National Commission on Teaching and America's Future (1996) found that regular classroom teachers as a proportion of all professional staff fell from 70 percent in 1950 to 52 percent in 1995, with 10 percent of the latter not engaged in classroom teaching. The financial implication is that a declining portion of the education dollar is being spent on the core activity of schools—teaching the regular instructional program.

Related research on the local use of new money from school finance reforms has found similar patterns of resource use. Poor districts get more money and use it for clear needs (facilities, social services, compensatory education), but little of the new money makes it into the regular education program (Adams, 1994; Firestone, Goertz, Nagle, and Smelkinson, 1994; Picus, 1994). The end result is a system in which money rises and services expand outside the regular classroom but results in terms of student achievement stay flat or improve by only small amounts.

These expenditure behaviors could be factors explaining the flat productivity of the education dollar.

The Case of Boston

Miles (1995) showed how this bureaucratic approach to organizing schools and using educational resources worked in Boston, which at the time of her study spent about $8,000 per child, a fairly hefty level of spending even for an urban school system with many needy students. Although the total staffing for schools provided sufficient resources for a student-teacher ratio of fifteen, the actual class size was closer to thirty. Specialist staff for pull-out compensatory, mildly disabled, and bilingual education programs was the major factor for this difference. But the propensity to hire specialist staff for special-needs students was not the only reason for the discrepancy between potential and actual class size: rigid class size restrictions combined with age grouping of students, fragmented planning and preparation time, and fixed forty-five-minute class periods also contributed to widening the gap between potential and actual class size.

For example, if the absolute maximum class size was thirty but thirty-two students were enrolled in a particular grade, the system had to provide two teachers, for an actual class size of sixteen and much higher per-pupil costs. This phenomenon occurred mostly in smaller elementary schools. Planning time was usually provided by hiring a regular education specialist to "relieve" the teacher for a period or two a day. Not only were there less costly ways to provide planning and preparation time, but most schools did not schedule the time in a way that allowed teachers with common interests to meet and plan together. Finally, most schools, particularly high schools, had teachers teaching five classes of about thirty students each day, thus requiring teachers to meet 150 students a day, a number hardly conducive to creating a personalized educational environment; longer class periods would have reduced this high daily student contact as well as allowed for improved teaching and more personal attention to each student (Miles, 1995).

In summary, the system was characterized by a high level of overall expenditure, large class sizes, a proliferation of fragmented special programs, uncoordinated planning time, widespread teacher dissatisfaction, and low levels of student achievement.

Although a large urban district, Boston is not unusual in this pattern of resource use. Studies in other states and local school districts reveal a similar pattern of school organization and resource use (Monk, Roellke, and Brent, 1996; Nakib, 1995; Picus, Tetreault, and Murphy, 1996; Speakman and others, 1995). Indeed, in the typical high school in America, teachers comprise only 60 percent of all staff, and academic teachers of mathematics, science, language arts, social studies, and foreign language comprise only 65 percent of all teachers; put differently, teachers of core academic subjects comprise just 40 percent of the total staff of the typical high school (Odden and Picus, 1992).

The Case of East Austin, Texas

Murnane and Levy (1996) describe an experiment in East Austin, Texas, that exemplifies why the spending behaviors described for Boston too often do not lead to higher student learning. The experiment involved sixteen elementary schools servicing minority, very low income students. For five years, each school received $300,000 above its regular budget; the goal was to improve results with an infusion of new money. But at the end of the five-year period, achievement rose in only two of the sixteen schools; results stayed flat in the remaining schools, and differences could not be explained by changes in student populations or any advantages afforded the two improving schools. In the fourteen nonimproving schools, the new money was used to hire more teachers both to reduce class size and to add special services but not to change the instructional program. Apparently because the additional money was used to purchase standard additional resources but the instructional program remained essentially the same, student achievement did not improve.

The two improving schools did use some of their money to reduce class sizes, but they did not hire more specialists. First, they mounted an ambitious reform effort, focused directly on improving the curriculum and instructional program, which, as we have argued, is fundamental to better results. Second, the schools engaged teachers and parents in analyzing the low levels of student achievement and in discussing instructional strategies to improve them. Third, they took the district's curriculum for the gifted and talented and extended it to all students in their schools. Fourth, they placed most special-needs students in regular classrooms and, rather than using the categorical program dollars for specialists, used them to hire more regular teachers to reduce class size across the board. Fifth, they spent the remaining funds on intensive, ongoing professional training to enhance the knowledge, skills, and capacities needed by all teachers to teach all their students to the higher standards of the tougher curriculum. They further provided incentives to everyone to engage in the hard work of restructuring and kept measuring results to give feedback and to determine whether the schools were moving forward. They applied other strategies as well, including more parent involvement and bringing health services from the social services department to the school site.

In short, they used both their new and their old funds more strategically to support a *schoolwide* effort to boost results. They guided the process by setting high expectations for greater student achievement. They concentrated their efforts on improving the curriculum and the instructional program. Then they used their resources to finance a cohesive whole-school strategy, reallocating resources from out-of-classroom specialist and support activities to more regular teachers and more training. More money helped, but not simply to expand the traditional approach either in staffing or in instruction; it helped because it was used to bolster major change in both the instructional program and in the staffing and training systems of the schools.

Summary and Conclusion

The discussion in this chapter about the education dollar should be somewhat disturbing. The good news is that the United States provides a large amount of money for public schools. But then two serious errors are made: the federal and state governments distribute the money in highly unequal ways, and the districts and schools use the money in traditional but ineffective ways. These behaviors must change.

The substantial investment the country has made in its public educational system needs to be restructured so the investment pays off in terms of large increases in student achievement over the next few decades. First, the dollars need to be distributed more equitably; this chapter has suggested a general strategy for doing so that would eliminate the most egregious spending disparities in the lowest-spending districts in the country.

Second, as we argue in the next chapter, the management of the education system must be redesigned to provide more power, authority, and accountability at the school level; financially, this means sending the bulk of education dollars to schools in a lump sum. Then the long-term task is to get schools, like the two in East Austin, to act more like producers of high levels of student achievement rather than mere consumers of educational resources or providers of traditional educational services. This means that schools need to adopt an instructional strategy designed to teach all students to high standards, deploy all fiscal resources (current and new, general and categorical) for the purpose of teaching this curriculum effectively to all students, increase the proportion of the budget spent on regular classroom teachers and decrease the proportion spent on specialists and thus reduce overall class sizes, and invest more in training and professional development. The remaining chapters show how these strategies could be implemented in most schools in this country.

CHAPTER TWO

THE CASE FOR DECENTRALIZED
SCHOOL MANAGEMENT

Improving the use of the education dollar does not begin with a new finance system. It more appropriately begins with identification of new and ambitious goals for the system, which today is students achieving at much higher levels, selection of the management strategy that has the best potential for producing this higher level of results, and then redesigning the entire system so that all elements—standards, curriculum, teaching, school organization, and teacher work design—fit with the new management approach. As we argue in this chapter, reworking the finance structure is a key element of this system redesign. And the system redesign is inherently creating a more professional decentralized site-managed education system (see also National Commission on Teaching and America's Future, 1996).

Most organizations in American today, not just the schools, are under pressure to dramatically improve results with existing or even fewer resources, especially organizations whose workers, like those in schools, are highly educated and produce the best results when they work collaboratively. These organizations have found that the most effective strategy to produce significant improvements in performance has been to set clear performance goals at the top, flatten the organizational structure, decentralize power and authority to work teams, involve employees in making key decisions about how to organize and conduct their work, invest heavily in capacity development, and hold teams accountable for results (Barzelay, 1992; Katzenbach and Smith, 1993; Lawler, 1986, 1992, 1996; Mohrman, 1994a; Mohrman and Wohlstetter, 1994). These organizations, as we will argue further for schools, have found that a key part of this strategy includes providing teams with power over their budget.

Standards- and school-based education reform is the embodiment of this strategy in the public school system (Fuhrman, 1993; Massell, Kirst, and Hoppe, 1997; Smith and O'Day, 1991). Such reforms seek to educate students to high achievement levels by setting goals, standards, testing, and accountability at the top (state or district) and decentralizing implementation to the school site by changing education management, governance, and finance.

A key issue is whether this strategy can and will work. Although it is too early to provide a definitive answer, this chapter summarizes evidence from several recent studies of situations in which the strategy did work, the conditions that helped make the strategy work, and—for this book—the importance of school control over the budget as one of the critical elements that helped make this strategy work.

The arguments in this chapter should not be construed to imply that standards- and school-based reform is the only way to dramatically improve the country's education system. Indeed, there may be other viable strategies. But standards- and school-based reform is the strategy that many states and districts are trying to implement; evidence is building that when fully designed, the strategy can produce spectacular results, and a school-based financing system is a crucial element of this strategy—an element that when present allows schools to use education dollars better and when absent constitutes a major obstacle to meaningful school restructuring (Bodilly, 1996a, 1996b).

To be sure, there is a substantial body of research that shows that poorly designed education decentralization has little, if any, positive effect (Malen, Ogawa, and Kranz, 1990; Murphy and Beck, 1995; Newmann and Wehlage, 1995; Summers and Johnson, 1996; Wohlstetter and Odden, 1992). These research findings need to be taken seriously and indicate that the legacy of past decentralization efforts in education is generally not encouraging.

One problem with many approaches to education decentralization is that they have been conceived as ends in themselves; the belief has been that involving teachers in making decisions or democratizing schools will automatically lead to better student performance. The research shows, however, that this type of decentralization has little effect. Education practitioners and policymakers should know that a similar absence of impact occurred in the private sector when decentralization was adopted merely to "democratize" the workplace (Mohrman, 1994a).

Another misconception of school-based management (SBM) is that the school council—its composition and activities—is the critical design element, and this has often triggered intense debate over the most effective composition of the council (Malen, Ogawa, and Kranz, 1990; Wohlstetter, Briggs, and Van Kirk, 1997). But the studies discussed in this chapter show that the council is not the only or even the most important decision-making group for helping school-based management work.

One chapter in a recent book from the National Academy of Science proposed that school decentralization should be combined with incentives for improved performance in order to make it work (Hannaway, 1996). The inclusion of incentives focusing on student performance is commendable, but incentives alone are insufficient for the task of improving school performance. As we will demonstrate in this chapter, because the proposal is not based on research, it lacks the array of strategic management conditions that ensure successful decentralization targeted at improved organizational performance.

In sum, decentralized school management will not automatically improve schools. Decentralized school management entails much more than just creating a school council and giving it some decision-making authority or just giving schools decision-making authority over the full site budget. Accountability and school-based management alone will not work.

Drawing on the findings from several recent research reports, this chapter argues that for school-based management to work, it must provide a series of organizational conditions at the school level. Schools must then use these conditions to work on and improve the dimensions of schools that most directly affect student achievement—curriculum and instruction. Further, school-based management must be coupled with school-level accountability for results. Finally, school-based management must provide schools with control over their budget (Beck and Murphy, 1996; Darling-Hammond, 1996; Joyce and Calhoun, 1996; Mohrman, Lawler, and Mohrman, 1992; Newmann and Associates, 1996; Newmann and Wehlage, 1995; Odden, Wohlstetter, and Odden, 1995; Robertson, Wohlstetter, and Mohrman, 1995; Smylie, Lazarus, and Brownlee-Conyers, 1996; Wohlstetter, 1995; Wohlstetter, Mohrman, and Robertson, 1996; Wohlstetter, Smyer, and Mohrman, 1994; Wohlstetter, Van Kirk, Robertson, and Mohrman, 1997).

Taken as a whole, these studies show that effective SBM must do all of the following:

- Use district and state goals, standards, and benchmarks to focus reform efforts on high levels of student learning and to funnel the energies of school professionals to the changes in curriculum and instruction needed to produce that level of learning
- Involve all of a school's teachers in decision making by establishing a network of teacher decision-making forums and work teams
- Allow schools to recruit and select staff so as to build a cohesive faculty committed to the school's mission, vision, and culture

- Focus on continuous improvement through ongoing schoolwide professional development in curriculum, instruction, and management skills
- Create a professional school culture committed to producing higher levels of learning for all students
- Create a well-developed system for sharing school-related information with a broad range of school constituencies
- Develop ways to reward staff behavior that helps achieve school objects and, we would add, provide sanctions to discourage behavior that does not
- Select principals who can facilitate and manage change
- Provide schools control over the budget and the power to reallocate current resources to more productive uses

The remainder of this chapter explores these key elements of school-based management and the research supporting them. Our purpose is to summarize the extensive recent research evidence, which shows that decentralized school management in the context of clear goals for high student achievement and accountability for results is a viable and potentially powerful education reform strategy and that it must be accompanied by each school's control over its own budget.

Center Change on Student Learning and a Rigorous Instructional Program

Not surprisingly, one critical research finding about school-based restructuring is that learning must be its core focus if it is to produce improvements in student achievement. One recent study termed this focus a learning imperative (Beck and Murphy, 1996), another "authentic learning" (Newmann and Wehlage, 1995), and a third an "instructional guidance" system (Wohlstetter, Smyer, and Mohrman, 1994).

"Authentic student learning," as defined by the Center on Organization and Restructuring of Schools (CORS), directed by Fred Newmann and Gary Wehlage (see Newmann and Wehlage, 1995; Newmann and Associates, 1996), is learning that is constructivist, includes discipline-based inquiry, and has a value beyond schooling. By constructivist, CORS means that learning entails more than memorizing facts and figures; constructivist learning requires students to seek out information, analyze that information, and draw reasoned conclusions from their analysis. The discipline-based element requires that students learn the content and constructs of subject areas (mathematics, science, literature, and so on) and have their inquiries structured around and informed by disciplinary knowledge, concepts, and facts. Finally, authentic learning requires that special value be placed on school activities and learning tasks that have real-world applications. The goal is to connect schoolwork to real-life issues in part to give substantive and more intrinsic meaning to school tasks and in part to signal that academic work is useful outside of school.

The importance of focusing on student learning was a central finding of the five-year CORS study. This ambitious study analyzed data from twenty-four schools in twenty-two primarily urban districts in sixteen states, information from a large sample of schools participating in the Chicago School Reform, and quantitative analyses of several large national databases. The research showed that although school restructuring could take many forms (including school-based management, shared decision making, block scheduling, multiage or multiyear student grouping, and schools within schools), the only time that it consistently led to improved student learning was when it focused on student learning. The study concluded that if the instructional focus was one of high standards, or "authentic learning" as defined by the study, students not only learned more than control groups but also learned more at all levels of achievement.

Student learning was also an important element of another study of school restructuring that included one hundred schools, three thousand teachers, and sixty thousand students. The primary focus of the reform initiatives studied was student learning; the key restructuring element was large-scale, long-term professional development; and learning about school renewal was actively encouraged (Joyce and Calhoun, 1996). These authors concluded that a concentration on student learning was critical and that it could improve student learning rapidly, even during the first year of program implementation. Indeed, these authors implied that if a school reform effort were to have a positive impact on student learning, its effects would be apparent by the second year at the very latest. The programs they analyzed produced impressively large effects—one to two standard deviations!

This claim of almost immediate results is supported by the extensive studies of the Success for All program. Not only does this program consistently produce large, positive effects on student achievement in reading (one standard deviation for the lowest achievers), but also students in nearly all schools experience improvements in reading in the first year of implementation, and the reading effect tends to increase in subsequent years (Slavin and others, 1996).

Ambitious Content Matters

The CORS study also concluded that the definition of student learning was important. CORS analyzed what it called "authentic student learning." That is the focus in school restructuring that CORS found produced higher levels of average student achievement and, even more important, higher levels of achievement for all types of students, including low-ability, low-income, and minority students (Newmann and Associates, 1996). CORS proclaimed this finding of great importance. CORS was interested in average learning effects as well as the distribution of learning impacts. The study sought to identify the type of restructuring and learning focus that specifically improved the achievement of "at-risk" students and concluded that a focus on "authentic learning" did have this result (Newmann and Wehlage, 1995; Secada, Gamoran, and Weinstein, 1996).

As would be expected, CORS found that a focus on authentic learning had to be accompanied by what CORS researchers called "authentic pedagogy," a reference to the curriculum and the program of instruction. CORS researchers even developed standards to identify whether the intellectual quality of the curriculum and instruction they observed in the schools studied met the requirements for authentic pedagogy (Newmann, Secada, and Wehlage, 1995).

Standards Help Too

Relatedly, several of the recent studies of successful restructuring and effective school-based management found that some combination of district and state curriculum content and performance standards (see, for example, Gandal, 1996; National Council of Teachers of Mathematics, 1989; and Hanushek and Jorgenson, 1996) helped focus the work of the school on the curriculum and the instructional program, including the notion of authentic pedagogy. An external set of such standards was one of four key elements of the supporting environment identified by the CORS study (Wehlage, Osthoff, and Porter, 1996). The standards could be developed at the state or district level, but in nearly every case, such a set of standards helped keep the site restructuring focused on the instructional program. Smylie, Lazarus, and Brownlee-Conyers (1996) reached the same conclusion from a study of a district-created shared-decision program in its schools; the district emphasis on reading and language arts helped focus the substance of site-based decision making on those aspects of the curriculum and the instructional program. The Consortium for Policy Research in Education (CPRE) international study of SBM also found that some version of district or state curriculum standards was one of eight key factors that made SBM effective (see, for example, Odden and Odden, 1996a; and Robertson, Wohlstetter, and Mohrman, 1995).

In sum, several recent studies of successful school decentralization have found that a focus on student learning and use of the decision-making authorities provided to the school to improve the curriculum and instructional program were critical in making the decentralization and restructuring process work. In addition, the existence of district or state curriculum content and student performance standards helped reinforce this use of school decision making.

These findings should not be surprising. It makes sense that funneling the energies unleashed in a school-based management and shared decision-making strategy to the key elements that determine student achievement—curriculum and instruction—and assessing the impact of the school's actions on student achievement are important aspects of what makes SBM work. The surprise is that so many SBM initiatives in education have *not* had this focus (Murphy and Beck, 1995; Summers and Johnson, 1996).

The importance of the focus on learning and instruction reinforces the appropriateness of the core design element of the increasing number of school reform networks. The whole-school designs provided by these national networks—Accelerated Schools (Finnan, St. John, McCarthy, and Slovacek, 1996), Coalition of Essential Schools (Sizer, 1996), Core Knowledge Schools (Hirsch, 1996), Edison Schools (Edison Project, 1994), and the New American Schools (1995)—have a high-quality, standards-based curriculum and instructional program at their core. Thus as would be expected, data indicate that they produce improvements in student performance (Comer, 1993–1994; New American Schools, 1996; Slavin and others, 1996; Edison Project, 1996a, 1996b, 1996c, 1996d).

Involve All Teachers in Decision Making

Recent studies have also shown that involving *all* teachers in school-based decision-making and restructuring work groups is another key element that makes school decentralization successful. This was a particularly strong and explicit finding of the CPRE's four-year international study of school-based management, which researched forty schools in thirteen districts in three countries. CPRE researchers concluded that the most effective school-based management strategies dispersed decision-making powers to all teachers through a series of horizontal and vertical teacher decision-making teams (see, for example, Odden and Wohlstetter, 1995; Odden and Odden, 1996a; Wohlstetter, 1995; and Wohlstetter, Van Kirk, Robertson, and Mohrman, 1997). CPRE also concluded that these types of decision-making arrangements were much more important than either school council subcommittees or school councils themselves.

This is not to devalue the effectiveness or usefulness of councils: councils were needed. Councils generally had the power to approve major school policies. Councils were often the key vehicle for directly involving parents in the processes of setting school policy. But CPRE found that councils tended to involve only a few teachers in decision-making roles; if the council became the major locus of decision-making activities, an "us versus them" dynamic often emerged—"they" were the few individuals who sat on the council and made decisions, and "we" were the teachers who toiled in the classroom every day. Although CPRE found that council subcommittees involved more teachers, the most effective SBM strategies devised ways to involve all teachers in multiple decision-making and restructuring activities. All teachers in schools were given decision-making power and were expected to work on the core issues of restructuring, providing valuable input in the process. Similar conclusions were reached by CORS in distinguishing between schools that "consolidated" decision-making power in a small group of school leaders and those using school-based management to create "shared power relationships" (King, Louis, Marks, and Peterson, 1996).

Horizontal decision making and work teams were primarily service delivery or instructional groupings—subschools, grade-level teams, houses within schools, or multigrade or multiage student-teacher groupings. Teachers in these decision-making and work groups collaborated on the curriculum and the instructional program, often creating curriculum units together, improving them over time. Vertical teacher groups performed coordination and development functions and often included schoolwide content teams for mathematics, science, language arts, social studies, a professional development team, a schoolwide curriculum committee (usually consisting of the chairs of the various teams), teams for various school priorities, and whole-school faculty groups. CPRE found that in the most successful school restructuring efforts, teachers were often members of two or more such teams (Odden and Wohlstetter, 1995; Wohlstetter, Smyer, and Mohrman, 1994).

The work of these various committees transformed the abstract and elusive notions of "teacher involvement" and "shared decision making" into the concrete specifics that were needed to make restructuring work—including changing the mathematics, science, reading, and social studies programs; developing curriculum units that were used in the school's classrooms; creating instructional practices that worked in the school; linking professional development to required new pedagogical strategies; reflecting on and assessing instructional practice; and continuously improving school strategies.

The various decision-making teams also functioned as a set of cross-school communication channels. Because all teachers participated on two or more teams, most teachers were aware of school goals and strategies, the specifics of curriculum and instructional changes, and the emerging norms of the school.

Joyce and Calhoun (1996) also found that the most successful restructuring strategies involved all teachers in the work of restructuring, again through a variety of within-school teams. The same was true in the most successful CORS restructuring sites (King, Louis, Marks, and Peterson, 1996) and in the district shared-decision programs studied by Smylie, Lazarus, and Brownlee-Conyers (1996) and Beck and Murphy (1996). These programs worked better if they involved all members of a school's faculty in the day-to-day, nuts-and-bolts, largely curriculum and instructional aspects of site management, shared decision making, and school restructuring. And when all teachers were involved, school-based management consistently led to an improved instructional program.

Allow Schools to Recruit and Select Staff

To build a faculty committed to the vision the school wants to implement, research also shows that schools need the authority to recruit and select staff who support that vision and want to contribute to the hard work of restructuring required to put that vision into practice. Building a cohesive faculty committed to a high-standards school vision is not easy. It is hindered both by district practices that place personnel in schools with little or no school input and by contract provisions that allow teachers to transfer into and out of schools based solely on years of experience and personal preference.

The essence of school-based management and school restructuring is clarifying a vision of what the school wants to be and then working over several years to change all features of the school—the instructional program, the organization of teaching and learning, the human resources system, and the decision-making processes—to achieve that vision. This requires extraordinary effort, best sustained by an entire faculty committed to the process. And it allows schools to "socialize" teachers into the norms and culture of the school. All of the studies we have mentioned found that site control over staffing was crucial to such effective school development (Beck and Murphy, 1996; Joyce and Calhoun, 1996; Newmann and Wehlage, 1995; Smylie, Lazarus, and Brownlee-Conyers, 1996; Wohlstetter, Van Kirk, Robertson, and Mohrman, 1997).

Thus another important element of a comprehensively designed school-based management or restructuring strategy is decentralization of the personnel function to school sites—in other words, providing schools with the authority to recruit and select their own staff. Changing rules, regulations, contract provisions, and other mechanisms to allow schools to recruit and select staff will take several years. One of the most vexing findings about this personnel element of successful decentralized school management is that too often it is given only superficial attention, and when it is taken seriously, it requires many years to implement fully (see, for example, Odden and Odden, 1996b).

Invest in Training and Professional Development

Professional development was another sine qua non of effective school restructuring and school-based management. All recent studies have concluded that substantial investment in ongoing professional development focused on the entire school and structured to develop both individual and organizational capacities is another critically important ingredient that makes school decentralization work

(Beck and Murphy, 1996; Guskey and Peterson, 1996; Joyce and Calhoun, 1996; Newmann and Associates, 1996; Odden, Wohlstetter, and Odden, 1995; Smylie, Lazarus, and Brownlee-Conyers, 1996; Wohlstetter, Mohrman, and Robertson, 1996). Indeed, the primary intervention in the Joyce and Calhoun study was on-going, intensive professional development. Broader studies of the implementation of standards-based reform also conclude that capacity development is essential to effective implementation (Corcoran, 1995; Corcoran and Goertz, 1995; Goertz, Floden, and O'Day, 1995).

A comprehensive professional development strategy helps teachers acquire the professional expertise they need to engage in successful school restructuring. Most teachers need to acquire new curriculum and instructional knowledge and skills if they are to deploy authentic pedagogy and successfully teach a high-standards curriculum program to diverse students. Because many restructuring objectives expand teacher roles, training may also be needed in counseling, advising, family outreach, and curriculum development. Most teachers also need skills to participate successfully in decision-making and work groups—coordinating decision-making teams, setting agendas, helping groups make decisions, ensuring that decisions are implemented, and following up on decisions made and work that needs to be done. When shifting from more hierarchically to more collegially run schools, most school personnel also need to learn collaborative skills, teamwork strategies, and leadership expertise. Additional expertise is needed for the new managerial responsibilities that accompany school-based management and restructuring, such as recruiting and selecting staff, developing and monitoring budgets, supervising peers, and assessing program effectiveness. In short, substantive school restructuring requires that teachers develop an array of new professional expertise that can be obtained only through ongoing, long-term professional development.

In part because this notion of professional development is expansive and engages teachers in a variety of developmental and inquiry activities—conversations about effective instructional practices, dialogues about the best grouping of students, debates about human resources policies, and discussions about continuous improvement—recent studies have found that professional development also helps create a professional school community and that one focus of a professional community is nurturing such professional development (Louis, Kruse, and Marks, 1996a, 1996b). Similarly, such professional development also contributes to professionalizing the work environment (National Commission on Teaching and America's Future, 1996).

The cost of investing in an appropriate professional development program can be substantial. The professional development required to participate in national school reform networks and obtain expert assistance during the three to four years required for full implementation can amount to 2 to 3 percent of a school's total budget (Odden, 1997b). This approximates the level of professional development funding in New York City's Community District 2, which has made extensive training a major feature of its reform strategy (Elmore, 1996). The previously cited studies did not tally the actual costs of the professional development provided, but their descriptions suggested hefty programs, the costs of which could easily total $50,000 per year in a school of five hundred students (Odden, 1997b).

Create a Professional School Culture

One more key element of effective school-based management, in part a result of the preceding teacher activities, is the creation of a professional school culture. As Louis, Kruse, and Marks (1996a, p. 179) write, "Cooperation alone does not guarantee adults' success in building intellectual capacity in children. . . . Community among adults, when focused on professional responsibility and the central tasks of education, can reinforce and augment the talent, knowledge, and insight that individual teachers bring to their work. While well-designed school restructuring efforts may stimulate teachers' enthusiasm and satisfaction in their work, without professional community, most individual teachers will find it difficult to sustain the level of energy needed to reflect continually on and improve their practice for the benefit of authentic student achievement."

The notion of creating a school-specific professional community or culture weaves together the numerous individual actions of professional teachers into a whole-faculty undertaking centered around the meaningful activities that underpin successful school restructuring. Here success means change in curriculum and instruction that produces "authentic" student learning, or students learning to high standards. To be sure, the broader notions of teacher professionalism—improving one's individual professional practice, developing a school-specific curriculum, and focusing on the needs of each student—remain important, as do the broader professional engagements in developing curriculum content and student performance standards and working toward National Board certification (Haynes, 1995; Shapiro, 1995). But the idea of a school-based professional community offers a more localized and powerful force of organizational support for a schoolwide effort that cuts across disciplines, individual elements of professionalism, and traditional notions of teacher autonomy in the classroom.

Professional community is created when teachers work together on common objectives, share the successes and failures of such efforts, and reflect together on the curriculum and instructional practices they deploy as a faculty in their school (Louis, Kruse, and Marks, 1996a). As a result of these efforts, teachers "own" both the product and the consequences of their work; professional community both creates and reinforces peer pressure and facultywide responsibility for effective pedagogy and student learning. Put differently, professional community creates a school culture characterized by collective responsibility for student learning and collective commitment to the school's strategies to produce that learning.

Louis, Kruse, and Marks (1996b) concluded that professional community includes five key dimensions of school culture: shared norms and values, a focus on student learning (which we identify as the important focus of school-based management), reflective dialogue about curriculum and instructional practices, deprivatization of practice, and collaboration.

Shared norms and values include assumptions about children, learning, teaching, teachers' roles, the importance of relations among individuals within the school, and commitment to the common goals and purposes of the school. When these assumptions are unclear or nonexistent, teachers fall back on their individual and autonomous definitions of these issues. In a professional school culture, these norms and values evolve collectively through discourse and collaborative efforts and over time are shared by everyone.

A focus on learning, in this context, means that the bulk of teacher discussions about schooling centers on student achievement to high standards, how students learn, how learning can be enhanced, and how achievement levels can be raised. "Teacher talk" is then professional discussion about curriculum, instruction, learning, and results (Rosenholtz, 1989; Talbert and McLaughlin, 1994).

Such talk includes "reflective dialogue," which is a means of analytical conversation about teaching strategies, analyses of why curriculum units or pedagogical approaches did or did not work with different types of students, and other collective discussions in which teachers reflect on and evaluate the results of their work.

Teacher talk requires "deprivatization of practice" so that each individual teacher's classroom practice becomes the subject of the reflective dialogue about what does and does not work with students in the school. To succeed in teaching more students to higher standards, each teacher must subject his or her own individual teaching practices to collective analysis in order for each teacher individually, and the faculty as a whole, to create curriculum and instructional approaches that successfully accomplish the challenging task of producing authentic student learning in their school. These tasks cannot be accomplished unless the traditional autonomy of the classroom is breached and the faculty's construction of good practices is adopted by each teacher.

Finally, the actions of a professional community are accomplished through collaborative effort, largely through the network of teacher decision-making and work teams described earlier, the specific structures of which can vary by school. To be sure, each individual teacher must practice new strategies independently,

but the majority of the efforts to create schoolwide instructional practices that succeed, schoolwide analysis of strategies, and collective responsibility for both practice and its effects are carried out through collaboration across common elements
that can often divide faculties by the grade level or subject matter teachers teach
or even by the age of the teacher (see also Rosenholtz, 1989).

At its core, professional community defines a culture that shares norms, strategies, and work; focuses on student learning; and takes joint responsibility for the
efforts of the school's faculty and their impact on student learning. Professional
community includes collective responsibility for student achievement—a characteristic that helps keep school-based restructuring continuously focused on student
performance.

Create a Comprehensive School-Based Information System

It should be clear that access to good information, particularly knowledge about
best practices, is critical to making conversations among teachers collaborating in
professional communities substantive and useful. To improve a school's instructional program, collegial discussions must analyze specific problems and issues
in light of the best professional knowledge available; otherwise discussions may
lack substance or import. A rich information system that includes data on best
practices and other aspects of the professional knowledge base of curriculum and
instruction and is accessible through computer technologies can help ensure that
when such professional conversations occur, they are based on knowledge and
craft, not opinion or ideology.

Providing schools with that information is important to creating school-based
management initiatives that work. Indeed, the economics literature on high-
performing organizations concludes that providing a comprehensive array of information to service delivery and management teams is one of the key elements
in creating organizations that are successful in reaching their goals (Cyert, 1988;
Cyert and March, 1963; Levin, 1996, 1997).

A short discussion of the importance of a school-based information system
might illuminate its importance. In most organizations, particularly bureaucracies,
information is provided to managers at the top of the system via a paper trail of
memos and reports. This paper trail is transmitted up through different channels
to the manager–decision makers at the top. Thus informed, managers are given
the responsibility to make key organizational decisions. Although managers can
make poor decisions, the connection between the locus of information and the
locus of decision making is at least rational—both reside at the same place in the
organization. One reason for the historical placement of information and decision

making at one point of the organization—the top—was that it was simply too expensive to have the information distributed throughout the organization.

Modern information technologies, however, have made it economically possible to distribute the wide array of information needed to make good decisions to more people in an organization by designing a systemwide (and in education, school-based) computerized information system. This possibility thus provides the opportunity to alter the locus of decision making to more arenas and to groups closer to the point of delivery: in our case, the classroom. Because these work teams—school faculties in education—can now have access to the information available only to managers in the past, it makes sense that they might also be allowed to make managerial decisions. Indeed, decentralizing information and creating multiple channels of information flow—up and down the organization as well as across various units and divisions within the organization—are new characteristics of high-performing systems (Lawler, 1992).

The CPRE school-based management study more generally found that the most successful SBM programs were those that through various mechanisms provided a vast array of information to teachers at individual schools. Moreover, the study found that the most advanced programs automated and made this information system interactive through some type of relational database, similar to many "intranet" systems that now are emerging in the private and nonprofit sectors (Wohlstetter, Van Kirk, Robertson, and Mohrman, 1997).

Victoria, Australia, created one of the most extensive school-based information systems we had seen (Odden and Odden, 1996a, 1996b). That state installed an automated system that provided schools with financial information, an electronic purchasing and invoicing system, personnel information, student attendance and achievement data, a system for tracking or "profiling" student achievement against the state's performance standards, and information on curriculum units, effective instructional strategies, and numerous other examples of best curriculum and instructional practices. The system was accessed through a personal computer in each principal's office. It gave schools access to data that had previously been available only at the state department of education.

Provide Rewards and Sanctions

Accountability is another key ingredient of successful decentralized school management. Unfortunately, one of the downsides of most efforts at school-based management has been the lack of any accountability system (Murphy and Beck, 1995; Summers and Johnson, 1996). But accountability matters, and unless decentralized school management is held accountable for results, the probability that it will substantially improve performance is low. Nearly all recent studies of school-based management and school restructuring have concluded that accountability is important (Joyce and Calhoun, 1996; Newmann, King, and Rigdon, 1997; Odden and Odden, 1996a; Smylie, Lazarus, and Brownlee-Conyers, 1996; Wohlstetter, Smyer, and Mohrman, 1994).

Consequences for the results of school actions help focus the purpose of decentralization and restructuring on student performance results and stimulate the reflection on practices and their effects that are characteristic of a professional community and that are needed to improve practices. Consequences include both rewards for succeeding (meeting improvement targets) and sanctions—negative consequences—for consistently not succeeding.

One of the most promising policies of the 1990s has been the design and implementation of school-based performance awards. Taking many forms, these programs have four common features:

- They are schoolwide, not individual—they provide rewards to everyone in a school if the school meets improvement targets.
- They are based primarily on student achievement in the core subjects of mathematics, science, reading, writing, and history or social studies.
- The performance measures used for providing awards are based on changes or improvements in performance and thus have schools competing with themselves, that is, with their level of performance in the preceding year.
- They are funded for several consecutive years.

Although school-based performance awards in education are controversial, research on motivation and the impact of such programs in other organizations, as well as the emerging research on their operation in education, suggests that they hold considerable promise (Elmore, Abelmann, and Fuhrman, 1996; Heneman, 1997; Kelley, 1997; Kelley and Protsik, 1997; Clotfelter and Ladd, 1996; Odden, Heneman, Wakelyn, and Protsik, 1996; Odden and Kelley, 1997). The research is not yet clear as to why these programs work. It may be that they require the education system to define the most valued school outcomes, thereby allowing teachers to focus their work, or that the money element of such programs provides symbolic signals that the specified results are important or that money motivates teachers to exert greater effort or some other reason. But these programs, unlike the past failed efforts of individual merit pay, represent new ways to provide rewards to entire faculties for accomplishing goals and thus are ways that the education system can provide rewards for producing results.

The flip side of rewards is sanctions, negative consequences for failing to produce results. Here, too, the education system has been aggressively experimenting in the 1990s. One version of sanctions is state takeover of unsuccessful schools or school systems. These programs have been complicated and often never get to the curriculum and instructional reforms needed to produce higher levels of student achievement (Elmore, Abelmann, and Fuhrman, 1996; Fuhrman and Elmore, 1992).

Another version of sanctions is the provision of technical assistance to struggling schools, which is the strategy used in Kentucky. Schools that consistently do not meet their improvement targets are labeled "schools in decline" and are assisted by "distinguished educators," educators identified as being knowledgeable and proficient or accomplished. Recent research suggests that this approach can have beneficial effects on schools: nearly all schools identified as schools in decline and given help by distinguished educators made substantial progress in subsequent years (Kelley, 1997; Kelley and Protsik, 1997).

School reconstitution constitutes a third intervention strategy. School reconstitution is a process in which consistently low-performing schools are redesigned and staffed with some combination of new management, new teachers, and new students. Although it appears to be a promising strategy, reconstitution efforts are in their infancy, and more information is needed to determine how they could work best. A variation of school reconstitution is a state or district requirement that consistently low-performing schools adopt a "high-performance" school design provided by the emerging numbers of school reform networks (Education Commission of the States, 1997; Hirsch, 1996; New American Schools, 1995, 1996).

One reason that rewards and sanctions are effective is that they communicate that results are important and thus reinforce a school's focus on the core and most valued results, those in the performance measure (which in most cases is student achievement in academic subjects). Both rewards and sanctions garner educators' attention and focus that attention on what the system has identified as the priority results. Further, rewards and sanctions seem to be more successful when used in tandem (the promise of a positive consequence for succeeding and the promise of a negative consequence for failing). These behavioral effects could well be more important than the money bonuses that accompany some programs.

Select Principals Who Can Facilitate and Manage Change

Decentralized school management also requires a new breed of principals. Effective school restructuring needs strong and expert leadership but not domineering leadership. School-based restructuring to higher-performance visions is aided by principals who can play the broader managerial roles that accompany more school self-management, can facilitate the work of teachers in a school's decision-making and work teams, and can manage a change process (Murphy and Louis, 1994).

Nearly all studies of school-based change find new, different, and more challenging roles and functions for principals (Bryk and others, 1997; Murphy and Louis, 1994; Newmann and Associates, 1996; Odden and Odden, 1996a; Wohlstetter and Briggs, 1994). Principals become responsible for more managerial tasks, such as budgeting, personnel, and local and office politics. These tasks require new skills and consume time, time a principal can devote to instructional leadership. Thus the more successful principals create strategies to involve more people in providing school-level instructional leadership, which usually entails elevating teachers into instructional leadership roles. For example, they create school curriculum content teams and professional development teams, all chaired and led by teachers. Principals stay in touch with the instructional program often by creating a curriculum council made up of the leaders of these different teams. To make these mechanisms work, principals need skills in designing a team-based school organization that elevates teachers into leadership roles and in selecting, training, and empowering teachers to lead those teams.

Principals are also charged with orchestrating the school processes of restructuring as the entire school works to transform itself into a new vision. Principals need to develop the expertise to design and manage such a large-scale change process, which is complicated and does not proceed effectively unless consciously coordinated (Mohrman, 1994b).

In short, school-based management and restructuring require principals with a new set of skills and competencies rarely included in current principal-training programs. Thus districts often need to change the standards for their principal recruitment mechanisms and to design training programs to develop their own principals, many of whom may be teachers who have performed leadership and coordination roles in site-managed schools.

Give Schools Control over Their Budget

Finally, all recent studies conclude that a school's control over its own budget was a key element of successful school-based management and restructuring. The CPRE study concluded that for school-based management to work, "schools would need to receive lump-sum budgets. School-based budgeting would also entail shifting authority from the central office to allow schools to determine the mix of professionals; how to spend or save money for substitute teachers and utilities; the source of supply; and how to spend unused funds" (Wohlstetter and Mohrman, 1996, pp. 81–82).

The CORS study articulated the importance of school control over resources in the following manner: "Staff testified that without the freedom to [hire] teachers who were both skilled and convinced of the school's intellectual purpose, [the school] could not have developed as it did. . . . An important factor contributing to [the school's] success was the financial support it [received, which] . . . gave the school important flexibility to develop its program" (Wehlage, Osthoff, and Porter, 1996, p. 276).

Joyce and Calhoun (1996) concluded that for schools to develop the learning communities that are key to large-scale education improvement, schools need to be "empowered by school-based budgeting to spend discretionary money for staff development and school improvement" (p. 179).

In the RAND study of first-year implementation of the high-performance school designs offered by the New American Schools, Sue Bodilly (1996b), the lead analyst, told a NAS leadership conference that "limited funds and lack of authority to reallocate school budgets impeded implementation progress" and that "schools reported stronger commitment when resources for transformation were clear and certain."

In more concrete terms, a principal in a school trying to restructure around a high-performance school design provided by the New American Schools and willing to reallocate resources already in the school to fund the design made this point: "We need control over our resources if we are to reallocate them toward our chosen NAS design. Until the district provides us with this authority, any discussion of school-based resource reallocation is interesting but academic" (Odden, 1997b).

Control over the budget is a core ingredient of decentralized management. This is true in other organizations (Lawler, 1986, 1992) and increasingly is a more explicit finding in education as well (Joyce and Calhoun, 1996; Newmann and Wehlage, 1995; Odden and Odden, 1996b; Wohlstetter, Van Kirk, Robertson, and Mohrman, 1997). Indeed, unlike the more tentative approaches in America to decentralized management, which often provides only small amounts of budget authority (Hess, 1995; Wohlstetter and Odden, 1992), other countries seeking to decentralize education management to the school site take much more seriously the imperative that decentralization must include *substantial* budget control (see Chapters Four and Five).

Odden (1997b) and Chapter Seven in this book show why control over the budget is so crucial. It turns out that many of the new, high-performance school visions that are part of the nearly two dozen school reform networks are staffed and structured very differently from most schools in America. They have more classroom teachers and fewer nonclassroom specialists. They spend more on professional development. They group students and teachers differently, often across age levels and for multiple years. Many have full-time instructional facilitator roles rather than discipline-oriented assistant principals. Many also have more computer technologies. In sum, they use money differently. Further, in most localities, these new uses of resources can be financed with dollars already in the system.

But to have schools reallocate existing resources to these new and, we hope, more productive uses, schools need control over their budget. As Lynn Olson (1997, p. 23) concluded in an article on district and school policy on budget devolution, "If teachers and principals are to call the shots at their schools, they also need control over the money. But the shift to school-based budgeting hasn't been easy," even though emerging research shows that when schools gain control over their budget, they begin to reallocate dollars to school-specific purposes quite quickly (see Odden and Odden, 1996b; see also Chapter Five).

To be sure, the most recent programs of school-based management have found that greater portions of the budget are being devolved to schools and that even full control of the budget is given to the select few schools that might be piloting fuller versions of school-based management within a district (Newmann and Wehlage, 1995; Wohlstetter, Van Kirk, Robertson, and Mohrman, 1997). But there are few examples in the United States of either states or large districts providing all schools with full control over their budget as part of a decentralization effort.

The major purpose of the remainder of this book is to encourage that next step and to suggest how school-based budgets can be constructed.

PART TWO

APPROACHES TO
SCHOOL-BASED FINANCING

CHAPTER THREE

THE CASE OF CHARTER SCHOOLS

Charter schools represent the clearest effort in the United States to develop and implement a policy that requires a school-based financing system. As this chapter shows, however, states have given much more attention to structuring the processes for becoming a charter school and to delineating their freedoms and authorities than they have to their financing. Nevertheless, understanding how states fund charter schools offers the best glimpse at how school-based financing is viewed in the United States today.

In 1990 there were no charter schools. But during the five years from 1991 to 1996, twenty-six states enacted charter school laws and many other states debated charter school legislation. The trend has been that if charter school legislation is not enacted during the first year it is debated, it usually is enacted in a subsequent year rather than being dropped as an issue. The rapid rise of charter schools is likely to continue now that incentive funding is available from the federal government to encourage groups and schools to engage in the planning necessary to create a charter school vision and initiate the process of applying for a charter from a designated charter-granting entity.

Charter schools were originally proposed as a strategy for improving the effectiveness of schools, with effectiveness defined as teaching students to higher levels of achievement. The idea was that charter schools would operate under a state-granted charter that included a student performance contract. Under this arrangement, the state would waive some rules and regulations, providing the charter school with greater autonomy than public schools, in exchange for the school's producing increased achievement as specified in the charter's student performance contract. The assumption was that a combination of local, state, and federal rules and regulations prevented public schools from deploying the strategies needed to improve student performance. The hope was that charter schools, having been granted relief from these alleged onerous constraints, would be able to restructure the teaching and learning process and thereby dramatically improve student achievement.

States have taken numerous approaches to creating and enacting charter school laws (Bierlein and Bateman, 1996; Finn, Bierlein, and Manno, 1996; Wohlstetter, Wenning, and Briggs, 1995). No two states' charter school laws are exactly alike. In some states, only public schools can apply for charter status; in others, groups of teachers or citizens, universities, and even regional education organizations can apply for a charter. States have created different entities for granting charters; in some states, only local school boards grant charters; in others, the state grants charters; and in some cases, both the state and the local school district must approve the charter. States have also provided different degrees of freedom, authority, and regulatory relief for charter schools. In some, the waiver of state rules and regulations is automatic and wholesale, while in others, individual charter schools have to specifically request each proposed waiver. In some states, charter schools are separate legal entities; in others, their legal status is linked to the local district in which they exist. And as the chapter will show, states also fund charter schools quite differently; some states finance charter schools directly, some require charter schools to negotiate the budget with the local board, and some—Arkansas, Georgia, and Kansas—do not even address funding!

Much has been written about charter schools, particularly how to increase charter school autonomy (for example, Bierlein and Bateman, 1996; Finn, Bierlein, and Manno, 1996; Wohlstetter, Wenning, and Briggs, 1995), but little has been written about how charter schools are financed. As we argued in Chapter One, budgetary responsibility is critical to the success of a school decentralization strategy, and charter schools are the country's most aggressive version of school decentralization. Without funding and authority over the budget, the school-based governance and management advanced by charter school laws are little more than political rhetoric and lack the substance required for school staff to target the site's resources to the strategies that best serve the needs of students (see Odden, 1994a; Odden and Wohlstetter, 1995).

This chapter discusses charter school financing by describing and analyzing the funding provisions in state charter school legislation. To set the stage, however, the chapter also describes the key overall elements of each state's charter school legislation, thus providing a broader context within which the funding provisions can be understood. Data were collected through telephone interviews, laws and information obtained from state Internet sites, and written documents. In the late summer and early fall of 1994, 1995, and 1996, state departments of education in all fifty states were telephoned to determine the status of each state's charter school laws. States with charter school laws sent copies of their legislation and other relevant materials. In cases where the legislation was not clear, state department of education, legislative, or executive staff members were interviewed over the telephone (depending on which entity had the strongest knowledge of existing charter school legislation). All data were updated to be current as of December 1996.

The review of legislation and interviews sought information in three general areas:

- *Development and status:* when the legislation was passed and became effective, the process for approval, availability of appeals, waiver provisions, and charter school legal status
- *Accountability:* performance requirements for charter schools
- *Financing:* the allocation of state unrestricted and categorical aid to charter schools and whether teachers' salaries remained within the school district's negotiated contract

The chapter is divided into three sections. The first describes the key nonfinancial elements of each state's charter school legislation, focusing on the issue of school autonomy, which has dominated the discussion of charter schools so far. The second section describes in detail the various ways in which charter schools are funded. The last section assesses the key features of state charter school finance policy and recommends ways that such school-based financing can be improved.

Substantive Features of Charter School Legislation

Table 3.1 summarizes the key elements of each state's charter school law as it pertains to the year the charter program was enacted, the process for becoming a charter, the degree of autonomy, legal status, and whether funding was addressed in the law. State charter school laws vary substantially across these dimensions. In 1991, Minnesota was the first state to pass a charter school bill; by the end of 1996, twenty-six states had charter school programs.

As the diversity apparent in Table 3.1 suggests, charter school legislation was not concentrated in any single region. The geographical dispersion of charter

TABLE 3.1. KEY ELEMENTS IN STATE CHARTER SCHOOL LAWS.

State	Year Passed or Operational	School Staff or Parent Vote to Become Charter	Final Approval at State or District Level	Appeal Available	Automatic Waiver of Rules and Regulations	Legal Status Distinct from District	Teacher Salaries in District Contract	Funding Specified
Alaska	1995	no	state[a] (either)	n/a	yes	no	maybe	yes
Arizona	1994							
Local		no	district	n/a	yes	yes	no	yes
State		no	state	n/a	yes	yes	no	yes
Arkansas	1995	yes	state	no	no	no	n/a	n/a
California	1992	yes[b]	state[a]	yes	no	yes	maybe	yes
Colorado	1993	no	district	yes	no	no	no	yes
Connecticut	1996							
Local		no	state	no	no	yes	maybe	no
State		no	state	no	no	yes	maybe	yes
Delaware	1995	no	either	no	yes	yes	no	yes
Florida	1996	yes	district	yes	yes	yes	maybe	yes
Georgia	1993	yes	state	no	no	no	maybe	n/a
Hawaii	1994	yes[c]	school	no	yes	n/a	yes	yes
Illinois	1996	yes[c]	state	no	yes	yes	no	yes
Kansas	1994	no	state[a]	no	no	no	maybe	n/a
Louisiana	1995	yes[c]	state	n/a	yes	yes	no	yes
Massachusetts	1993	no	state	n/a	no	yes	no	yes
Michigan	1993	no	district or sponsor[d]	yes[e]	no	yes	yes[f]	yes
Minnesota	1991	yes[c]	state	yes	yes	yes	no	yes
New Hampshire	1995	no[e]	district	yes	yes	yes	n/a	yes

	Year							
New Jersey	1996	yes[c]	state	yes	no	yes	yes[c]	yes
New Mexico	1993	yes	state	n/a	no	no	yes	yes
North Carolina	1996	yes[c]	state	yes	yes	yes	no	yes
Oregon	1995	no	district	yes	no	yes	maybe	yes
Rhode Island	1995	yes[c]	either	n/a	no	yes	yes	yes
South Carolina	1996	yes[c]	state	yes	yes	yes	no	yes
Texas	1995		(either)					
Home rule		no[e]	district	n/a	no	yes	n/a	n/a
Campus		yes	district	no	no	yes	n/a	n/a
Open enrollment		no	state	n/a	no	yes	n/a	yes
Wisconsin	1993	yes[b]	state[a]	n/a	yes	no	yes	no
Wyoming	1995	yes[b]	district	no	n/a	no	yes	n/a

Note: n/a = not addressed.

[a] State rejects only if the maximum number of charters is reached.

[b] Or total districtwide teacher vote.

[c] Existing schools only.

[d] In addition to school districts, sponsors include intermediate school boards, community college boards, or state universities.

[e] Districtwide, not school vote.

[f] Only if sponsored by a local school board.

school legislation suggests that it is viewed as a general education reform strategy and not as a strategy particular to a state's education system.

The Charter Approval Process

The process that schools undergo to become a charter school varies by state and is often the most detailed part of charter school legislation. In some cases, the legislation begins by outlining processes starting with the school building. In other cases, the legislation begins after a school decides it wants charter school status. In all states, the legislation specifies whether the state, the local school district, or some other entity is responsible for granting final approval to become a charter school.

Involvement of School Staff and Parents. The first area where states differ is in specifying the process for how an existing or proposed new school would gain charter status. Some states address this process quite substantially; others do not. Arkansas, California, Florida, Georgia, Hawaii, Illinois, Louisiana, Minnesota, New Jersey, New Mexico, North Carolina, Rhode Island, South Carolina, Texas, Wisconsin, and Wyoming require school staff and parents in existing schools (either teachers or all staff and parents) to decide whether or not they want to be a charter school. The decision is usually made by a vote with the required level of support ranging across these states from a simple majority to a two-thirds majority of all school staff and parents. A few states (Connecticut, New Hampshire, and home-rule charter schools in Texas) even require *districtwide* votes or polling to ascertain community interest in charter schools. These states also allow for new schools to be created as charter schools. But for this situation, the states generally require that the proposed charter school demonstrate through some mechanism that parents support the charter school application and that there is some level of demand for the proposed charter school.

In the other states in which the law does not address the decision to seek charter school status, there is the assumption that charter schools are a desired commodity; the law does not specify a process or require a vote either for existing schools converting to charter status or for new schools becoming charter schools. These states' legislation addresses the approval process for schools only *after* a decision, however determined, is made to seek charter status.

Final Approval from the State. After the decision has been reached to become a charter school, states vary substantially regarding the entity that is empowered to provide final approval and grant the charter. Sometimes this is a state function, sometimes it is a local district function, sometimes it is both a state and local function, and sometimes the legislation empowers other public entities to grant a charter. The vast majority of states (Alaska, Arkansas, California, Connecticut, Georgia, Illinois, Kansas, Louisiana, Massachusetts, Minnesota, New Jersey, New Mexico, North Carolina, South Carolina, and Wisconsin) require a state agency, usually the state board of education, to provide final approval for a charter school application. However, the bulk of these states also require school districts to initially approve the charter school application, thereby having the state essentially ratify a local decision. For example, in Connecticut, charter status can be granted either by the state board of education or the local school district board, but the state board of education has the final say in accepting or rejecting all applicants, regardless of the initial sponsor. And in Massachusetts, negotiations for charter school status occur *only* between the proposed charter school and the state. In stark contrast, Alaska, California, Kansas, and Wisconsin all provide the state with very little power in approving charters. All four states set a statutory limit on the number of charter schools allowed in operation at any given time. The state simply receives the charter school applications that have been approved locally and automatically approves them at the state level unless the state limit on the number of charter schools would be exceeded.

Final Approval from the Local School District. Colorado, Florida, Michigan, New Hampshire, Oregon, and Wyoming empower local school districts to provide the final approval for charter school status. In Oregon, charter schools can be sponsored by both school districts and education service districts (regional education districts). The state merely receives copies of proposals and notifications of approval; it has no approval authority. However, a school can appeal to the state board of education if charter school status is denied at the local level. Importantly, in the six states that allow school districts to provide the final approval for charter schools, three—Colorado, Florida, and Oregon—provide an appeal process to contest local school board decisions. The others either expressly deny appeals by prospective charter schools or neglect the issue in their legislation. Thus even when the law gives initial grant-making authority to local school districts, the governmental authority that has the last word in approving charter schools is not always clear.

New Hampshire has the most elaborate approval process; it eventually ends back at the school district level, having taken a somewhat circuitous route. First, district voters must decide whether they want any charter schools within their district. Then a school must apply to and receive approval from the local school board for charter status. Next the state board must approve the local board's decision. Finally, if approved at all these levels, the charter has to be approved yet again by *another* districtwide vote.

Hawaii stands alone in allowing schools to declare charter school status all by themselves. However, Hawaii is an unusual state in that it has no school districts. Education is solely a state responsibility, and schools have no local school district to which to apply for charter status. The state could, but did not, require application to the state department of education. Hawaii simply, and in a sense boldly, decided to allow schools to make the charter school decision themselves.

Final Approval from Either the State or the Local School District. Arizona, Delaware, Rhode Island, and Texas allow *either* the local school district *or* the state to approve charter schools. Delaware and Rhode Island give schools seeking charter status the option of applying either to the district or to the state; if approved, the school simply becomes a charter school. These states do not identify the *type* of charter school by the level that provides the charter. However, Arizona and Texas distinguish the type of charter by whether it is approved locally or at the state level. For example, Texas created three different types of charters: home-rule charters, which are districtwide and voter-approved; campus charters, for which a majority of the school's parents and teachers apply to the local school board for charter status; and open-enrollment charter schools, for which the school or the entire district applies directly to the state for the charter. In Texas, the entity that provides the charter determines the type of charter school that is created.

Waiving State and Local Rules and Regulations

One of the main rationales for charter schools was to exempt them from numerous state and local education rules and regulations. School districts and their public schools are required to comply with a series of state rules and regulations. Receipt of state funding is usually contingent on such compliance. The breadth and scope of state rules and regulations for school districts varies by state, but examples range from the general, such as professional development plans and the provision of safe and healthful facilities, to the specific, including maximum class size and minimum beginning teacher salaries. A key assumption behind charter school laws is that these types of requirements limit a school's ability to teach its students.

But of the twenty-six states that have enacted charter school laws, only twelve provide for automatic waiver from state rules and regulations, generally excluding those related to health, safety, and desegregation requirements. Put a different way, in fourteen state charter laws, each charter school must apply for a waiver from specific state rules and regulations. In most of these states, charter schools have to request waivers of each individual rule and regulation. In some of these fourteen states, the issue of waiving state rules and regulations was not even addressed in the state charter school legislation. However, some of these states allow waivers through other processes and make that procedure available equally to all schools, charter or not.

Legal Status Separate from the School District

A surprising finding in the charter school legislation is that the legal status of charter schools is inconsistent. Legal status refers to whether a charter school is considered a distinct legal entity by the state. As a distinct legal entity, a charter school can sue and be sued and enter into contracts with outside vendors aside from the school district. Without distinct legal status, the prerogatives of a charter school are limited and the performance of the charter school necessarily remains a concern of the resident district, because the resident district can be held accountable for the actions of the charter school. Legal autonomy ensures that the onus of the charter school's commitment to educating students remains at the school site.

In sixteen states, charter schools are designated as distinct legal entities, and in several cases, charter schools are specifically designated as nonprofit corporations under state law. In nine states, charter schools are not considered distinct legal entities. In these states, charter schools are considered to be legally a part of the school district within which they are located. Again, Hawaii's charter school laws are somewhat different in that charter schools are no different legally from other schools in the state, but the legal status of schools in Hawaii is unlike schools in most other states.

Authority over Personnel

Given that teacher salary and other professional staff costs account for roughly 75 percent of all education spending, the ability of charter schools to hire teachers through independent means outside the district-negotiated contract may provide important administrative, organizational, and financial flexibility. But again, charter school authority over teacher salaries, as well as terms and conditions of employment, varies widely in state charter school legislation.

Nine states require charter schools to determine teacher salaries and do not allow those salaries to be negotiated with the district or to be included in the district's teacher salary contract. Seven states *permit* charter schools to be a part of the local district contract but do not require teacher contract participation. Seven other states *require* charter school teachers' salaries to be included in the district contract. Interestingly, Arizona, New Hampshire, and Texas do not address the issue of teacher salaries and working conditions in their charter school laws, leaving the status of that issue unresolved.

Performance Requirements

All state charter school statutes except Oregon's require that charter schools meet student performance requirements. These vary from statewide tests conducted for all students to assessments defined by the school in its charter. Generally, all charter schools must discuss in their application the student performance criteria under which they will be held accountable. At the same time, research has not been conducted on the specific nature of these student performance contracts. Anecdotal evidence suggests that the contracts might not be as specific or as clear as many educators would like.

Summary

In short, states have taken many different routes in structuring their charter school laws. Some states have created a process that stimulates existing and new schools to apply for charter status and provides them with significant management and organizational autonomy—automatic regulatory relief, ability to negotiate their own salary structures, and distinct legal status. Other states have created a relatively onerous process for obtaining charter school status and often do not provide the autonomy that motivates the creation of charter schools in the first place. Still other states have structured their programs in between these extremes. Just as for state education policy that is enacted on a state-by-state basis, charter school policy shows great variability; one idea has a different manifestation in each state where a specific charter program has been created.

Financing Charter Schools

Most, but not all, charter school laws address the issue of charter school funding. But before we discuss the specifics of charter school financing, we must look into the general features of kindergarten through twelfth grade (K–12) education funding because that has implications for charter school financing. States must decide if and how charter school financing will be linked to the overall school finance system, including the additional funds some districts raise beyond those provided according to the state's standard funding formula. As states have addressed this issue, they have struggled with the dilemma of how to handle local school district revenue in the charter school financing scheme. States have resolved these issues using many different strategies and, as we will argue, have not linked charter school financing as closely to the overall K–12 finance structure as is possible and have made the issue of how to handle "local" revenues much more complex than necessary. The result is that charter school financing—the country's only school-based financing policy—could be substantially improved.

Background

In most states (the exceptions are Delaware, Hawaii, North Carolina, and Washington), state funding for K–12 education includes a local school district contribution. Whether the state uses a foundation formula, a guaranteed tax base (GTB), or a combination of the two, state financing of education generally assumes that school districts will contribute some specified amount of local revenues. For example, under a foundation formula, a state might support a minimum level of expenditure per pupil, say, $5,000, and require local districts to fund a portion of that expenditure with a minimum tax rate on property, say, 10 mills. Thus District A, with taxable property of $100,000 per pupil, would generate $1,000 per pupil in local revenues, and District B, with $200,000 per pupil, would generate $2,000 per pupil. Under a foundation formula, the state would make up the difference between the local revenue raised and the foundation base of $5,000 by allocating $4,000 per pupil to District A and $3,000 per pupil to District B.

Under a GTB education financing system, the state guarantees a given property value per pupil for districts; all districts with property value under the guarantee can operate as if they had the state guaranteed tax base. Using districts A and B again, if the state guaranteed a property value of $350,000 for up to $5,000 of district spending, each district would need to levy 14.3 mills to produce that level of spending ($5,000/$350,000 = 14.3 mills). At that rate, District A would raise $1,430 in local revenues and District B would raise $2,860, with the state making up the difference between $5,000 and the locally raised revenues. (Some states use a similar approach known as "percent equalization." Under percent equalization, with the state role pegged at one-third and a state average tax base of $200,000, District A, spending at $5,000 per pupil, would receive $3,333 in state aid—$5,000 minus one-third of $5,000. Even though the math is different, the end result is the same as a guaranteed tax base at $300,000. Consequently, we will treat percent equalization states as if they were guaranteed tax base states for the remainder of this discussion.)

In addition to the local contribution required for most state school financing formulas, most states also allow local districts to raise *additional* local revenues above those assumed in the state school funding formula. In our districts A and B, each district might raise additional local revenues to produce per-pupil spending levels of $5,100 and $6,500, respectively. These additional revenues are problematic when designing charter school financing laws; the issue is whether or not a charter school will receive its share of the additional revenues. The resolution is important for charter schools. For example, if a state funds charter schools using the regular statewide formula at the minimum expenditure of $5,000, a charter school in District A spending at $5,100 for each "regular" district pupil would be only slightly disadvantaged by receiving $100 less than other schools in the district. However, a charter school in District B would be *significantly* financially disadvantaged because it would receive $1,500 less than "regular" schools in the district. Thus as states devise their funding mechanisms for charter schools, they must decide whether to make allowances for funding differentials between school districts resulting from local revenues and spell out who will pay for what.

In policy conversations about charter school financing in the United States, the issue has often been defined as how the state will handle the "local" revenues from the school district in which the charter school is located and whether the state will cover the full cost of financing charter schools solely with "state" funds. States with charter schools further struggle to decide whether the state will contribute all funds directly to the charter school or will funnel charter school funds indirectly to charter schools through local school districts.

One problem in addressing these issues is that many states have failed to realize that student enrollment decisions automatically shift levels of both state and local resources. Take the case of District A in a state with a foundation expenditure level of $5,000. In our example, it sounds as if there is $1,000 of local and $4,000 of state revenues for each student. But if one student moved out of the district or to a fully state-funded charter school within the district, the decrease in state revenues would be the full $5,000! This is true because the foundation assumes a minimum tax rate applied to all taxable property, and local revenues remain unchanged despite the student transfer. However, though the local level of funding remains constant, the state aid is reduced, based on the number of students attending schools within the district multiplied by the foundation level and deducting the local revenues. So if there were ten students in District A and one transferred to a charter school, the local effort would remain $10,000 in total (10 mills times $1 million in property) and the state would give the district $35,000 ($5,000 times nine students minus $10,000 in local property tax revenues). If the student had not transferred, District A would still raise $10,000 in local revenues, but it would receive $40,000 in state revenues ($5,000 times ten students minus $10,000 in local revenues). The state revenue shifting would also be true in most cases for the GTB system.

This means that a state could decide to fund each charter school student directly from the state and that it would cost the state no more to cover the full $5,000 for each student (assuming that each student came from a converted public school). Similarly, the state could funnel the dollars through the local district and require it to send the full $5,000 for each student to the charter school. To be sure, if students now attending private schools decided to enroll in a charter school, more money would be needed—$5,000 for each student. But this would also be true if a private school student decided to attend a public school, and in that case the entire $5,000 would be provided by the state.

These examples show that there is no reason to make a distinction between state and local revenues in funding charter schools, at least up to the level of the school finance equalization formula. The algebra of the school finance equalization formula will make all the adjustments to revenue flow. If states understood these behaviors of formulas, they likely would conclude that the least complex way to fund a charter school would be to consider the charter school as a distinct district with zero property wealth and treat it as a district in the school funding formula. For students in public schools converting to charters, this would require no extra state or local cost; for students entering the system, the state would pick up the entire additional cost, just as it would if the students enrolled in regular public schools. Yet only a few states have adopted this more straightforward approach to financing charter schools.

This strategy does not address the local revenues some districts raise above those included in the school funding formula. Whether or not those revenues should also be available to charter schools is essentially a political question, which states have addressed in very different ways. States that require districts to provide charter schools with the average district per-pupil revenues have decided that charter schools deserve their fair share of these local additional dollars. In Chapter Six we explain how a single school-based financing policy could include these additional revenues in charter school financing as well.

Table 3.2 presents the key characteristics of the school financing system for each state with charter school legislation as of December 1996. It shows the K–12 education funding system employed, whether state categorical aid is distributed by weighting pupils in the state formula or through a separate categorical structure, whether states restrict local funding above that in the state financing formula, and the share of local funding in combined state and local funding.

Column 4 identifies only states with strict local funding limits; in other words, it indicates whether funding is absolutely or virtually prohibited above a given defined amount (percentage of budget or millage rate). It thus excludes states that have cost controls but allow districts to exceed them if the voters approve. Colorado is an example of a strict limit: it allows districts to raise local funding only 20 percent above the formula funding level and then only with voter approval. California is included because districts essentially cannot raise any additional local revenues.

TABLE 3.2. PROFILE OF K–12 EDUCATION FINANCING SYSTEMS IN STATES WITH CHARTER SCHOOL PROGRAMS.

State	K–12 Education Financing Type	Categorical Aid	Strict Limits on Local Funding	Local Funding, 1995–96 (percent)
Alaska	foundation	weighted pupil	yes	23.9
Arizona	foundation	weighted pupil	yes	49.3
Arkansas	foundation	weighted pupil	yes	26.1
California	foundation	separately allocated	yes	34.2
Colorado	foundation	separately allocated	yes	48.7
Connecticut	foundation	separately allocated[a]	no	55.2
Delaware	combination full state funding[b] and guaranteed tax base	weighted pupil	no	26.7
Florida	foundation	weighted pupil	yes	43.3
Georgia	combination foundation and guaranteed tax base	weighted pupil	no	23.9
Hawaii	full state funding	separately allocated	n/a	2.0
Illinois	foundation	separately allocated[a]	yes	61.3
Kansas	foundation	both[c]	yes	33.8
Louisiana	foundation	within the foundation[d]	yes	32.5
Massachusetts	foundation	both[e]	yes	58.2
Michigan	foundation	separately allocated[a]	yes	37.6
Minnesota	foundation; small guaranteed tax base	both[a, f]	no	44.9
New Hampshire	foundation	weighted pupil	no	89.0
New Jersey	foundation	weighted pupil	yes	56.0
New Mexico	foundation	weighted pupil	yes	14.9
North Carolina	full state funding[b]	separately allocated	no	24.9

Oregon	foundation	weighted pupil	yes	36.4
Rhode Island	guaranteed tax base	separately allocated	yes	55.0
South Carolina	foundation	weighted pupil	no	44.2
Texas	combination foundation and guaranteed tax base	weighted pupil	yes	47.7
Wisconsin	guaranteed tax base	separately allocated	no	52.5
Wyoming	foundation	separately allocated	yes	44.5

Note: n/a = not addressed.

[a]State weights only students in poverty in its foundation formula.

[b]State uses a funding formula (flat grant) that does not include local revenues.

[c]State allows weights for transportation, vocational, and bilingual education but not for special education.

[d]State funds special education within the foundation level but without using weights.

[e]State does not weight students requiring categorical services but includes them in "enrollment categories" and allocates funding separately.

[f]State weights only for disabled prekindergarten and kindergarten students in its foundation formula and allocates funding separately.

Source: Gold, Smith, and Lawton, 1995; National Education Association, 1996, p. 39.

Table 3.2 demonstrates that local revenues play a major role in school district finance. This highlights the difficulty states have in discussing charter school financing; if funds are identified as "state" and "local," it seems that a large portion of "local" revenues will flow to charter schools. Second, local funding limits indicate whether or not there will be local funding above the level in the formula, and that needs to be addressed in the charter school financing mechanisms. If significant variability in funding is produced by additional local funding, states not wanting to place charter schools at a financial disadvantage may have to make up or require that such additional local per-pupil funding be provided to charter schools—at least up to the district per-pupil funding level so that the charter school can reasonably "compete" with other schools in the district.

Third, in addition to issues of local funding, Table 3.2 shows the different methods states use to provide additional funds for students with particular educational needs (such as compensatory, bilingual, or special education). Some states fund such programs as "add-ons" to the state foundation or guaranteed tax base funding. Other states weight students with additional educational needs so that funding may reflect that some students require more resources than others. Charter school financing should also include these additional funds to enable charter schools to provide the additional educational services these students need.

Charter School Financing Methods

As they do on most other governance and management issues, states vary in the way they fund charter schools. In general, however, states employ one of four strategies for determining the funding for each charter school: direct state-to-school funding; specific state formulas or procedures that determine funds for charter schools but provide them through school districts; funding negotiated locally between the charter school and the district; or leaving funding out of the law entirely. Table 3.3 identifies each of these approaches and the states using them. Note, however, that some states use two methods simultaneously. For example, Arizona allows for two types of charter schools—local and state—and each type is funded differently. If a charter school is approved locally, the funding is provided through the school district, and it must be *at least* the district's average per-pupil expenditure. If the charter is state-approved, funding is provided directly from the state according to the state funding formula for all schools.

Funding Directly from the State to the Charter School. Arizona, Connecticut, and Texas have different types of charter schools (local or state-sponsored), and direct state-to-school funding is only used for the state-sponsored charter schools. In Arizona (state-sponsored charter schools), Hawaii, Michigan, and Minnesota,

TABLE 3.3. CHARTER SCHOOL FUNDING APPROACHES.

Funding Mechanism	State
Funding directly from the state to the charter school	Arizona[a], Connecticut[a], Delaware[b], Hawaii, Michigan, Minnesota, Texas[a]
Funding specifically targeted through the school district to the charter school	Alaska, Arizona[a], California, Colorado, Delaware[b], Florida, Illinois, Louisiana, Massachusetts, New Hampshire, New Jersey, New Mexico, North Carolina, Oregon, Rhode Island, South Carolina, Texas[a]
Funding negotiated locally between the charter school and school district	Connecticut[a], Texas[a], Wisconsin[c]
Funding not addressed in state law	Arkansas, Georgia, Kansas, Wyoming

[a]Different funding methods are allowed.

[b]Charter schools receive funding from both state and local sources separately.

[c]A maximum per-pupil funding level is set by law.

charter schools are funded fully and directly from the state. These states all use their regular school finance foundation formulas to determine the base funding for charter schools; they also use the state formulas for special education and other categorical funding to provide additional dollars for students who are eligible for those services either by way of weighting students within the foundation or by separately allocating categorical aid. In these states, charter schools do not receive any of the local revenues that a district might spend above that provided by the base school finance foundation and categorical aid system.

In general, these states treat the charter school as a district with no local property wealth. As we stated earlier, this is the most straightforward way to fund charter schools directly from the state. The only disadvantage is that this approach does not provide charter schools with the additional local revenues that schools in the same district might have if the district spends above the base amounts guaranteed in the school financing equalization formula.

For these four states, this is a smaller rather than a larger problem. Arizona severely restricts additional local funding for education to just 10 to 15 percent of the foundation expenditure level. Thus for state charter schools in districts spending over the foundation level, using only the state foundation formula does not serve as a great disincentive because expenditure differences between schools will be at most 15 percent. All schools in Hawaii are funded under the same formula, so charter and noncharter schools receive essentially the same level of resources. In Minnesota and Michigan, where local spending is not restricted to a specific percentage or millage rate, variability in school district per-pupil funding could be larger. Charter schools funded only at the foundation level in districts spending over the state foundation level may not compare favorably to other schools in the school district. If large, this could represent a real disincentive for charter schools in high-spending districts in these two states.

Regarding categorical programs, Arizona weights students with additional educational need and thus includes the extra money in the regular foundation formula. For example, a student requiring special education services is weighted more than a regular education student to reflect the additional resources required. Because these weights are built into the state foundation formula, state categorical aid necessarily follows the student to the charter school. Michigan and Minnesota use extra weights for compensatory education in their foundation formulas but provide other state categorical aid through separate funding formulas. Thus in Michigan and Minnesota, the supplemental resources necessary for students with additional educational needs (beyond compensatory education) is added onto—not built into—the state foundation. Hawaii, as a full-state-funding state without local school districts, simply uses the statewide average per-pupil funding for charter schools (adjusted for special-needs students). In addition, Arizona, Hawaii, Michigan, and Minnesota make charter schools, like local districts, eligible for other federal or state grants.

Again, we would conclude that the strategy of these states is the most straightforward way for the state to finance charter schools, with the exception of the issue of local revenues above the school financing equalization formula. Recall that, assuming that all students in charter schools are in regular public schools that convert to charter schools, this system subtracts the full amount of spending in the foundation or GTB formula from the district and provides it to the charter school, just as would happen if the student left the district and attended school elsewhere.

The systems in Delaware and Texas (for state-sponsored charter schools), both of which have foundation programs with GTBs covering spending above the foundation, are different and more complex. These states have revenues "tagged" as "state" or "local" and provide only the "state" share for the district in which the charter school exists directly to the charter school. The charter schools receive the remaining portion of their funding from the average per-pupil local revenues for the school district in which the student resides. In Delaware, this works as a simple shifting of funds within the state treasury because the state treasurer serves as the treasurer for the state and all local school districts.

Although more complicated than the other strategies, this policy ensures that charter schools receive any local revenues that districts spend beyond those supported in the state school financing formula. But by tagging dollars as state and local, the system injects a complication into the funding system, and as we argue in Chapter Six, there is a more straightforward way to structure charter school financing. Nevertheless, allowing charter schools to receive state *and* local funding addresses some of the concerns over inequality *within* districts between charter schools and district schools when only the state foundation formula is used.

Connecticut provides state-sponsored charter schools with 105 percent of the state-supported foundation expenditure level, in part because many Connecticut districts spend above the foundation level. Connecticut also weights children from poverty in the foundation formula and thus provides these extra dollars to charter schools as well.

Charter schools in Connecticut, Delaware, and Texas are also eligible for the appropriate state and federal categorical funds for which their students qualify.

In sum, these seven states provide base funding largely from the state directly to the charter school, two of the states also ensure that charter schools receive the additional local revenues spent above the level supported in the school financing formula, and all seven states make charter schools eligible for all other state and federal categorical programs. To a significant degree, they treat the charter school as a district with no local property wealth for the purpose of funding and in this way ensure that charter schools receive the full funding to which they should be entitled.

Funding Specified by State Law but Provided by Local Districts. The second approach to funding charter schools is to specify by state law how the funds for charter schools are to be calculated, requiring that the calculation be conducted by local districts and that local districts send the funds to charter schools. This has become the most common approach to funding charter schools, with seventeen states following this strategy. Nevertheless, although representing a single, general strategy, the specific mechanisms states have designed vary widely among the states using this approach. Some states specify that charter schools receive their local school district's average per-pupil funding level (along with additional categorical aid where appropriate); other states require districts to provide a percentage (less than 100) of the district's average per-pupil funding; one state links charter school funding to district figures for the preceding year. Each state's chosen approach to allocating funds to charter schools is identified in Table 3.4.

Of the seventeen states specifying that charter schools will be financed through local school districts, seven require that charter schools receive the average amount the district spends from state and local sources for students in noncharter schools. In a slight variation, three states, California, Florida, and Oregon, require charter schools to receive the state-determined foundation expenditure level, per

TABLE 3.4. STATUTORY APPROACHES TO SPECIFYING CHARTER SCHOOL FUNDING THROUGH DISTRICTS.

Approach	State
District average per-pupil state and local funding	Alaska[a], Arizona, Louisiana, Massachusetts[b], New Mexico[a], North Carolina, Rhode Island
State foundation expenditure	California, Oregon, Florida[a]
Previous year's funding adjusted for inflation and enrollment	South Carolina
Percentage of district average per-pupil funding	Colorado (80%), Illinois (95% to 105%), New Hampshire (80%), New Jersey[b] (90%)
District average per-pupil local funding	Delaware, Texas[b]

[a]Minus indirect costs retained by the school district.
[b]From the student's district of residence.

regular student in California and per weighted student in Florida and Oregon. South Carolina essentially requires use of the average district spending figure but, for charter schools, has the district use the previous year's average per-pupil expenditure level (from state and local revenues) adjusted for inflation and enrollment. In a slight twist, Massachusetts requires funding to be provided by the school district in which the student attending the charter school resides.

As discussed earlier, Delaware and Texas take the allocation process a step further by simply requiring that both the state and the school district allocate their proportion of funding directly to the charter school.

Alaska, Florida, and New Mexico specifically allow school districts to retain an undesignated portion of district funds for "indirect" or district management tasks, thus providing an expenditure figure less the average per-pupil amount for such indirect costs. None of these states identifies the functions that constitute district management or indirect expenses. Interestingly, several districts in California also hold back a portion of the foundation, or revenue limit, amount that is supposed to be allocated to charter schools, even though this "holdback" is not mentioned in the charter school financing provision of state law.

Four states require districts to provide charter schools with a percentage of their average per-pupil costs, with the percentage below 100 percent in all states except Illinois, where the percentage can vary from 95 to 105 percent. In Colorado and New Hampshire, the percentage distribution is *at least* 80 percent of the charter school's resident district's per-pupil funding, while in New Jersey it is set at 90 percent of the student's resident district. The percentage distribution method recognizes that districts might need to continue to provide some services to all schools, including charter schools, and that it is reasonable to allow funds for these services to be retained by the district. The percentage approach also ensures that charter schools receive a portion of local revenues above the foundation level. This can be a considerable amount for many districts in these states. In the case of Colorado, New Hampshire, and Illinois, the language stating that charter schools receive *at least* a given percentage allows the charter school and school district to negotiate beyond the minimum.

Funding policies not reflected in the table but of great importance due to their equity implications are that the charter schools in all seventeen of the states where charter schools are funded through the local school district also receive state, federal, and other special grants for which students or the school are eligible (as for special education) through the local school district.

Allowing charter schools to receive their proportionate share of local funding from school districts means that similarly situated charter and noncharter schools in the same district will be funded at the same level and that charter schools will receive local revenues above the spending level supported by the state school financing formula. Thus state financing of education remains mostly the same, with no shifts in the responsibility for financing charter schools—charter schools receive the same proportionate share of state and local funds as the school district. By designating funds for charter schools on the basis of average per-pupil state and local revenues (or a percentage thereof), the state allows schools within school districts—charter or otherwise—to be funded similarly, thus confronting and resolving a *districtwide* equity issue. However, this also permits similar charter schools in different school districts to receive different per-pupil funding, thereby creating a problem for *statewide* equity.

Other Charter School Funding Strategies. In Connecticut (locally sponsored) and Oregon, charter school budgets are negotiated locally between the school and the district. This is also true in Wisconsin, but Wisconsin sets a cap on revenues available for charter schools. The cap in Wisconsin is the average per-pupil funding from *all* revenue sources in the local school district, including categorical aid. Although these three states leave the budgeting to local districts, at least the state laws raise the issue of finance.

By contrast, state charter school laws in Arkansas, Georgia, and Wyoming do not even mention charter school financing. Thus, by default, these three states leave the charter school budget up to local negotiations.

In all of these cases in which charter school financing is ignored in the state law or left to local negotiations, charter school laws are also weak; they designate only local boards as having final approval, they allow no appeal processes, and waivers are not automatic. Similarly, these same states assign charter schools a mixed legal status. Arkansas and Wyoming both ignore the issue of legal status; in Texas (home-rule and campus schools) and Oregon, charter schools are distinct legal entities but without clear access to funding.

Assessment and Analysis of Charter School Financing

Charter school laws vary not only in their substantive and programmatic aspects but also in the methods they prescribe for financing charter schools. Until recently, the driving issue in charter school financing has been who gets what. Is the money allocated directly from the state, through the district, or both ways? How can "state" and "local" dollars be treated differently? What dollar amount is distributed to charter schools? Is local funding included? These are important issues, and current charter school funding policies are simpler and better developed than the original financing mechanisms for public school choice policies (Odden and Kotowski, 1992), which often allowed only what were considered state dollars to follow a child to the school of choice.

Although the details vary, states have tackled two major issues in deciding how to finance charter schools. The first is whether charter schools will receive their funding directly from the state or directly from the local school district in which they are located. The second is whether charter schools will be supported at the level of the school finance equalization formula (either the foundation level or the GTB expenditure level) or the actual expenditure of the district in which the school is located. Nearly all states make charter schools eligible for state and federal categorical programs, particularly for those focused on special student needs, and there is little variation on this issue.

If there were no spending disparities across school districts, the key issue would be whether to have the state or the district funnel dollars to the charter school. But there are spending disparities, due to revenues that districts raise above those supported by the school financing formula. States have taken different tacks in deciding how these additional dollars will be treated for funding charter schools.

The simplest overall approach for charter school financing, and the one that ensures that charter schools receive the full level of state-supported spending, is for the state to treat the charter school as a school district and make it eligible for all state programs, including the school finance equalization formula. The major downside of this strategy is that it does not include the local revenue add-ons or includes them in a cumbersome way.

Our proposal for school-based financing described in Chapter Six addresses both of these issues, as do the school-based financing policies in England described in Chapter Five. The strategy would be for school districts to calculate the level of charter school funding and then have a state agency provide the funds to the charter school. This strategy combines the best of the two major strategies that states currently follow.

The one major issue that states have not addressed in any substantive way concerns the "indirect" services that districts must or should provide even under a school decentralization policy. The states that allow districts to provide a percentage of their overall funding to charter schools have recognized this issue, but by simply stating that the percentage should be at least 80, they have not responded to the many and complex substantive issues of what should or should not be included in "indirect" or required district activities.

As England has done, and as we suggest should be done in the United States, school-based financing, including charter school financing, should be determined by what roles and functions work best at the site level and what should remain at the district level. England (Chapter Five) provides an important example of how these issues could be conceptualized. England reconfigured education financing so that a significant proportion of funding is devolved to the school site through local education authorities. In addition, England has schools—grant-maintained (GM) schools—that are very similar to American charter schools. GM schools are autonomous from their resident local education authority. However, by law, local education authorities retain some funding for central services provided regionally for *both* GM schools and local education authority schools.

Some state charter school laws have hinted at these issues by suggesting or requiring that expenditures for transportation and food services be retained at the district level. But there are many other functions that could be retained and many that should be devolved. What is needed is a substantive analysis of these issues both as part of school-based financing policies generally and for charter schools as well. So far, no such careful consideration of state versus district versus school roles has been included in any charter school legislation in the United States.

Charter schools in this country—and schools in districts interested in further supporting site-based management—would do well to consider the roles and responsibilities of states, districts, and schools within the context of education finance. Some states have taken the first steps down this road in their charter school legislation by specifically mentioning the provision of transportation to students as a district responsibility (as in Connecticut and New Jersey) or excluding bond indebtedness from charter school funding (as in South Carolina). However, a more comprehensive analysis and discussion of appropriate roles and responsibilities between the school district and school is necessary to ensure adequate funding for meeting the educational needs of children. Systematically tracing resources and their use from the learning environment, school, and district would prove beneficial for a multitude of important school financing concerns, including adequacy and equity in funding.

CHAPTER FOUR

A STATE-TO-SCHOOL MODEL
FROM AUSTRALIA

School-based financing policies have been designed and implemented for
several years in four English-speaking democracies outside the United States:
Edmonton, Alberta, Canada; England; New Zealand; and Victoria, Australia. All
are excellent examples of how to decentralize education finance to the school site,
but they do not all use comparable systems. Edmonton is a single large school district. New Zealand is a country without local school districts, so it has a national-
to-site funding structure. England, discussed in the Chapter Five, is more like a
U.S. state, with local school districts. Victoria, discussed in this chapter, is a state
without local districts, so the funding system reflects a state-to-site structure.

Victoria, Australia, began implementing a school-based financing system in
1993 as part of its Schools of the Future program, which combined decentralized school management with standards-based education reform. Victoria is a
state with a population of approximately 4.5 million people. As of August 1996,
some 770,000 students were in school education, 515,000 in government schools.
The Victorian education system is about the size of that in Wisconsin or Missouri. Though primarily Australian, students in Victoria's government schools
are ethnically diverse; about 25 percent are children from non-English-speaking

Portions of this chapter are drawn from Odden and Odden (1996a, 1996b) and Caldwell and others (1996).

backgrounds, the offspring of immigrants from Asia, Southeast Asia, southern Europe, the Middle East, and Latin America.

Victoria began decentralizing power and authority to schools nearly thirty years ago. In the 1960s, the education system was highly centralized; the state made all key decisions on curriculum, budget, and personnel. It had a state-required, uniform classical curriculum designed primarily to prepare students for university. The state selected, hired, and placed all principals, teachers, and non-professional school staff including secretaries and janitors. The budget was controlled centrally. Students' residential address largely determined the school they attended. The local community, parents, and teachers had almost no say in school operations. Only 25 percent of students graduated from secondary school.

Decentralization was initiated in the late 1960s. A 1970s law created school councils as legal entities for each school site; in 1983, the councils were given several powers to set policy and approve budgets. Each year, decentralization was enhanced. By the end of 1992, all school sites were governed by a school council that had power and authority over almost all but the professional staff portions of the budget. The council selected the principal, who in turn selected all support staff. The council also approved school policy on all aspects of the curriculum, although curriculum was guided by state frameworks developed in the 1980s with broad teacher involvement. Students had the choice of virtually any school in the state. The local community, parents, teachers, and administrators had substantial input into all aspects of local school operations through the school council. School councils generally had several collaborative decision-making structures. The state also eventually eliminated separate vocational schools, merged them into more comprehensive secondary schools, and created the Victorian Certificate of Education (VCE), which replaced the old comprehensive examination for graduation from secondary school with a mixture of examinations and performance tasks. Over the intervening thirty years, secondary school graduation rates increased to nearly 80 percent, with the most substantial increases occurring in the period 1986–1992.

In 1993, a new administration proposed that school decentralization should be accelerated in response to a task force proposing full decentralization for "Schools of the Future." In March of that year, the government asked for applications to place one hundred of the state's schools into a pilot program that would provide virtually full authority over the budget and personnel function to the school site. Within a six-week period, over seven hundred schools applied, and in July 1993, more than three hundred schools entered the first phase of the Schools of the Future program. Another five hundred schools entered the program in early 1994 and an equal number in July 1994. By mid-1995, virtually all Victorian schools were in the Schools of the Future program.

Along with this decentralization of power and authority, Victoria also revised its curriculum content and student performance standards and created the Curriculum and Standards Frameworks (CSFs); developed and administered a new student testing system called the Learning Assessment Program (LAP); expanded professional development for principals and teachers; created a school-based information system with financial, student, achievement, and teacher data; designed a new school-based funding structure; and revised the principal and teacher compensation and career structures.

In sum, Schools of the Future is an ambitious school decentralization initiative. It is designed to set curriculum content, student performance standards, and measurement of school results at the top of the education system and to decentralize accomplishment of goals and objectives to each school site. It also includes a series of results-based accountability mechanisms, created to shift the orientation of the education system from inputs to outputs.

Schools of the Future did not emerge all of a piece. Most of its key decentralization elements were advancements on initiatives that had been created and implemented under both Labour (1982–1992) and Liberal governments in earlier years, for example:

- School councils had been given increasing roles and responsibilities that culminated in Schools of the Future.
- Whole-school improvement plans evolved into school charters.
- Councils and schools had also been given increasing authority to select staff, which culminated with the ability to select all staff, including teachers.
- Responsibility for ever-larger portions of the budget evolved into responsibility over the entire global budget; curriculum frameworks evolved into the CSFs.
- Profiling of student achievement according to the national and Victorian profiles evolved into profiling against the CSF performance standards and were augmented with the LAP.
- The new compensation system for teachers had its roots in an earlier effort to add a "pay for knowledge" element to the teacher salary structure.

Although the elements of Schools of the Future were more focused and sharper than their predecessors, it must be acknowledged that the program did not start from scratch in 1993 but rather was an evolutionary culmination of a twenty-year trend in Victorian education policy.

It is also important to note that the Schools of the Future program represents perhaps one of the most sweeping and comprehensive strategies at school decentralization for higher student performance attempted anywhere in the world.

Stated most succinctly, Victoria is implementing a relatively complete form of high-involvement school-based management (Mohrman, Wohlstetter, and Associates, 1994; Odden and Odden, 1996a, 1996b) within the context of a standards-based education reform structure. As such, the Victorian reform includes most of the key components of standards-based reform (Fuhrman, 1993; Smith and O'Day, 1991) and decentralized school finance (Odden, 1994a, 1994b). More information on the design, implementation, and effects of the Victorian education decentralization strategy can be found in several studies (Odden and Odden, 1996a, 1996b; Cooperative Research Project, 1994, 1995, 1996).

This chapter describes the funding structures that were used through 1996 to provide schools with full control over their budget and summarizes proposals that were made in late 1996 to improve the funding structure. A key element of the Schools of the Future decentralization program was devolving the budget to the school site. In 1994, schools received their budget in three categories: salaries and benefits, operations, and facilities and maintenance. In 1995 and 1996, schools were given a "global" lump-sum budget that covered all elements of school operations—salaries and benefits of teachers, administrators, and other school professionals; salaries and benefits of all nonprofessional school employees (secretaries, bookkeepers, janitors, and so on); instructional materials and supplies; operations and maintenance; and minor facilities upkeep.

The Australian Context of Victorian School Finance

The financing of education is primarily a state function in Australia, although the federal government is the primary collector of tax revenues and provides each state with the bulk of its revenues for state-operated functions. Table 4.1 shows the number of students and average expenditures per pupil for each Australian state. Victoria is the second largest and spends just a bit more than the Australian average expenditure per pupil.

Two important additional aspects of Australian and Victorian school finance are not indicated in the table. First, each state tends to spend considerably more on secondary than on primary schools. The differential in Victoria is approximately 45 percent. Second, a significant portion of students attend nongovernment church-related or independent schools; the average is about 29 percent across Australia and close to 33 percent in Victoria. Further, the federal government provides aid to nongovernment schools. The aid varies according to a twelve-category factor based on need and ranges from $200 to $774 (Australian) per primary pupil and $300 to $1,131 per secondary pupil.

TABLE 4.1. STUDENTS AND EXPENDITURES IN AUSTRALIA, 1993–94 (AUSTRALIAN DOLLARS).

State	Students	Expenditure per Pupil ($)	Total Expenditure ($)
New South Wales	755,771	$3676	$2,778,214,196
Victoria	520,328	3855	2,005,864,440
Queensland	403,234	3556	1,433,900,104
Western Australia	223,105	3794	846,460,370
South Australia	181,640	4369	793,585,160
Tasmania	64,061	3911	250,542,571
Australian Capital Territory	39,865	4235	168,828,275
Northern Territory	26,934	5596	150,722,664
Australia	2,214,938	3806	8,430,054,028

Note: $1.00 Australian = approximately $0.80 U.S.

Source: Data from Ministerial Council on Education, Employment, Training and Youth Affairs, 1996, p. 36.

The Global Budget

As shown by the data in Table 4.2, Victoria has devolved the bulk of recurrent funding for government primary and secondary schools to the school site. Of the total expenditure of just over $1 billion for 1996, fully 86.7 percent was budgeted to the school site in the global budget. Only 5.3 percent of the total was spend on central administration, which included the salaries of the state and six regional offices, associated administration and office costs, and a proportion of the operating costs for the Victorian Board of Studies, which is a statutory body responsible for setting curriculum standards for all students in government and nongovernment schools in all years of schooling and for assessment and certification of all students in years 11 and 12 and now years 3, 5, and 10 as well.

Exclusions represent costs spent on school-level activities but under the control of the center and not the school site. Exclusions comprised 8 percent of the recurrent budget and included such items as student home-to-school transportation (actually the responsibility of the transportation department), assistance to poor families for the costs of such school items as uniforms and books, salary costs for teachers on long-term leave, and support services such as speech therapists and psychologists who serve more than one school.

The resultant global school budget represented 86.7 percent of total operating components. It had six major categories: (1) core funding, the largest portion,

TABLE 4.2. EDUCATION FUNDING AND THE GLOBAL SCHOOL BUDGET IN VICTORIA, 1996 (AUSTRALIAN DOLLARS).

Expenditure Category	Amount ($ millions)	Share of Total (percent)
Total recurrent funding for government schools	$1,020.0	100.0%
Nonschool expenditures Administration	54.0	5.3
School-level expenditures	966.0	94.7
Exclusions	82.5	8.0
School global budget	885.0	86.7
Core funding	739.5	72.5
Premises	55.5	5.4
Disabled students	31.5	3.1
Special learning needs	12.0	1.2
Non-English-speaking backgrounds	13.5	1.4
Rurality and isolation	8.0	0.9
Priority programs	24.0	2.3

Note: $1.00 Australian = approximately $0.80 U.S.

Source: Caldwell and Hill, 1996.

comprising 72.5 percent of all operating funds and 84 percent of the global budget; (2) disabilities and impairment, which is funding for the disabled; (3) students with special learning needs, which is similar to compensatory education in the United States; (4) students from non-English-speaking backgrounds; (5) adjustments for rural and isolated schools; and (6) categorical programs from both the state and federal governments, called priority programs. By 1996, nearly 90 percent of all funds appropriated for school education in Victoria was budgeted to the school site (Caldwell and others, 1996).

Core Funding

Core funding was the largest component of the budget. In 1996, core funding had four separate components: teaching and administrative staff, instructional and administrative support, benefits, and operations and maintenance, called premises support. For 1997, premises was separated from core funding and provided as an additional school budget element.

Teaching and Administrative Staff. For 1995 and 1996, Victoria provided each school with a staffing and administrative allocation for the teaching and administrative functions for each school. As will be discussed later, the state is considering switching to a dollar-per-weighted-pupil funding formula, but during the first years of implementing the school-based budgeting strategy, it provided this component of the budget via a staffing formula.

The same general formula structure was used for both primary and secondary schools, but secondary schools were allocated higher levels of staff. Primary schools were allotted one teacher position for every twenty-one students. Secondary schools were allowed one teacher position for every sixteen students, in addition to a base staff of four. Adjustments in these staffing allowances were made for schools with small enrollments, below two hundred students for primary schools and below five hundred students for secondary students.

Each school was also given an additional amount so that 30 percent of its teachers could be placed in leadership positions, at principal class Levels 2 and 3 of the state's new teacher compensation structure. Of this 30 percent, half, or 15 percent, of teacher slots were funded at Level 3 of the principal class, and half at Level 2. To formally elevate teachers into leadership roles, schools were required to have a minimum of 25 percent and a maximum of 35 percent of their teacher positions in these leadership classes; any funds saved by placing fewer than 30 percent of teachers into leadership positions could be used for any other purpose. In addition, the budget provided an extra $600 for special-duties payments for each teacher and an extra $200 for recognition incentives, again for each teacher. Finally, an amount of $148 per day for seven days was provided for each teacher to pay for substitute teachers.

Within these parameters, schools were given complete authority to "tag" their teaching slots for the staffing arrangement and structure they selected for their school. Nearly every school selected a principal to fill one of the teaching slots. Schools could allocate the rest of their teaching slots to any combination of regular classroom teachers, specialist teachers (teaching art, music, computer technology, or reading or serving as librarian), and pupil support professionals. By providing schools with a number of undesignated teacher slots, the state was not signaling any particular school staffing structure; it was merely providing each school with the numbers of its core staff and encouraging each school to staff itself according to its own selected educational strategy.

Schools could easily convert staffing slots to budget figures. Indeed, for 1996, each teacher position was worth $39,000 on average. Schools could "cash in" their teaching positions for dollars that would be used to meet other education-related needs for the school. In this way, the staffing allotment was mathematically quite similar to a per-pupil funding formula. The primary reason the state used this strategy was because that was the way schools had been resourced before the Schools of the Future program was implemented. Continuing that strategy and also allowing schools to trade teaching slots for cash provided a way to move to school-based funding without radically changing the school budgeting process. As we shall see, however, Victoria is considering changing to a per-pupil funding system for the 1998 academic year.

An important additional point is that on the expenditure side, each school was charged only for the average teacher salary in the state, which was $39,000 for 1996. Although there were different mixes of teacher experience across schools, and thus different average salaries, the state nevertheless decided to charge only for the average salary, a practice that had been used in Edmonton, Canada, a school system that had been implementing school-based budgeting for several years (Caldwell and Spinks, 1992). This policy also was under debate in late 1996, with advocates recommending a gradual transition to charging for the actual teacher's salary, thus requiring each school to manage its mix of teachers and their actual salaries.

Staffing Flexibility. Although the goal was to provide each school with a staffing allotment that could be converted to a lump sum of dollars, several items in the global budget were actually provided as staff "credits." But during the first three years of implementation, schools that wanted either to "trade in" some of these credits for cash to be used for other purposes or to spend some cash items on locally identified needs had to obtain approval for staffing "flexibility." But by early 1996, only about 250 of Victoria's schools had been given full staffing flexibility. As a result, many schools had considerable constraints placed on their use of the teaching slots in their global budget.

The major reason so few schools had staffing flexibility was that when Victoria committed to reducing its teaching staff, it sought not to fire any teacher and not to force any teacher out of the system. First, the state offered a quite attractive early retirement package that many teachers took advantage of. But many "excess" teachers remained in the system. Victoria then required that new hires at any school be taken from a list of "excess" teachers. In 1994 and 1995, the state department of education also created a cadre of substitute teachers (classroom replacement teachers) that comprised another group of excess teachers. Any teachers still in excess were paid by the state and remained at their school, as teachers over and above the regular allotment.

In 1996, the state shifted financial responsibility for all excess teachers to each school site. Although this relieved the state of the financial burden of "carrying" excess teachers, it significantly strained the global budgets of schools with excess teachers. Schools without staffing flexibility were required to continue to recruit for new positions from the excess teacher list. Further, to receive full staffing flexibility, which allowed a school to recruit statewide and to spend its global budget as it saw fit to meet local needs, schools had to submit a workforce plan that showed that they could financially cover any teacher who was on leave and might decide to return to the school (in part as a protection against declining enrollments). The workforce plan also had to show that no more than 70 percent of their teachers were under a currently valid full-time contract.

Needless to say, these personnel transition constraints caused considerable consternation at the school level. Schools with or near staffing flexibility were able to enjoy both the staffing and the financial freedoms envisioned by the Schools of the Future program. Those that did not have staffing flexibility were significantly constrained and quite unhappy about those constraints. One lesson learned is that it takes more than three or four years to fully phase in a school-based financing system that provides sites with complete flexibility over staffing.

In late 1996, hoping to eliminate the frustrations associated with the staffing constraints, the state department of education decided to provide all schools with staffing flexibility beginning with the 1997 school year. To do so, it redistributed all remaining "excess" teachers evenly across schools without staffing flexibility and augmented those schools' budgets to cover the salary costs. The budget augmentation was reduced as natural teacher attrition occurred; the goal was to have all schools at the normal staffing level by the 1997 or 1998 school year.

Instructional and Clerical Support. Instructional and clerical support, called teaching support, covered instructional assistants, office support such as clerical staff and bursars, other administrative positions, and instructional materials and related costs. Prior to 1996, these costs, a relatively small portion of the school budget, were funded through numerous and complicated formulas (Department of School Education, 1994). In 1995, however, a school finance task force recommended that these many formulas be combined into one per-pupil formula (Education Committee, 1995). Thus in 1996, this category was funded in a more straightforward manner: $280 per child for primary schools and $470 per child for secondary schools.

Benefits. A common benefit rate, known as "on costs," was added to dollar amounts for salaries. Further, when schools "traded" staffing slots for cash, they received not only the salary equivalent but the benefits dollar equivalents as well.

Premises Support. A common set of formulas based on the number of buildings on a site, the average size of the building and land area, and the number of students in the school was used to provide funds for premises support, or operation and maintenance expenditures. The formulas were also sensitive to the condition of each school site. For example, the formula for minor facilities maintenance was based 50 percent on the land area, 25 percent on the type of material used to construct the building, and 25 percent on the condition of the physical plant. For some formulas, there were a variety of small size, rurality, and isolation adjustments. This became an important funding adjustment, from the school perspective, because Victoria has numerous very small schools.

Special Student Needs

There were three major funding categories for special student needs: students with special learning needs (SLN) (the equivalent of U.S. compensatory education), students from non-English-speaking backgrounds (NESB), similar to limited-English-proficient students, and students with disabilities and impairments (D&I).

Students with Special Learning Needs. In the past, the SLN category included a number of different state (Victoria) and federal programs, focused mainly on low-income students. For 1996, nearly all of these state and federal programs were combined into one new approach. A new SLN index was created for each school, the goal being to identify schools that had the largest concentration of students at risk of failing to meet national standards in reading. The index was developed by regressing student achievement on several demographic characteristics including proportion of students from families receiving an educational maintenance allowance (a poverty measure), proportion from families speaking a language other than English, proportion who had changed schools recently (known as "transiency"), and proportion of Koorie (aboriginal) students. The results were used to determine an index that identified schools with concentrations of students at risk of not achieving proficiency. All variables were weighted equally, except for speaking a foreign language at home, which was weighted 50 percent extra. Thus a school with 80 percent of students receiving educational maintenance, 50 percent from a non-English-speaking background, 10 percent Koorie, and 15 percent transient would have an SLN index of $0.80 + 0.50(0.50) + 0.10 + 0.15 = 1.30$.

The SLN funding structure provided financial assistance to the schools most in need of such help. Only schools with an SLN index above a threshold of 0.48 were eligible for SLN funding. The funding equaled the school index minus the threshold times the school's enrollment times $457. In other words, the school in our example received the following amount: $457 times (1.30 minus 0.48) times the school enrollment, or $375 extra for each student in the school. The SLN index formula concentrated financial assistance in the most needy schools. In addition, SLN funding in 1996 included an extra $20 for each primary school child; the funds were to be used to ensure that all students entered grade 3 reading at the required levels in the Curriculum and Standards Frameworks.

Students Learning English. The NESB category provided funds for both multi-cultural educational aides and for teachers to provide instruction in English as a Second Language (ESL) and other needed services. Funding for each student reflected the number of years the family had lived in Australia (under two years, two to five years, five to seven years), with greater funding going to schools with newer immigrants and with NESB students in the upper primary and secondary grades.

Disabled Students. D&I funding was provided for students with disabilities, who were placed in six different levels according to the additional resources needed for their specific needs; the extra dollar amounts at the six levels were $2,348, $5,460, $8,588, $11,723, $14,835 and $17,963. The state also supported several state-run schools for the disabled, but these were funded according to special criteria.

Rurality and Isolation

Although most students in Victoria attend schools in metropolitan areas, primarily surrounding Melbourne, the state also has numerous schools in rural and isolated locations. The school formula has a substantial rurality and isolation factor to address the higher costs related to curriculum provision, administration, and access to student support services that schools in rural and isolated areas face. The rurality and isolation factor adjustment includes a location index that is calculated on the basis of the following three conditions: (1) distance in kilometers from the Melbourne metropolitan area, (2) distance from the nearest provincial center with more than 20,000 population, and (3) distance from the nearest primary or secondary school, as appropriate, that is not eligible for funding as a rural or isolated school. The additional aid is then equal to $182 + (location index times student enrollment times $24).

Small schools in rural areas also receive an adjustment to their core funding. Like the adjustment for staff funding, this adjustment is provided to primary schools with an enrollment below two hundred and to secondary schools with an enrollment below five hundred students.

State and Federal Categorical Programs

Finally, there were several state and federal priority (categorical) program categories, including such issues as instrumental music, Koorie teacher aides, gender equity programs, science, technology, physical and sport education (a new Victorian priority), and language other than English (LOTE). LOTE was important because the Victorian government recently required that all students learn a language other than English. However, this program became something of a problem for many schools for two reasons. First, there were an insufficient number of teachers who spoke a second language, so it was hard to staff schools with teachers who could teach a LOTE. Second, schools with students speaking twenty or more different languages were required to teach a LOTE that was different from any of those native languages, thus requiring NESB students not only to learn English but concurrently to learn a third language as well. Many observers questioned the wisdom of this policy, believing that educating such students to proficiency in English should have been a higher priority.

Additional Factors

As mentioned earlier, in 1995, Victoria began providing to each school an extra $240 per teacher for professional development. Although this represented a smaller investment in state-funded professional development than prior to 1993, it was a welcome addition when provided in 1995, the same year the state required schools to implement more rigorous curriculum content and student performance standards (Odden and Odden, 1996b).

Each school was allowed to raise funds locally. Nearly all schools engaged in a wide array of fundraising activities that included charging parents voluntary fees (from $30 to $350 per child) for books and instructional materials, fundraisers and fairs, net receipts from running the student cafeteria, rental of the facilities to community and other groups, and contributions from the local community including local businesses. On average, the total of locally raised funds was significantly below 10 percent of the overall global budget, although economically advantaged communities tended to raise more such funds, including voluntary parent contributions, than schools in economically depressed locales.

Implementation of the Global Budget in 1996

Odden and Odden (1996a, 1996b) have conducted extensive qualitative analyses of the local implementation of Schools of the Future. Here we briefly summarize the major features of local response to the global budget described more fully in Odden and Odden (1996b). Schools generally, and particularly primary principals, strongly supported the budgetary power provided under Schools of the Future. Indeed, even in the first two years of the program's implementation, when schools had only partial control of their budgets, principals embraced the levels of budgetary authority that had been devolved at that time. This section reports on findings for primary schools studied in 1996, as that was the first year in which the full lump-sum global budget was provided and the new teacher compensation program was implemented.

The Core

Principals generally supported the way the global budget distributed dollars to each school and its providing the dollars in a lump sum. Principals felt that the elements in the new core formula were "transparent"—they understood how the formula worked and why different schools received different levels of funding. The major problem identified by primary school principals was the difference in staffing and therefore funding between primary and secondary schools: they agreed that the differences should be reduced, not by decreasing secondary school funding but by increasing primary school funding.

Special-Needs Funding

All schools studied had many students with special needs. Although principals suggested that the special-needs portions of the global budget needed higher funding levels, they generally supported the three categories of D&I, SLN, and NESB—including their ability to use the extra funds in ways they deemed best for the students in their schools.

Each school had a few D&I students, and the principals expressed no criticism of the amount of funding provided once it was received. However, some principals had difficulty getting the state to approve students as D&I. Principals generally supported the new SLN index used to distribute what we in the United States would call compensatory education money. They felt that using characteristics of students rather than using sociodemographic characteristics of communities, the earlier practice, made the formula more accurate in identifying school needs. They also supported the elements that had been used in constructing the SLN index; student mobility was specifically mentioned by principals of schools with a significant number of transient students. Principals also supported elimination of the previous $120,000 cap in SLN funding, as the new formulas allowed the amount of money to rise to whatever level was appropriate for a given school. There was limited understanding of the "threshold" aspect of the formula, which funneled SLN funds into schools with the highest concentration of SLN students.

Several comments were made about inadequate funding of the LOTE program. Many of the schools had diligently sought to add a foreign-language program but had run into funding and personnel shortfalls. Although the principals understood the problems, they suggested that the state mandate to teach LOTE may have been premature and promulgated before there were adequate personnel or financial resources to support complete implementation.

Principals also approved of separating the special-needs funds for the disabled, students with special learning needs, and students from non-English-speaking backgrounds. Principals said that these categories sent a message to schools that the different needs of these three categories of students should be assessed separately and matched with appropriate site resource allocation. Although principals appreciated the funding flexibility the global budget provided even for these dollars (there were no audit requirements to spend those dollars on the eligible students), they still said that by providing the dollars according to three separate formulas, the state highlighted the need for schools to understand the special educational circumstances of these three categories of students.

Professional Development

There was strong, universal praise for the $240 per teacher in professional development funds. Most schools were involved in creating professional development plans for their school and for each of their teachers and had budgeted funds from their global budget for professional development, but they had not been able to budget sufficient local funds to finance all desired activities. The state professional development grant allowed schools to proceed in a more comprehensive way in implementing what they considered a core school function. One principal stated that the funds helped his school sustain a culture that supported ongoing professional development.

Staffing Flexibility

Only one of the schools we studied had received full staffing flexibility. Two of the schools were close to being granted such flexibility, and one school was far from gaining flexibility and was still funding excess teachers. Not surprisingly, the first three schools had already begun to engage in resource reallocation and to spend their global budget in ways different from past practice. The school without staffing flexibility was simply unable to engage in substantial budgeting changes. Chafing under its constraints, this school had minimal discretionary funds left after paying its excess teachers. The school was also upset at what it considered conflicting messages from the state department of education about staffing flexibility and the financing of excess teachers. Its principal was wary of staffing flexibility and greater freedom in spending the budget because of concern that school council pressure could result in significantly lower expenditures for teacher staffing.

The two schools that were close to staffing flexibility had also experienced some staff turnover, which provided opportunities for implementing budget changes even within the constraints of not having full staffing flexibility. One school had recruited three new teachers and, after vociferous pleading by the principal, was required to hire just one new teacher from the "excess" list. But both schools were cognizant of the additional freedoms they would enjoy with full staffing flexibility and were in the final processes of submitting their official request for that status. Their regional general managers, through whom the request was submitted to the state department of education, had reviewed their documents and had given strong indications that the applications would be approved. Thus the schools knew that the constraints they faced in the near term would probably soon be alleviated.

Evidence of Resource Reallocation

Principals identified numerous examples of how their schools had taken advantage of their budget freedoms to reallocate resources. Each school had identified several priorities and numerous examples of how they were able to reallocate their budget to the school's identified priorities:

- Certain primary schools had taken funds from several areas to strengthen their early literacy program. These schools used the funds to hire Reading Recovery teachers, instructional aides to provide remedial reading instruction, and instructional materials.
- Several schools combined the extra funds for the teacher leadership positions and the special payments funds and used them to expand the number of teacher leadership positions. The common goal was to have more teachers in formal leadership roles.
- One school created extra funding by replacing a teacher who had been a librarian with a lower-paid librarian technician while simultaneously automating the library.
- Nearly all schools also found increasing amounts of money in their budgets for professional development, beyond the $240-per-teacher state grant, as well as for purchasing computers and related technologies.
- During the first three years of implementing Schools of the Future, most schools also invested funds in their physical plant, providing long-overdue renovations.

In short, we found several specific instances of resource reallocation in the schools we visited and also at least two different instances in each school studied.

These results suggest that schools were taking advantage of the budget flexibility embodied in the vision of Schools of the Future and the global budget and were tailoring their resource use to perceived school needs. Most encouraging, the main focus of primary school resource reallocation in 1996 was on a priority education need: early literacy. Schools tried to hire at least one and sometimes two Reading Recovery tutors to help ensure that all children reached grade 3 performing at proficiency in literacy, in the belief that intensive early intervention with tutoring was the most effective strategy in accomplishing this goal. The other foci of resource reallocation—computers, leadership development, and overall professional development—were equally encouraging.

Recommendations for Change in Calculating the Global Budget

In 1994, the minister of education in Victoria set up an education committee to analyze the global budget that was being used to determine the budget for each school site, to monitor implementation in 1995 and 1996, and to make recommendations for system improvements. The committee was asked to analyze the potential for shifting from determining the global budget through a staffing allocation to a more straightforward dollar-per-weighted-pupil formula.

In its interim and final reports, the Education Committee (1995; Caldwell and others, 1996) proposed that eight key principles should guide development and use of the school-budgeting formula:

1. *Preeminence of educational considerations:* Educational considerations should be the most important in determining the factors and their relative weightings that ought to be in the school budget formula.
2. *Effectiveness:* Relativities among primary and secondary school allocations in the school global budget should reflect knowledge about school and classroom effectiveness.
3. *Efficiency:* Allocations in the school global budget should reflect knowledge about the most cost-effective ways of achieving desired outcomes in schooling.
4. *Fairness:* Schools with the same mix of learning needs should receive the same total per-pupil resources in the school global budget.
5. *Transparency:* The basis for allocations in the school global budget should be clear and readily understandable by everyone with an interest in the budget, and the basis for allocating resources to each and every school should be made public.
6. *Subsidiarity:* Decisions on resource allocation should be made centrally only if they cannot be made locally. Items of expenditure should be excluded from

the school global budget only if schools do not control expenditures, if there is excessive variation of expenditure, if expenditure patterns are unpredictable, if expenditures are one-time, or if schools are mere payment conduits.

7. *Accountability:* A school that receives resources because it has students with a certain mix of learning needs has the responsibility to provide programs to meet those needs, has the authority to make decisions on how those resources will be allocated, and should be held accountable for the use of those resources, including outcomes in relation to student learning.

8. *Strategic implementation:* When new funding arrangements are indicated, they should be implemented progressively over several years to eliminate dramatic changes in the funding levels of schools from one year to another.

The committee spent the bulk of its time seeking to determine how to structure the formula in a way that actually made educational considerations pre-eminent. The clearest implication of that principle was that the extant differences between primary and secondary school funding, about 45 percent on average, had to change. To ascertain how the changes should be determined, the committee sought to identify the most effective school practices at three different stages of schooling: kindergarten to grade 4, the middle school years of grades 5 through 8, and the high school years of grades 9 through 12. They sought to determine best practices through a review of the literature on these stages of learning in Australia, England, and the United States; an analysis of effective school practices at these stages in Victoria; and a series of consultations with the leading educational researchers and practitioners in Victoria.

The committee then linked its conclusions about best practices to the relative differences in resources needed in these different stages of learning. The goal was to link the calculation of each school's budget to the resources needed to teach its students to the standards specified in the state's Curriculum and Standards Framework. Thus rather than just identifying effective practices and resource differences for the two types of Victorian schools—primary and secondary—the committee identified a more detailed set of best practices that matched these three different stages of learning. The following summarizes the conclusions the Education Committee reached about effective educational practices and their implications for the funding formula.

For *kindergarten and grades 1 and 2,* the committee concluded that the key issue was literacy and the need for all students to learn how to read well. For reading and writing classes, resource requirements related to the need for smaller student groupings and the need for accurate and early diagnosis of reading and writing problems and other learning needs, in particular allowing for implementation of an appropriate early childhood education curriculum (Blachford and Mortimore,

1994). The committee suggested that every school use some version of a Success for All/Reading Recovery program that included one-to-one tutoring for students not reading at proficiency (Pikulski, 1994; Slavin and others, 1996; Wasik and Slavin, 1993). For the average school, this required resources for a full-time reading tutor, a school facilitator for the early literacy program, and reduced class sizes for the daily ninety-minute language arts instruction. For most schools, the smaller class sizes for the language arts period could be produced by having the reading tutors, literacy coordinator, and even other specialist staff teach reading. To produce the extra resources for the tutor and facilitator, the committee recommended a 20 percent increase in resources for each kindergarten child, a 30 percent increase for each first-grade student, and a 10 percent increase for students in grade 2. Schools with larger concentrations of students at risk of reading failure, usually indicated by poverty concentration, would receive additional resources for a potential second, third, and fourth tutor through the SLN program.

Grades 3 and 4 became the referent with a relative weighting of 1.0.

The committee reviewed the literature on *schooling for young adolescents (generally grade 5 or 6 to grade 8)* and concluded that the middle school design seemed to produce the best results (Braddock and McPartland, 1993; George and Shewey, 1994; Lee and Smith, 1993). This approach requires, among other things, student assignment to teachers for at least two years, allowing teachers and students to develop longer-term relationships and help reduce adolescent alienation in school; an interdisciplinary team organization for teachers; more teacher planning time; flexible scheduling, often in a block-schedule format; a curriculum emphasizing balanced exploration and solid academics; and other appropriate middle school activities. The committee identified these key elements in many of the best Victorian middle school programs. Although the specific ways in which these principles were implemented varied among Victorian schools, suggesting that there was no best way to structure a good middle school, the committee concluded that the major aspect of more effective middle school programs was "interdisciplinary teams of teachers working with as few students as possible in as many subjects as possible" (Caldwell and others, 1996, p. 37).

To provide this type of program, including some of the nonacademic elective courses typically offered in middle schools, the committee concluded, dependent on results from ongoing research, that grades 5 through 8 might need a 20 percent higher resource level compared to the referent grade 4. The committee also concluded that resourcing across the middle school grades was generally quite similar, with minimal differences between grade 8 and grade 5. Thus the committee recommended that the long-term goal should be to fund grades 5 and 8 at about the same levels, and closer to 20 percent rather than 45 percent above grade 4.

The Education Committee's recommendation for the *upper secondary grades 9 through 12* tended to reflect the particular structure and emphases of Victorian education at those grade levels. The state had invested considerable effort and resources into grades 11 and 12, had required each secondary school to provide a series of rigorous academic classes including many advanced classes, and had required schools to administer a common set of assessment and academic tasks that students needed to complete to earn the important Victorian Certificate of Education (essentially the high school diploma). At these levels, class sizes were substantially smaller, and support services and investments in technology and equipment were substantially higher. The result was that resourcing was significantly higher.

Table 4.3 indicates the current weightings in the Victorian funding structure and the changes that the Education Committee recommended in December 1996. Three features of the table need to be noted. First, the proposed new weightings are more detailed than the current system and reduce the current 40 percent differential between grade 6 and grade 7. Second, the proposed new weightings are connected to the three different stages of schooling and the six different bands of the state's Curriculum and Standards Framework. Third, the committee hoped that by having schools increase retention in grades 11 and 12 and use other strategies to reduce the inefficiencies (very small classes) in providing the grade 11 and 12 VCE curriculum, the grade 9–12 weights could be reduced further, thus allowing the system to reallocate some resources from secondary to primary schools.

In this way, the committee attempted to connect key elements of the funding structure directly to the educational goals of the system, a practices-funding link that few states have ever tried in such an ambitious way. Although one could disagree with some of the conclusions the committee reached about effective practices at different levels of schooling, the important fact about the committee's approach was its serious effort to determine funding differentials by identifying best educational practices and their relative costs.

Two other points should be made about the foregoing recommendations. One is that the committee proposed that the weightings be used for a dollar-per-weighted-pupil funding structure, one that would replace the staffing element of the core funding formula Victoria used in 1996. If adopted, this would mean the state would need to identify the dollar amount for the base student at grades 3 and 4, and then that amount, together with the weights and the number of students at each stage of learning, would determine core funding for all schools. Second, although the proposed weights were developed and rationalized on understandings of best practices at different schooling levels, the committee did not recommend that schools be required to spend funds in those proportions. The committee expected that schools, especially secondary schools, would expend funds in rough proportion to the weights but stated that the formula should be used only

TABLE 4.3. CURRENT AND PROPOSED WEIGHTS FOR SCHOOL FUNDING IN VICTORIA.

Grade Level	Current School Level	Current Funding Weight	Stage of Learning	Band in the Curriculum and Standards Frameworks	Proposed Funding Weight
Kindergarten	Primary	1.0	Primary	1	1.2
1	Primary	1.0	Primary	1	1.3
2	Primary	1.0	Primary	2	1.1
3	Primary	1.0	Primary	2	1.0
4	Primary	1.0	Primary	2	1.0
5	Primary	1.0	Middle	3	1.2
6	Primary	1.0	Middle	3	1.2
7	Secondary	1.4	Middle	4	1.2
8	Secondary	1.4	Middle	4	1.2
9	Secondary	1.4	Secondary	5	1.5
10	Secondary	1.4	Secondary	5	1.5
11	Secondary	1.4	Secondary	6	1.8
12	Secondary	1.4	Secondary	6	1.9

to budget dollars to the schools and that the state should hold schools accountable for producing student achievement to the desired standards, not for spending money in any predetermined pattern.

If adopted and with a base 1.0 student grant of \$2,500, a primary school with 350 students (50 students in each of grades K–6) and 68 percent of its students at risk of achieving below proficiency would receive the following budget:

$$\$2,500[50(1.2) + 50(1.3) + 50(1.1) + 100(1.0) + 1.2(100)]$$
$$+ \$457(0.68 - 0.48)(350)$$
$$= \$2,500(60 + 65 + 55 + 100 + 120) + \$457(0.20)(350)$$
$$= \$2,500(400) + \$457(70)$$
$$= \$1,000,000 + \$31,990$$
$$= \$1,031,990, \text{ plus extra amounts for premises, ESL and disabled students,}$$
rurality and isolation, and federal and state categorical programs

With the same base 1.0 student grant of \$2,500, a secondary school of twice the size with 700 students (117 students in each of grades 7–12) and 68 percent of its students at risk of achieving below proficiency would receive the following budget:

$$\$2,500[234(1.2) + 234(1.5) + 117(1.8) + 117(1.9)] + \$457(0.68 - 0.48)(700)$$
$$= \$2,500(280.8 + 351.0 + 210.6 + 222.3) + \$457(0.20)(700)$$
$$= \$2,500(1064.7) + \$457(140)$$
$$= \$2,661,750 + \$63,980$$
$$= \$2,725,730, \text{ plus extra amounts for premises, ESL and disabled students,}$$

rurality and isolation, and federal and state categorical programs

Note that for the core funding, this would have reduced the current secondary-primary differential from a formal 40 percent and actual 45 percent to 33 percent, a smaller differential that is within the range of U.S. high school versus elementary school spending differentials (Odden and Picus, 1992).

Finally, the Education Committee also appeared to be moving in the direction of recommending that Victoria begin phasing in a policy of charging schools for actual teacher salaries. There were three reasons for this recommendation. First, it recognized that by charging the average teacher salary, the state was resourcing some schools at higher levels than others. Second, it acknowledged that especially with ongoing professional development, more senior teachers were more skilled than less experienced teachers, thus advantaging schools with larger percentages of more experienced teachers. Third, providing schools with an actual dollar budget but not charging for actual teacher salaries introduced unnecessary confusion into local budget management, one set of books for actual costs and another set for charged costs. Thus the committee believed that a gradual five- to seven-year shift to charging schools for actual teacher salaries would be an additional improvement to the Victorian school finance structure.

Conclusions

The Victorian Schools of the Future program shows that a school-based funding system can be designed and implemented and that with appropriate training, schools can quickly learn how to manage their fiscal affairs. Indeed, no instance of fraudulent spending occurred at the seventeen hundred school sites in Victoria during the first three years of implementation of the decentralized financing system, and thanks to centralized and computerized controls on total spending, no school overspent its budget or sank into bankruptcy. Further, as noted, when schools received their budget in a lump sum, they spent the dollars in different ways. Finally,

Victorian principals and even most teachers strongly supported local management of schools, including local management of their budget (Cooperative Research Project, 1995, 1996; Levacic, 1995; Thomas and Martin, 1996). Whatever opinions individuals might hold before devolution of the budget, after experiencing receipt of the budget dollars and using those opportunities to make financial decisions and to deploy resources to identified school needs, strong support for budget devolution tends to emerge. Yes, principals reported that their workloads rose (Cooperative Research Project, 1995, 1996), but they felt the extra effort was worthwhile for they were able to make their own school spending decisions.

CHAPTER FIVE

SCHOOL-BASED FINANCING IN ENGLAND

This chapter describes the school-based financing system that has been used in England since their education reforms in 1988. We studied England because it is comparable to a large U.S. state. It has a population of 49 million and a student population of 8 million in government schools. Education is provided through local education authorities (LEAs), which function much like school districts in the United States, although the English LEAs are larger and fiscally dependent on local government authorities. (The present 109 LEAs are scheduled to increase to 119 in 1996–97 and 132 in 1997–98 as the size of certain large LEAs is reduced.) The relationship between England and its LEAs can be reasonably compared to American states and school districts—especially fiscally dependent school districts, as in New York City or in the southern United States. Further, although England has changed its education funding policies to ensure that most funds are budgeted in a lump sum to the school site, it has done so through the LEAs. Thus England represents a state-to-district-to-site financing strategy, the type of strategy that would likely have to be implemented in all U.S. states (except Hawaii) if decentralized education funding to the schools were to be widely adopted.

In addition, there is an integral relationship between the school financing changes in England and the programmatic education reforms of 1988 that make the combined policies quite similar to a fully designed and implemented version of standards-based reforms. The 1988 English education reforms included a national curriculum, a performance-based testing system linked to the national curriculum, student choice of school, and local management of schools (LMS) that decentralized the bulk of the budget to school sites and provided schools with the authority to recruit and select staff (Levacic, 1995; Thomas and Martin, 1996).

The 1988 education reforms also created an even more aggressive form of school decentralization, called grant-maintained (GM) schools. To become grant-maintained, a school, through a vote of its local site council and parents, may decide to "opt out" of the LEA system and become quasi-independent. The proposal is submitted to the LEA for comment, and the case is forwarded to the secretary of state, who subsequently decides whether the school may become grant-maintained. Even if the school is granted GM status, it remains technically a government school. At that time, GM schools receive 100 percent of their site budget. Beginning in 1994, GM school funding was provided through a new entity called the Funding Agency for Schools (FAS), which essentially created a state-to-site funding system. Since the level of GM school funding is still linked to the LEA in which it is located and since there are some differences in per-pupil spending across LEAs, GM school funding has created several equity issues about differences in school funding when numbers and characteristics of students are similar.

All of these developments make the English approach to school-based financing well worth understanding as states and districts move toward designing U.S. approaches to school-based financing. The remainder of the chapter describes and discusses the English approach to financing schools, primarily the LEA-affiliated schools. First we review national policies for funding education, including the English state-level policies both for equalizing the ability to fund education (as well as all local services) across local government authorities and for budgeting funds to each school site. Then we describe in detail how four diverse LEAs have transformed these general requirements into more specific policies and procedures for funding each of their schools. Next we summarize perspectives on the funding systems as articulated by primary and secondary "headteachers" and their budget officers who were interviewed as part of this research. This discussion also includes findings from several other larger research projects on the impacts on schools of the decentralized finance structures. Finally, we identify lessons that can be learned from the English education finance reform experience, with specific implications for designing a school-based funding system in the United States. For interested readers, Appendix 5.1 describes the mechanisms for financing GM schools, similar to U.S. charter schools, and how those policies have evolved over the past several years.

The Central Government's Role in Funding Local Education Authorities

In England, most local services, including education, are provided by local government authorities; each local government has within it a fiscally dependent, local education authority (LEA) through which education services are provided. Historically, the funding of local services has been shared by central government taxes and local taxes, exclusively local domestic property taxes. As in most countries, including the United States, the ability to raise local taxes varies among local government entities. As a result, over the years, the central English government has sought to "equalize" the ability of local governments to finance these services. The general strategy has been to provide a fiscal equalization grant based on expenditure need for each local service function minus the yield from a uniformly applied tax rate on the local tax base; technically, the central government equalization aid is provided as one overall grant, but it is determined through a separate calculation of need for each local service function, called a standard spending assessment (SSA).

Until recently, the central government equalizing strategies helped reduce but did not eliminate spending variations across local government authorities; indeed, fifteen years ago, local resources still comprised nearly 50 percent of local government funding, resulting in sizable differences in local government per capita spending. But today, through a variety of mechanisms, including an increase in the central role, a decrease in the local role, and caps on local spending and spending increases, the central role in local government financing has risen to about 80 percent and the local role has dropped to about 20 percent. Further, through related changes in how the central government provides aid for each of the local service functions, the differences in spending per capita and on many specific functions, including education, have been reduced significantly. Thus one major state element of English school finance is the equalization system for central financing of local education services.

As stated earlier, the 1988 education reforms included requirements for LEAs to send the bulk of their funding in a lump sum to each school site. The legislation required the Department for Education and Employment (DFEE, formerly the Department of Education) to create a set of policy regulations that would provide the macro structure for the LEA fiscal devolution. Thus the second major state element of English school finance is the central government policy umbrella for the LEA school funding systems. Let us examine these two key central government roles.

The Standard Spending Assessment

Similar to an American state, England's central government provides education equalization aid to each local authority through a formula using an education standard spending assessment as the measurement of need. England calculates SSAs for all local service areas, including social services, capital spending, housing, and highways. Education is the largest service bloc. In fact, education represents over 44 percent of all central funding for local services (Hale, 1996).

The sum of all the various service area SSAs is called the general government revenue grant. This "grand total" is the amount that the central government identifies as the expenditure need for all individual service areas, using a common approach to calculating need. The actual amount of the grant is determined by the grand total of all the SSAs minus the proceeds from a national uniform tax rate on business (nonresidential, non–individually owned properties) and the central government's assessment of the local authority's tax proceeds (termed council tax).

In addition to the general revenue grant, local government authorities may raise extra revenues by levying a separate and smaller tax on residential property. However, these local taxes have been severely limited by the central government. Today, the secretary of state caps local property taxes at two different tiers of higher spending: (1) local authorities spending over their SSA but under 12.5 percent, and (2) local authorities spending more than 12.5 percent above their SSA (Hale, 1996). In the first tier, a local authority's increase in local property taxes may not exceed the annual increase in the local authority's general government revenue grant *or* a percentage increase ranging from 0.5 percent to 3 percent, depending on the type of authority (shire district, inner London borough, and so on), whichever is greater. Local authorities in the second tier are not allowed increases above their previous year's budget requirement. Thus local property taxes may serve to disequalize funding across English local government authorities, but the amount of such funding is so restricted that the inequities from local taxation are unlikely to be severe.

The SSAs allocated as revenue to local government authorities for each service area are intended to serve as rough proxies for local expenditure needs in each service area. However, local government authorities do not have to spend their SSA for each function and can move funds from one service area to another and so spend above or below their functional SSAs. Furthermore, the additional revenues local authorities raise by taxing residential property can also be used to increase spending for any specific service area. Indeed, a key element of the local budgeting process is the determination of the spending amount for each service area. Recent changes in government spending, however, particularly the caps on local spending, have created a situation in which most authorities are moving in the direction of spending the SSA amount for each service area because local governments' overall budgets are so tightly constrained. Thus the authorities we visited said that over the past five years, education spending had moved closer and closer to their education SSA.

Table 5.1 gives the figures for each element and highlights the differences between primary and secondary students. The education SSA is composed of five parts, based on student ages: (1) under five, (2) five to eleven (primary school, grades 1–6), (3) eleven to fifteen (secondary school, grades 7–11), (4) sixteen to nineteen (sixth form, grades 12 and 13), and (5) other (youth, community, adult education, and the like). For 1995–96, the total education SSA for all of England was approximately £20 billion, with the amount for primary and secondary education (parts 2 and 3 of the five) coming to approximately £17 billion, or 85 percent of the total.

The SSA for primary and secondary education is calculated largely on the number and characteristics of students enrolled in government schools within each LEA (including both LEA and GM schools), but it has five factors for each of primary and secondary students. The education SSA includes (1) a flat or foundation amount for each student, (2) extra funding for additional educational needs (the proxies for which are the number of students from single-parent families, the number of students from low-income families as indicated by students eligible for free school meals, and the number of students of non-English ethnicity within the LEA), (3) a sparsity factor, (4) funding for the costs of providing free school meals, and (5) for some LEAs, an area cost adjustment. (Some additional funding is provided to assist LEAs in supporting the needs of students who are not attending a government school. Services supported through these additional funds are generally transportation and special education students. The formula for these monies is similar in structure to that for students in government schools; the monetary parameters are simply much lower.)

The basic formula works as follows:

1. The LEA receives £1,477 ($2,290) for each primary student and £1,964 ($3,044) for each secondary student to provide the basic education program.

2. The LEA also receives extra money for additional educational needs (AENs)—extra funding to provide services for the disabled, students achieving below standards or from low-income backgrounds, and students with limited English proficiency. The factors used to predict the level of additional education need are the percentage of students living in single-parent families, low-income families as measured by the percentage eligible for free school meals, and the percentage of students from outside the United Kingdom. Each of these three factors is weighted (2.4, 2.4, and 1.0, respectively) and multiplied by a fixed monetary amount—£158 for primary students and £215 for secondary students.

TABLE 5.1. ELEMENTS OF THE EDUCATION STANDARD SPENDING ASSESSMENT FOR ENGLISH LOCAL EDUCATION AUTHORITIES, 1996–97.

Factor	Primary	Secondary
Base level per pupil	£1,477	£1,964
Additional educational need (AEN) adjustments		
Single-parent family	2.4 times the percentage of students from single-parent families	2.4 times the percentage of students from single-parent families
Poverty	2.4 times the percentage of students from families receiving income support	2.4 times the percentage of students from families receiving income support
Limited English proficiency	1.0 times the percentage of students born outside the United Kingdom[a]	1.0 times the percentage of of students born outside the United Kingdom[a]
Total AEN	£158 times the sum of the AEN factors	£215 times the sum of the AEN factors
Sparsity	£82 times the sparsity factor for primary students	£106 times the sparsity factor for secondary students
Cost of providing free meals	£126 times the percentage of students qualifying for free meals	£171 times the percentage of students qualifying for free meals
Area cost adjustment	54.5% for London 23.77% inner London boroughs 12.27% outer London boroughs 4.64%–11.97% fringe London boroughs 75% for Isles of Scilly	54.5% for London 23.77% inner London boroughs 12.27% outer London boroughs 4.64%–11.97% fringe London boroughs 75% for Isles of Scilly

Note: £1 = approximately $1.55 (U.S.).

[a]A student may also qualify if a parent was born outside the United Kingdom.

So if in a particular LEA, 20 percent of primary students were from single-parent families, 30 percent from families in poverty, and 10 percent of non-U.K. background, the extra amount would be £158[2.4(0.20) + 2.4(0.30) + 1.0(0.10)] = £158(0.48 + 0.72 + 0.72) = £158(1.92) = £303.36 for each primary student in the LEA. The formula works the same way for secondary students, with the AEN factor multiplied by the higher secondary figure of £215.

Each of the three proxy variables, their weights among them, and the £158 and £215 figures have been determined by regression analysis of historical spending patterns. Although there is debate about the precise variables, weights, and figures, the point is the SSA system includes a substantial adjustment for additional education needs.

3. The sparsity factor is a monetary amount times a factor based on sparsity of population in the local education authority.

4. The free school meal amount is provided for the costs of serving free school meals to eligible students from low-income families. The amounts differ by education level: £126 for each primary student and £171 for each secondary student.

5. Finally, the total monetary figure for each student is multiplied by an area cost factor, which is designed to indicate the varying purchasing power of the educational pound. Although there is controversy over the specific cost factors used in the SSA formula, as there are in the U.S. states that use education price adjustments, the cost factor adjustments themselves are within the range of education price adjustments in the United States (Chambers, 1995; McMahon, 1994), except for a particularly high value for the Isles of Scilly.

As should be evident, for almost every category (excluding the cost factor), all monetary figures are higher for secondary students than they are for primary students. Although this reflects a worldwide practice (Organization for Economic Cooperation and Development, 1995) and a general trend in the United States as well (Odden and Picus, 1992), the primary-secondary differences are much larger in England than in the United States. As England has moved to a pupil-weighted formula for funding each of its schools (to be discussed shortly), the large difference in funding for primary versus secondary students has become a contentious issue.

An additional factor that is not included in Table 5.1 is a scaling factor. Although important legally, the scaling factor is simply an adjustment that, after final appropriations have been made, ensures that the total amount of the central government grants is exactly the amount that was appropriated for education. The scaling factor usually ranges from a figure larger than 0.99 to a figure just under 1.01 and therefore does not significantly alter the totals noted here. The scaling factor is applied equally to all LEA revenue grants. It should not be confused with what would be called a pro rata factor in the United States, which is used to adjust actual aid amounts to the amounts appropriated. Pro rata factors in the U.S. are often much below 100 percent and used because the amounts appropriated are significantly under the levels required to fully fund a formula. By contrast, the scaling factor in England is simply to ensure that the revenue grant totals equal the exact amount appropriated—to the final penny.

In short, the English SSA calculation is generally comprehensive and sophisticated: a base amount augmented by amounts for extra educational needs, sparsity, and the cost of free meals, with the total adjusted by a factor that accounts for the varying purchasing power of the educational pound. Indeed, the English SSA calculation, if used in many U.S. states, would be viewed as one of the most complete in the country.

Although the SSA provides the same base amount of money for each student in each LEA, the final per-pupil totals are different because of the need, sparsity, meal, and cost factors. Nearly everyone interviewed noted the unequal total figures and characterized the overall system as therefore providing inequitable amounts of per-pupil education funding. Although one could argue with any of the particular adjustments, these tended not to be the focus of the claims that the differences represented inequities. Rather nearly everyone criticized the system for providing different and therefore inequitable amounts per primary and secondary pupil.

Many of the people interviewed at both the national and LEA level generally did not understand in detail how the SSA formula worked, and this lack of specific knowledge could help explain their characterizing the resultant differential amounts as inequitable. Those interviewed also tended not to be familiar with the U.S. methodologies for adjusting final totals for differences in need, cost, and price (Berne and Stiefel, 1984; Odden and Picus, 1992). If the English system were subjected to a U.S. type of equity analysis to determine the degree of "unjustified" differences in per-pupil figures across LEAs, the final total figures would be adjusted at least for the extra amounts provided for educational needs and price, and we expect that the system would be judged quite equitable. Even recognizing legitimate issues that can be raised with any particular variable, weight, or pound value in any part of the SSA, we conclude that the education SSA is nevertheless conceptually sophisticated and comprehensive.

The major legitimate limitation of the SSA could be that it does not provide adequate levels of education funding, a criticism we also heard expressed quite often. The decreases in local government taxing authority and the caps on local spending increases, combined with very small recent increases in central government education funding, means that education revenues per pupil did not increase much from 1990 to 1996 and probably did not keep pace with inflation. Nevertheless, a criticism of inadequate levels would suggest that the pound parameters in the formula need to be increased, not that the structure of the SSA formula itself is flawed.

Centrally Determined Budgetary Requirements for Local Education Authorities

When England decided to require LEAs to decentralize the bulk of education funding to schools as part of its 1988 reform program, it did not simply allow LEAs to design a system on their own. The strategy of the central government was to create a policy umbrella that prescribed the broad outlines for fiscal decentralization and allowed each LEA to tailor the specifics to its local context. The central requirements not only ensured that significant proportions of LEA budgets were delegated to schools but also required each LEA to follow a centrally determined framework in creating the LEA formula for sending the money to schools. The central policy is called the Budgetary Framework, and the LEA policy is known as the LMS Scheme.

The Budgetary Framework begins with the overall LEA budget for primary and secondary schools. The framework defines several budgetary levels: the general schools budget (GSB), the potential schools budget (PSB), and the aggregate schools budget (ASB). The policy sets the limits and the structure for each LEA to determine the pound amounts for each of these budget categories.

The GSB is the total amount appropriated by each local government authority to its LEA for financing educational expenditures for all schools. The GSB covers both capital and operating costs for the schools. There are no central requirements for how local authorities determine the GSB although, as mentioned, the trend has been for the GSB to be close to the standard spending assessment used to determine the central fiscal equalization grant. But technically, determining the GSB is simply a political determination of the local government authority.

The next set of budgetary policies is guided by the Budgetary Framework. The PSB is the next lower budget level; it is the GSB minus a set of services and functions that are retained as centrally or LEA provided. The ASB is the next lower budget level; it represents the actual amount of money that is budgeted to school sites in a lump sum. Over the years, England has required that an increasing percentage of the PSB be identified as the ASB. Today, at least 85 percent of the PSB must become the ASB; the nationwide average is nearly 90 percent, and a recent government white paper has proposed that the minimum proportion be increased to 95 percent.

The Potential Schools Budget (PSB).
The central government requires that certain educational functions and their revenue streams be retained by the LEA, rather than devolved or delegated to the school. These are called mandatory

exceptions, and they are deductions from the GSB to determine the size of the PSB. Mandatory exceptions include only six functions: (1) capital expenditures and financing; (2) educational welfare; (3) educational psychology services; (4) statutory assessments for disabled students requiring statements (individual education programs), referred to as "statemented" students; (5) premature retirement and dismissal costs; and (6) central government and European Union (EU) grants for special purposes.

Education welfare services are essentially student attendance services; they are activities related to ensuring that all students within the LEA attend some government or nongovernment school. Educational psychology services are provided to a small number of students. "Statements" for disabled students correspond to individual education programs in the United States. Teachers in England have developed a professional code of practice providing services to children who need extra help. The code covers both students who are low achievers but need extra help to achieve to the standards in the national curriculum as well as students who are more severely disabled. Statements are developed for the top two of the five different levels of extra educational need. Developing statements has been identified legally as an LEA responsibility, and the LEA therefore retains funding for the administrative costs of statementing students. Premature retirement and dismissal costs are held by the LEA because the LEA is the compensating authority and hence all costs associated with compensation should be retained by the LEA. Finally, central government or EU grants for specified purposes legally must be retained by the LEA but may later be devolved to the schools within the ASB, with explicit grant requirements driving spending patterns (as on professional development) accordingly.

These six functions are all responsibilities that England has determined are best handled by the LEA either because of statutory responsibility (as is the case of statements for disabled students) or economic efficiency (such as capital expenditures). They include only a small portion of the overall budget and, interestingly, are few in number. Technically, *all* other functions and services can be delegated to schools, and some LEAs have devolved nearly all other functions.

The umbrella policy of the Budgetary Framework also allows LEAs to identify additional functions that *can* be excluded from the PSB; thus the central government allows LEAs to decide if six additional functions and services should be centrally provided or devolved to the schools. These six functions are (1) providing school meals (free or not), (2) transportation between home and school, (3) pupil support (such as financial aid for children from low-income families to purchase uniforms when these are required by the school), (4) school council governors' liability insurance (since council members can be sued and held liable for damages), (5) LEA education initiatives (restricted to no more than 0.5 percent of the GSB), and (6) contingencies (unexpected damage to buildings, unpredicted enrollment changes, and so on).

Using national averages for England, Table 5.2 lists the twelve mandatory and discretionary exceptions under the PSB and the percentage of the total GSB that each represents. The PSB averages 81 percent of the GSB. Mandatory exceptions represent about 11 percent of the GSB, and discretionary exceptions, 7 percent.

The Aggregated Schools Budget (ASB). The aggregated schools budget (ASB) is the amount provided to the site in a lump sum. The central government Budgetary Framework policy umbrella specifies two major requirements for the ASB: first, that it must be at least 85 percent of the PSB, and second, that at least 80 percent of the ASB total must be determined by a pupil-weighting formula. The central government does not specify what remaining functions the LEA can retain or how much funding can be retained. These decisions are completely devolved to each LEA. The only central requirement is that at least 85 percent of the PSB total be sent to the school site. Although 85 percent is the currently required statutory level of devolution of the PSB, the percentage was 75 percent when the plan was first implemented, the actual LEA average is much closer to 90 percent, and in June 1996 the government proposed that it be increased to 95 percent. Thus

TABLE 5.2. GENERAL SCHOOLS BUDGET AND POTENTIAL SCHOOLS BUDGET IN ENGLAND, 1996–97 (ESTIMATED).

	Budget (£ thousands)	Share of GSB (percent)
General Schools Budget	£15,090,680	100.0%
Mandatory exceptions		
Capital expenditure and financing	1,029,089	6.8
Education welfare service	60,210	0.4
Education psychology service	58,150	0.4
Statementing costs	33,389	0.2
Premature retirement compensation	127,761	0.8
Specific grant-related expenditures	413,459	2.7
Discretionary exceptions		
School meals and milk	599,767	4.0
Home-to-school transport	334,629	2.2
Pupil support	33,670	0.2
Liability insurance	23,107	0.2
LEA initiatives	35,278	0.2
Contingencies and other	68,488	0.4
Potential Schools Budget	12,273,683	81.3

Source: Calculations based on data from the Chartered Institute of Finance and Accountancy.

the practice has been to send an increasing proportion of PSB funds to the site; in mid–1996, the majority of LEAs delegated well above the minimum required by law, and the general sense of the education and political community seems to be to increase the proportion delegated even further.

LEA behavior is varied as to the specific services retained at the LEA within the PSB. Although the major school-level functions such as instruction, school administration, school operations, and minor maintenance are devolved, data are collected nationally that highlight the various other discretionary exceptions that are retained by the LEA under the PSB. Table 5.3 illustrates the most common categories of expenditures and services retained by the LEA under the PSB (in other words, items subtracted from the PSB to create the ASB). As should be evident from Table 5.3, LEAs already devolve just under 90 percent of the PSB to schools, thus reflecting the policy objective of greater delegation of budgets directly to the school site.

After establishing the ASB, LEAs must then construct a formula to determine the actual monetary amount sent to each school. According to the Budgetary Framework, the general goal of formula funding is to ensure that within each LEA,

TABLE 5.3. POTENTIAL SCHOOLS BUDGET AND AGGREGATE SCHOOLS BUDGET IN ENGLAND, 1996–97 (ESTIMATED).

	Budget (£ thousands)	Share of PSB (percent)
Potential Schools Budget	£12,273,683	100.0%
Typical functions retained by LEAs		
Management and administration	271,908	2.2
Curriculum advisory and inspection services	78,042	0.6
Special education provisions for statemented students	292,781	2.4
Other special education	88,804	0.7
Peripatetic staff services	52,313	0.4
Library and museum services	18,414	0.2
Operational units (excluding special needs)	24,515	0.2
Substitute teachers	58,310	0.5
Salary safeguarding	13,446	0.1
Professional development	16,155	0.1
Insurance	74,562	0.6
Structural repairs and maintenance	195,332	1.6
Other	52,750	0.4
Actual Schools Budget	11,036,351	89.9

Source: Calculations based on data from the Chartered Institute of Finance and Accountancy.

"schools with the same characteristics and the same number of pupils . . . receive the same level of resources under the formula" (Department of School Education, 1994). The requirement to fund schools via formula funding was intended to transform "historical" funding of schools, which often followed no particular pattern, was sometimes biased, and in a few cases had little or no rationale, to a system that was fair, clear to all parties, predictable, and not subject to administrative whim or bias. Indeed, the Budgetary Framework regulations required each LEA not only to design the specific mechanisms, or scheme, it would use to fund each school but also to publish those local policies to make them public.

The central government policy umbrella for the LEA school funding scheme works the following way. First, the formula must distribute at least 80 percent of ASB money via pupil-led factors. The pupil-led aspect of the funding formula is commonly referred to as age-weighted-pupil units (AWPUs). The notion is that AWPUs must determine how at least 80 percent of the ASB is provided to schools. Using AWPUs, LEAs generally identified a base or norm student who received the base amount of money and a weight of 1.0; usually students around grade 4 were 1.0 students. Sometimes younger students had higher weights, particularly students in preschool and kindergarten, and secondary students always had higher weights, but these weight differentials were not required by national law. The national requirement was merely that 80 percent of the ASB be distributed according to some pupil-weighting scheme.

Within the 80 percent that is pupil-led based on the AWPUs, 5 percent may be pupil-led based on additional education needs. This allows LEAs to provide extra weights for various student characteristics, such as when the student is from a low-income family or if the student needs additional education services according to the Code of Professional Practice. LEAs may use funding formulas that distribute more than 80 percent of the ASB based on pupil-led factors. In fact, the average estimated proportion of the ASB allocated on the basis of pupil-led factors was roughly 84 percent in 1995–96, clearly indicating that many LEAs exceed the 80 percent minimum.

The remaining percentage of the ASB that LEAs allocate to schools must also be based on objective factors, but not necessarily related to student counts. The funding formulas commonly included a variety of non-pupil-related budgetary factors such as small school size, salary protection, premises-related funding, transitional adjustments, and additional special-needs funding (portions that exceeded the 5 percent allowed as pupil-led or portions that were place-led, such as a special resource room). Figure 5.1 provides a visual depiction of the sequence of school-based financing structured by the central LMS framework.

In reviewing the figure, note that the English education finance reform addressed the issue of what services should remain controlled by the LEA and what

**FIGURE 5.1. SEQUENCE OF SCHOOL-BASED FINANCING
ACCORDING TO THE CENTRAL LMS FRAMEWORK.**

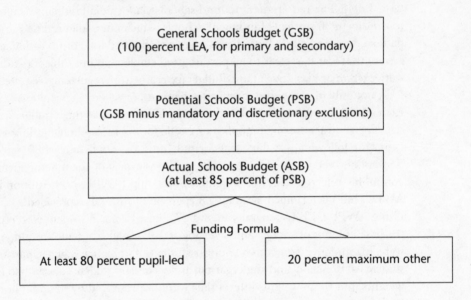

could be delegated to the school. As noted, the central government provided detailed descriptions of mandatory items that LEAs must retain centrally and also allowed for discretionary items under both the GSB and PSB so that LEA-specific factors could be accommodated within LMS. In addition, given the LMS goal to devolve a very high proportion of funding to the school, the requirements surrounding the ASB clearly signaled to the LEA that it should delegate the highest possible degree of funding to the school. Also, the emphasis on a primarily pupil-led formula to distribute the ASB ensured that spending between similar schools in an LEA would not vary more than 20 percent on nonpupil factors. Indeed, the Budgetary Framework ensured that the LMS goals of distributing resources more equitably among schools in a given LEA and providing greater school autonomy over education resources were achieved.

Case Studies: How Four LEAs Translated State Policy Guidelines into a School Funding Plan

We studied how four LEAs—Birmingham, Cambridgeshire, Kent, and Wandsworth—implemented the central policy for funding their schools. The LEAs represented a range of LEA contexts, but no LEA was predominantly rural. Birmingham is in the industrial midlands of England. Wandsworth, an urban authority in south-central London, was formerly a part of the Inner London Education Authority. Kent, on the southeastern fringe of London, is one of the largest LEAs but has many small rural schools as well. Cambridgeshire is an LEA just forty minutes by train north of London and thus represents a mostly suburban LEA, although it also has many schools in rural areas.

The LMS Schemes of these four LEAs show the decisions each has made about the mandatory and discretionary items retained by the LEA in determining the PSB, as well as the formulas used for distributing the ASB to schools. The data presented here reflect each LEA's 1996–97 Section 42 Budget Statement and Scheme required under LMS.

From the GSB to the PSB

This section describes how each LEA constructed the potential schools budget from the general schools budget. Table 5.4 shows the specific services each LEA retained under the mandatory and discretionary categories and the percentage of the GSB represented by each. On average, the LEAs retained 16.9 percent of the GSB for these services, compared to the average of 18.7 in all of England. Table 5.4 also demonstrates how the LEAs varied both in which services were retained and in the budgetary amounts. Birmingham retained the least overall total (15.6 percent of the GSB), and Wandsworth retained the most (18.8 percent). There were wider differences for each particular service. For example, Kent, a growing LEA, retained 7.9 percent of its GSB for capital and major repairs, in part to build new schools for rising enrollments, while Birmingham retained only 2.2 percent. As might be expected, discretionary exclusions retained from the GSB to the PSB also varied. For instance, Birmingham did not retain any funds centrally for pupil support, but both Kent and Wandsworth did. Interestingly, LEA initiatives (as for improved literacy) hovered around 0.23 percent of the GSB in all of the LEAs. All four LEAs, as is typical across England, retained the transportation service as centrally provided. Nevertheless, the LEAs studied made quite different decisions about which services would be retained centrally and the resource levels that would finance them.

From the PSB to the ASB

The potential schools budget is the general schools budget minus the sum of all mandatory and discretionary exceptions. Within the PSB, LEAs make a series of additional decisions about functions they retain centrally. When the decisions about these functions are made and their revenue streams are identified and subtracted

TABLE 5.4. FOUR LOCAL EDUCATION AUTHORITY APPROACHES TO DETERMINING THE POTENTIAL SCHOOLS BUDGET FOR 1996–97.

Category	National	Birmingham	Cambridgeshire	Kent	Wandsworth
General Schools Budget	£15,090,680,000	£409,441,000	£202,087,000	£412,467,500	£66,203,000
Portion retained for both mandatory and discretionary exclusions	18.7%	15.6%	22.8%	16.4 %	18.8%
Mandatory exclusions (percent of GSB)					
Capital and major repairs	11.70%	2.23%	11.36%	7.90%	4.64%
Education welfare (attendance)	0.34	0.73	0.34	0.18	0.60
Education psychologists (for advising students and helping with statements)	0.58	0.31	0.34	0.33	0.40
Statementing (writing and administration)	0.27	0.11	0.58	0.30	0.56
Premature retirements and dismissals	0.53	0.90	0.80	0.55	0.44
Specific central government and European Union grant programs	2.67	2.93	2.67	2.01	4.52
Discretionary exclusions					
Home-to-school transportation	2.22%	1.91%	2.46%	3.06%	2.57%
School meals	3.97	5.64	3.66	1.48	3.58
Liability insurance for LEA and school governors	0.15	0.04	0.14	0.03	0.52
Pupil support	0.22	0.00	0.25	0.04	0.12
LEA initiatives, such as literacy for African and Caribbean students	0.23	0.36	0.03	0.38	0.45
Contingencies (changes in student counts, school emergencies such as fire or theft loss or vandalism, exceptional education needs largely for Levels 4 and 5 statemented students)	0.34	0.40	0.19	0.05	0.40

Sources: Calculations based on data from the Chartered Institute of Finance and Accountancy and on LEA Section 42 Budget Statements for 1996–97.

from the PSB, the result is the aggregated schools budget, the amount that is actually provided to schools. This section describes how each of the four LEAs constructed the ASB from the PSB.

Table 5.5 provides data on the ASB, PSB, and GSB for the four LEAs studied and England as a whole. The first row identifies the percentage that the PSB is of the GSB. Row 2 identifies the percentage that the ASB is of the GSB. Row 3 then shows the percentage that the ASB is of the GSB, that is, the proportion of the total LEA budget that is devolved to schools in a lump sum. Recall that the Budgetary Framework requires that a minimum of 85 percent of the PSB be sent to the school, but the PSB represents only a locally defined portion of the GSB (total LEA budget for schools). Thus all schools received well over the statutorily required 85 percent of their LEA's PSB, but the percentage of the GSB that was actually allocated to schools (ASB) varied more widely, as did the PSB as a proportion of the GSB. As Table 5.5 notes, of the four LEAs studied, all delegated at least 68 percent of their GSB, thus retaining a maximum total of 32 percent. Across all of England, the average of the GSB actually devolved to schools was 73 percent. The fact that 73 percent of the overall education budget is actually delegated to schools should be highlighted because it indicates that even in a system that has devolved substantial funding to school sites, about a quarter of education resources are still retained by the LEA.

One of the key issues in England has been the percentage of the PSB that each LEA must devolve to schools. In the first years of the 1988 reforms, LEAs had to devolve only 75 percent of the PSB. Today, that requirement is 85 percent, but as stated earlier, the average across all of England is closer to 90 percent. The four LEAs in Table 5.5 delegated at least 89 percent of their PSBs to schools, and Birmingham delegated just over the overall England average of 89.9

TABLE 5.5. POTENTIAL SCHOOLS BUDGET AND AGGREGATE SCHOOLS BUDGET AS A PERCENTAGE OF THE GENERAL SCHOOLS BUDGET FOR 1996–97.

	National	Birmingham	Cambridgeshire	Kent	Wandsworth
PSB as a percentage of GSB	81.3%	84.4%	77.2%	83.6%	81.2%
ASB as a percentage of GSB	73.1	77.1	68.9	74.4	72.7
ASB as a percentage of PSB	89.9	91.3	89.2	89.0	89.5

Source: Calculations based on data from the Chartered Institute of Finance and Accountancy and on LEA Section 42 Budget Statements for 1996–97.

percent. Cambridgeshire, Kent, and Wandsworth exceeded the 85 percent required by law but were just shy of the average by which all LEAs in England exceeded that minimum.

Table 5.6 provides additional details regarding the items that are generally retained by the LEA when determining the ASB from the PSB. The PSB serves as the starting point, and all percentages are noted from the PSB. Just as for the discretionary exceptions, the LEAs made quite different decisions both about which functions to retain and the level of revenues for each function.

The management and administration function, which includes fiscal and payroll services, has been one of the most scrutinized services. Each LEA retained some portion of this function, but the percentage of the PSB for this service ranged from 1.66 percent (£37 per pupil) in Birmingham to 4.28 percent (£86 per pupil) in Kent. The pound figures are interesting in themselves but also because many LEAs sought to keep the figure for this service below £100 per pupil, and in mid–1996 the Labour party proposed to limit this amount to £50 per pupil. Management and administration together with special education students that are statemented constituted the largest revenue totals for services retained within the PSB. Indeed, most of the remaining services were quite small, nearly all below 1 percent of the PSB.

In sum, the numbers show that of the total (operating and capital) LEA education budget (GSB), England devolved about three-fourths to schools. Of the smaller, PSB, England devolved about 90 percent to schools. Further, all the revenues that were retained and the functions they supported were clearly identified and made public.

Distributing the ASB to School Sites

As indicated earlier, the aggregate schools budget is the amount that is ultimately sent to each school but is not sent as a simple per-pupil amount. Each LEA uses a comprehensive and in some cases fairly complicated set of formulas and objective strategies to determine the monetary amounts each school receives. Table 5.7 identifies the key formula elements that are used to determine each school's budget, for each of the four LEAs studied.

As discussed earlier, the Budgetary Framework requires that 80 percent of the ASB be distributed through a pupil-led formula. The various pupil-led formula categories for each of the LEAs are noted in Table 5.7. The age weight category indicates whether weights were linked to the key stages of learning in the national curriculum or to the age of students. Two LEAs weighted by key stages of learning and two weighted by age.

TABLE 5.6. LOCAL EDUCATION AUTHORITY APPROACHES TO DETERMINING THE AGGREGATE SCHOOLS BUDGET FOR 1996–97: PORTIONS OF THE POTENTIAL SCHOOLS BUDGET RETAINED BY THE LEA (PERCENT).

Functions Retained	National	Birmingham	Cambridgeshire	Kent	Wandsworth
Management and administration including fiscal services	2.22% (£44 per pupil)	1.66% (£37 per pupil)	1.82% (£30.87 per pupil)	4.28% (£86 per pupil)	3.23% (£87 per pupil)
Advisory and inspection services	0.64%	0.28%	0.46%	0.43%	1.04%
Special education (statemented)	2.39	1.79	4.25	3.30	3.44
Special education (nonstate-mented)	0.72	0.47	1.19	0.77	0.72
Traveling instru-mental music	0.43	0.06	0.16	0.31	0.00
Library and mu-seum services	0.15	0.10	0.10	0.10	0.04
Operational units, excluding spe-cial needs	0.20	0.49	0.20	0.00	0.00
Substitute teachers	0.48	0.49	0.49	0.23	0.44
Salary safeguarding	0.11	0.07	0.19	0.13	0.00
Professional development	0.13	0.22	0.28	0.03	0.00
Insurance	0.61	0.43	1.06	0.43	0.21
Structural repairs and maintenance	1.59	2.21	0.11	0.51	0.57
Other	0.43	0.42	0.43	0.51	0.83

Sources: Calculations based on data from the Chartered Institute of Finance and Accountancy and on LEA Section 42 Budget Statements for 1996–97.

The other elements of the pupil-led categories note how nonstatemented students were treated in the LEA formulas. Proxies for social deprivation (a term used in England for what would be termed compensatory education in the United States) are noted (all of the four LEAs used free school meals). Table 5.7 also shows whether students requiring language support and students with low academic achievement received additional funding at the school site. The formula factors for nonstatemented students, students requiring language assistance, and students living in poverty are all related to the supplementary 5 percent of funding that may be allocated for additional educational need (within the 80 percent of funding that must be pupil-led).

Non-pupil-led factors included how costs for buildings (premises) and operations were funded, as well as extra amounts for small schools or schools with multiple sites. Transportation costs delegated to schools are also listed, as are how student transiency and enrollment projections versus actual student counts were handled for school budgets. New schools, newly merged schools, and school swimming pool costs were included in one LEA, as noted in Table 5.7. Details relating to each of these LEA formula factors are discussed next.

Pupil-Led Factors: Age-Weighted-Pupil Units (AWPUs). Of the four LEAs in Table 5.7, two, Cambridgeshire and Wandsworth, funded their age-weighted-pupil units primarily by key stages. Birmingham and Kent used a formula that included a different weight for ages within each key stage. Key stages of learning are outlined in the national curriculum and testing programs. Key stages of learning are logical weighting factors when considering possible variations in educational needs that would be reflected in the national curriculum requirements for English, mathematics, science, history, geography, and languages. As mentioned earlier, key stages of learning are divided by age ranges: key stage 1 is for ages five to seven; key stage 2 is for ages seven to eleven; key stage 3 is for ages eleven to fourteen; and key stage 4 is for ages fourteen and fifteen; sixth form and other high school curricula are for ages sixteen and over.

Table 5.8 provides the details of the AWPUs used in allocating the ASB formula for each LEA. As the table clearly shows, pupil weights varied by LEA. First, consistent with the differential funding found in the education SSA, LEAs weighted secondary students much higher than primary students. However, the range in disparities between the extreme high and low weights of secondary and primary students varied by LEA. Cambridgeshire had the greatest disparity between its weight for five-year-olds and its weight for sixteen years and older, and Wandsworth had the smallest disparity. Across all LEAs, seven-year-olds generated the lowest weights (or pound amount). Cambridgeshire had the highest weight for students sixteen years and older. Wandsworth had the highest weights (1.5) for chil-

TABLE 5.7. MAJOR FUNDING FORMULA FACTORS IN FOUR LOCAL EDUCATION AUTHORITIES FOR 1996–97.

Factor	Birmingham	Cambridgeshire	Kent	Wandsworth
Pupil-led factors				
Age weights	age-specific	key stage	age-specific	key stage
Nonstatemented students	merged with social deprivation	n/a	funded on basis of school district audit	n/a
Social deprivation	free school meals	free school meals	free school meals	free school meals
Language support	n/a	n/a	n/a	funded
Pupil attainment	n/a	n/a	n/a	funded (scores from achievement tests)
Other factors				
Premises and fixed costs	funded	lump sum	funded	lump sum
Split sites	funded	n/a	funded	n/a
Transport	funded	funded	funded	n/a
Small school	n/a	funded	funded	n/a
Predicted roll	n/a	adjustment	n/a	adjustment
Pupil turnover	n/a	funded	funded	n/a
New schools	n/a	based on forecast for next two years	n/a	n/a
Merged schools	n/a	protection against large drops in funding	n/a	n/a
Swimming pools	n/a	funded	n/a	n/a

Note: n/a = not applicable.

Source: LEA Section 42 Budget Statements for 1996–97.

dren aged three and four, ages for preschool and kindergarten, and for children aged five and six (1.2), year levels 1 and 2.

The large differences in funding between primary and secondary students became well known when England required LEAs to adopt explicit funding formulas for primary and secondary school students via the age-level weights. The differences also became controversial, with many educators believing that more resources should be devoted to primary students. Several LEAs desired to increase the primary student weights, thereby reducing the secondary-primary funding differentials. However, given the overall limited funding increases for education and little ability to raise additional money locally or shift funds from other

TABLE 5.8. AGE-WEIGHTED-PUPIL UNITS FOR FOUR LOCAL EDUCATION AUTHORITIES FOR 1996–97.

Age	Year Level	Learning Stage	Birmingham (age)	Cambridgeshire (stage)	Kent (age)	Wandsworth (stage)
4			1.4365	1.45	1.2994	1.5
5	1	1	1.3514	1.04	1.2994	1.5
6	2	1	1.0042	1.04	1.0399	1.2
7	3	2	1.0136	1.04	1.000	1.2
8	4	2	1.0000	1.04	1.000	1.0
9	5	2	1.0094	1.04	1.000	1.0
10	6	2	1.0232	1.23	1.1996	1.0
11	7	3	1.0000	1.60	1.5979	1.2
12	8	3	1.3396	1.60	1.5979	1.2
13	9	3	1.3559	1.60	1.5879	1.2
14	10	4	1.3396	2.03	1.8275	1.2
15	11	4	1.5639	2.03	1.8275	1.9
16+ (A-levels)	sixth form		1.6800	2.66	2.4961	2.15
16+ (other)			2.1169	2.66	1.9971	2.15

Source: LEA Section 42 Budget Statements for 1996–97.

local authority services, altering student weights proved to be largely a zero-sum game. And if secondary schools perceived themselves to be at risk of losing funding, the concern among LEA staff was that secondary schools would opt out to become GM schools, which would result in the LEA's losing most authority and funding for the school. As a result, there have been only very modest increases in primary school weights and commensurate decreases in the primary-secondary differentials.

Pupil-Led Factors: Additional Educational Need. LEAs also provided extra funds for additional educational needs. These funds could be for statemented and non-statemented disabled students; for students scoring at different levels on reading or other achievement tests; for students with other proxy indicators of additional educational need, such as eligibility for free school meals, one-parent family, non-English ethnicity, limited English proficiency, or student transiency. These factors are at the discretion of the LEA. Up to 5 percent of these extra funds could be counted toward the 80 percent of funds that must be pupil-led in the LMS distribution formula.

The four LEAs implemented different approaches to funding extra programs for students from low-income backgrounds. Each child eligible for free school meals generated £127 for schools in the Birmingham LEA. In addition, Birmingham had a "concentration factor" for schools with high densities of students in poverty (eligible for free school meals). Schools with above the LEA average (38 percent) of students eligible for free school meals received an additional £104 for each pupil. Thus a school with 300 students, 48 percent of whom (144 students) were eligible for free school meals, would receive funding for this category according to the following equation: £127(144 eligible students) + £104(30 students above the LEA average) = £18,288 + £3,120 = £21,408. By contrast, Wandsworth used a simpler approach and provided £217 per child eligible for free school meals but did not apply a concentration factor. Wandsworth also provided an extra £529 for each student who scored below a specified reading and mathematics level. Kent provided a social deprivation factor (similar to Birmingham's concentration factor) of £204 for each free-school-meal child in a school above a 32.5 percent threshold. Cambridgeshire set aside 2 percent of its total budget and distributed the funds according to each school's proportion of students eligible for free school meals.

Because statemented students are the responsibility of LEAs, devolving funding for statemented students was a significant issue in the LEAs visited. Three (Cambridgeshire, Kent, and Wandsworth) were planning to devolve the funding for statemented students. Birmingham was not devolving funding to schools, nor did its Scheme or Section 42 Budget Statement indicate an intention to do so anytime soon.

Other Factors. A collection of other factors were included in LEAs' formulas for funding to schools, including operation and maintenance costs, local council rates taxes, small size adjustments or minimum base allocations, transitional salary protection, and transportation for field trips. Each LEA had a very different set of strategies for these other factors.

For example, LEAs varied by how they funded premises and related costs. Wandsworth assumed that premises costs (operations and minor maintenance) were included in its AWPU and base allocation; Birmingham and Kent used formulas that included factors for repairs and maintenance, energy, business rates, and other expense items. However, the premises formulas used by Birmingham and Kent were very different from each other.

In all LEAs studied, staff interviewed were searching for ways to streamline the LEA formulas. Streamlining suggestions included simplifying the pupil-led formula or the premises factors. Several staff felt "trapped" in more complicated formulas because of resistance to change, scarce resources, and initial efforts to include many "objective" factors that reduced differences in formula funding from historical funding. Scarce resources meant that any major distributional change that might occur from streamlining the funding formula could likely result in some schools losing funding. In addition, as one LEA began implementing its LMS, the tension between historical precedent and scarce resources meant that every penny had to be accounted for *through* the formula as it was developed. Great care was taken to cause as little change to historical funding as possible, so the resulting formula proved fairly complicated in most aspects. In fact, some LEA schemes reviewed even include maintaining historical funding levels for schools as a goal. All LEA staff considered significant changes in funding levels unlikely for the future, and several were postponing efforts to streamline and simplify their LMS formulas. Those working to simplify their LMS formulas focused on the more detailed and less costly factors, such as premises, and not the redistributive factors of primary and secondary student weights.

Wandsworth had created one of the most streamlined LMS funding systems. It basically weighted (generally only to one decimal point) students by each stage of the national curriculum (not by every age and therefore year level). For additional education need, it provided an extra £217 for each free-school-meal student and extra amounts for students scoring below standards on reading, mathematics, and language tests. Finally, it provided a lump sum (£50,000 for each primary school and £100,000 for each secondary school) for operations, maintenance, scale diseconomies, and other nonteaching costs. Although the formula had a few other small factors, the point is that rather than a long, complicated, detailed formula, Wandsworth had simplified its system to a more compact and, its administrators felt, quite fair one. "After all," one individual interviewed stated, "the formula is simply a way to distribute funds. If a simpler formula distributes funds in essentially the same pattern as a lengthier and more complicated formula, the simpler formula should be preferred."

Charging for Site Expenditures

Under LMS, individual LEA schools are charged for expenditures according to an "averages in, actuals out" scenario. As already discussed, schools were apportioned revenue on the basis of their number of age-weighted pupils and other LEA-determined factors. School revenues continued to be held centrally by the LEA, but schools controlled the expenditure of those revenues. Schools determined their own spending needs, then passed the bill along to the LEA, whereby the LEA paid the bill and accounted for the expenditure to the appropriate school. This scenario also played out with salary expenditures. The LEA paid all salary checks, and each school was charged according to the *actual* salary for each individual employed at the school. Some schools were called "checkbook schools" and had the ability to pay for their own bills (excluding payroll) from their own school account, essentially cutting out the LEA as an entity with which vendors contended. Thus schools were funded on the basis of general (average) LEA principles and charged for their *actual* expenditures.

In comparison, Victoria, Australia, and Edmonton, Alberta, Canada, charged schools the *average* teacher salary costs. So schools had little incentive to keep their actual salary costs down and in fact had an incentive to hire more experienced (expensive) teachers than the average teacher salary. (Victoria is currently considering a shift to charging actual costs.) In England, by contrast, schools were charged their actual salaries, and this meant that schools with higher percentages of experienced teachers had higher salary costs. Since the budget distribution formula did not include adjustments for such higher salary costs, the 1988 reforms allowed LEAs to provide transitional budget augmentations over a five-year period to help schools phase in actual salary charges. But most districts needed six to eight years to fully implement such a strategy, and by the 1998 school year, all transitional budget augmentation for charging actual salaries will have been eliminated, except for a special allowance for small schools.

School-Level Perspectives on LMS

In summarizing the perspectives of primary and secondary headteachers and budget managers on school funding policies in England, we draw on our own interviews as well as findings from other research on the same topics. We do not address the wider issue of local response to local management of schools in general, although many other studies have done so (Levacic, 1995; Thomas and Martin, 1996). Five issues emerged in the local interviews: (1) overall reactions to budget devolution, (2) fiscal equity issues, (3) adjustments for extra educational need, (4) adequacy of overall education funding, and (5) the freedom to make resource allocation choices.

Overall Reactions to Budget Devolution

First, school heads and budget managers generally supported LEA school-based funding formulas, or LMS Schemes, that determined the budget totals that would be sent to each school. They believed that the formulas provided budget distributions that were objective and generally fair and that the formula structures were more justifiable than the historical funding of schools. They also believed that formula funding made school funding more "transparent," more public and open.

Second, headteachers and school budget managers strongly supported site authority over the budget. Several of the headteachers we interviewed stated that they had been skeptical at the beginning—both because the LMS reforms were rationalized on a "market-oriented," conservative political basis and because they wondered whether they could handle many of the new functions that would be devolved to them. But after six years of experience having their school receive a lump-sum budget that could be allocated any way the school wished, all headteachers and budget managers said that they strongly supported the system and would be loath to return to the former structure under which the LEA made the bulk of resource allocation and use decisions.

Our findings are similar to those in other studies of England's new system as well (Levacic, 1995; Thomas and Martin, 1996). Indeed, it would be hard to overstate the strong site support for school-based budgeting and devolution of fiscal authority. Although headteachers raised numerous questions about specific aspects of the funding formulas, those questions were subsidiary to the overwhelmingly strong support for the policy of providing schools with their budget in a lump sum and allowing schools to tailor spending to their own needs.

We also asked headteachers and budget managers if they would prefer that LEAs decentralize functions that had so far been retained. The answer was positive, especially in the case of secondary schools, even if the responsibility—such as managing the teacher payroll or managing the entire funding function—was substantial and even if the revenue stream that would follow was small. Most schools preferred to manage their own affairs, to as great an extent as possible. Most schools also believed that they could improve the quality of their service either by providing it themselves or by contracting for it in the private market. Further, most schools believed that they could provide the service and save money, even if the additional revenue stream was not large.

Most headteachers and budget managers believed that money would be spent more effectively and efficiently when the decisions about allocations and expenditures were made at the site level. This belief undergirded their general support for the budget devolution that had already occurred and for additional functional and fiscal devolution that could occur in the future. This strong support is reflected by their stated willingness to take on even more functional responsibilities for many of the items that still remained at the LEA level regardless of the size of the funding stream that would accompany them.

Our study did not assess the validity of site claims either as to the more effective or more efficient use of fiscal resources. Our comments relate only to local perspectives on budget devolution in England. The bottom line is that such devolution is now supported by headteachers and their budget managers.

Equity Issues

Two major equity issues were raised by headteachers and budget managers. One concerned funding differentials between primary and secondary schools. The second concerned the funding of grant-maintained schools.

Although primary schools in England (indeed, nearly all primary schools in the world) have been and continue, under LMS, to be funded at a lower level than secondary schools, the move to school-based formula funding seemed to make this policy more public and more questionable. Everyone we interviewed mentioned that one major debate that erupted as LEAs constructed their school-based funding schemes concerned primary-secondary school funding differentials. Most LEAs not only weighted secondary school students at a higher level than primary school students but sometimes at weights 100 percent or more higher. Although the consensus was that primary school funding should be increased without cutting funding for secondary schools, primary headteachers generally did not favor any funding differences between the two levels of schools, whereas secondary headteachers believed their schools should have extra funding. Primary school educators were concerned about this issue because they felt that primary schools were underfunded, and secondary school educators were concerned because they felt that secondary school funding might be decreased in the pressure to increase funding for primary schools.

The second equity issue that emerged concerned funding differences between LEA locally managed (LM) schools and grant-maintained (GM) schools. The parallel U.S. issue would be between districts and charter schools, an issue that is problematic (Bierlein and Fulton, 1996; Wells, 1996; see also Chapter Three). Initially,

GM schools received more than their appropriate share of LEA fiscal resources. This occurred because the revenues associated with several functions that were retained at the LEA level for LM schools but devolved to GM schools were initially overestimated, sometimes substantially. Further, GM schools also initially received additional funding in part to assist them in their transition to full autonomy. Both overfunding policies were questioned.

More recently, several other funding equity issues between GM and LM schools have emerged. One concerned the lack of GM access to capital funding. Another concerned the alleged LEA ability to "jigger" LMS funding schemes in ways that advantaged LM schools and disadvantaged GM schools. As discussed earlier, all of these issues led to the creation of a separate agency to handle financial affairs for GM schools, the construction of a common funding approach that each LEA must follow in determining both LM and GM funding, and separate appropriations for capital costs for GM schools.

Finally, the issue of equity of funding has been raised for all schools in England. Many observers wonder not only why similarly situated GM schools should be funded at different levels but also why *any* similarly situated school should receive more or less funding per pupil than any other school. This overarching fiscal equity issue is beginning to dominate education funding policy discussions in England today, and proposals for a national funding formula for all schools are starting to emerge. It seems that a move to school-based financing puts fiscal equity across schools squarely on the policy agenda. Although funding differences among LEAs may be justified on the basis of local choice and local control, funding differences between schools (not counting those based on additional educational need or different educational prices) seem less justified, particularly since schools do not have revenue-raising authority.

Adjustments for Extra Educational Need

Headteachers and business managers raised several issues related to LEA adjustments for extra student needs. Recall that the Code of Professional Practice requires teachers to identify all students who need extra educational support, those with mild needs and those with more substantial needs. Extra needs are identified at five levels. LEAs were legally responsible for fully funding the extra needs identified for Levels 4 and 5. Fiscal issues were raised about the mild disabilities or mild levels of additional education need, Levels 1 through 3.

Many schools felt that resources were not sufficient for them to provide the services needed for Levels 1 through 3. Although one LEA, Kent, tried to establish a funding system that provided resources for all students according to the level of extra need that was identified, the system needed substantial monitoring to ensure that local educators did not overestimate the level of extra educational need. Schools in districts that did not have particular adjustments for students in Levels 1 through 3 felt that the LEA formulas did not provide adequate funding for the necessary services.

At the same time, school practice in England was not to have funding for special-needs students "encroach" on the school's overall budget, as often happens in U.S. schools (Murphy and Picus, 1996). At the school level, the basic and regular education program had the first draw on a school's budget. Students identified as needing Level 4 or 5 services received them, either directly from the district or with LEA funds that had been devolved to schools. Services required for Levels 1 through 3 were fully funded only if there were adequate funds for the "regular" program—and often there were not. Although both the state-to-district funding scheme and most LEA-to-site programs addressed additional need, this area demanded further attention, if only to determine whether school claims of underfunding were accurate.

Adequacy of Overall Education Funding

Headteachers and school budget managers raised concerns about the overall level of education funding, which included issues specifically addressing revenues for education, class size, professional development, and facilities. First, the level of funding for government schools was considered inadequate and had to increase. To some degree, this response was expected, since most individuals in most work settings in both the public and private sectors would like funding levels to be higher. But nearly everyone interviewed raised this issue. There were several reasons for the intense articulation of this particular concern about England's government schools. For one thing, funds were deemed inadequate because the central government had provided only small funding increases to the SSA over the past six years. Another consideration was that local governments' ability to raise funding for schools—or any other locally provided service—had been capped. In addition to small increases provided centrally and strict constraints on local revenues, the central government also agreed to a teacher salary increase that was larger than the overall education budget increase, forcing LEAs to compensate by cutting staff or other budgetary items to finance the required salary hikes. In short, funding increases had been small (generally less than inflation) and costs had been rising (generally faster than inflation) for over four years, and headteachers were feeling the squeeze in constructing their school budgets.

The second set of issues relate to class size. Actual class size in most schools had risen over the past several years to around thirty in nearly every school visited (although class sizes in sixth-form programs, grades 12 and 13, tended to be small—between fifteen and twenty). Nearly everyone believed that classes were generally too large, that they should be decreased, and that the only way to decrease them was to add money to hire more teachers.

But some headteachers were a bit tentative on this issue. These headteachers sought to maximize their overall school budget by seeking to enroll the maximum number of students allowed for their school—even if that meant increasing class size to accommodate them. Although these schools had higher budgets than other schools with similar enrollment levels, they obtained them at the cost of larger classes. The headteachers in these schools believed that the positive potentials afforded by the larger budget more than offset the negative aspects of larger class size. If we had interviewed teachers in such schools, we might have unearthed an opposing set of opinions.

In a few schools, headteachers had increased class size to obtain the budgetary flexibility to provide pay supplements for some teachers who assumed additional responsibilities. For a variety of reasons, these headteachers had decided to pay some teachers above the minimum required by the national teacher salary schedule. To do so, they had to find money for the differentials within their overall school budget. Increasing class sizes by small amounts often generated the funds required. Again, these headteachers had decided that such an expenditure of funds provided more than sufficient benefits to compensate for slightly larger classes.

In short, the issue of class size emerged as a "problem" in many interviews, but the nature of the problem varied substantially. In some cases, large class sizes were seen as problematic and caused by insufficient overall government funding, but in other cases, large class sizes were acknowledged as the result of budget policies at the site.

A third issue concerned professional development. Nearly every school believed that there was insufficient investment in the ongoing training of teachers and, in some cases, of headteachers as well. Interestingly, unlike the case in Victoria, Australia, where most schools took the opportunity provided by school-based management to add money from the school budget to teacher professional development (Odden and Odden, 1996b), few schools did so in England. Most schools spent the national funds for professional development but added little school money even though they might have believed that more training was needed. There was a belief that such funding should be provided from the central government, not from already squeezed local budgets. The schools wanted to increase funding for professional development but "couldn't afford to," many interviewees said.

Finally, nearly all headteachers identified the issue of facilities maintenance and capital construction as a major financial problem that needed more attention. There was unanimous agreement that the country and LEAs had underinvested in facilities in the past and that many schools needed major rehabilitation and some needed to be rebuilt completely. Most headteachers identified several facility enhancements that they funded from their operating school budget and could identify even more costly facility enhancements that were needed. GM headteachers also raised the facilities issue, even though it was beginning to be addressed for GM schools via a separate capital appropriation. But all headteachers agreed that more attention to the capital budget side of education finance, similar to the attention and policy initiative that had been given to the operations side, was needed.

Freedom to Make Resource Allocation Choices

Without exception, all of the headteachers interviewed discussed with enthusiasm and pride numerous examples of choices made that directly affected their budget. Most common were improvements made to the school building and grounds. Most headteachers argued that a good learning environment was important to both students and staff and improved the "marketability" of the school. And as already mentioned, headteachers generally felt that LEAs had historically been remiss in their facilities maintenance. Importantly, several headteachers noted that they felt more confident handling their own contracts for building maintenance. They felt that the school was the most appropriate level to handle such services because it allowed for fostering personal relationships and, subsequently, lower prices with the contractor. Other examples of resource allocation decisions included hiring more classroom assistants to support the teachers; one headteacher chose to pay all the school's teachers above the national salary scale. In addition, several headteachers pointed to areas in their school's curriculum that were being emphasized and how they attempted to focus funding there by purchasing professional development or additional educational material in the subject area.

Significantly, no headteachers interviewed complained of being charged actual salary costs by the LEA. In fact, budget decisions in general proved invigorating to headteachers—including decisions over personnel and salary costs. However, some headteachers expressed concerns over being able to hire and retain the best-quality teachers, given the perceived inadequacy of overall funding.

Lessons Learned

Eleven major lessons emerged from our study of England's approach to school-based financing, and all of them can help guide the design of a school-based financing system in the United States. Certainly, other important issues were and continue to be raised that can inform U.S. policy, but these eleven proved the most compelling.

First, a site-based finance system can be developed and implemented within an education governance structure that includes local education agencies, the structure already in place in every state except Hawaii. The experience in England from 1988 to 1996 shows that the mere existence of LEAs is not an obstacle to designing and implementing a school-based financing system; nor do LEAs need to be dismantled in order to shift to an education funding system in which most of the monies flow to school sites in a lump sum. Indeed, one could argue that a site-based funding system might be better in a system that included LEAs rather than in a state-to-site system; the ability of the LEAs in England to tailor a funding formula to the different contexts of schools within their jurisdiction was a strong element of the overall site-based funding strategy. The bottom line is that the widespread existence of local school districts in the United States is not an obstacle to creating a school-based education financing structure and could even be an advantage.

Second, from the English experience, the statewide policy framework that structured the key features of how an LEA-to-site finance system would function seems to have been an effective policy choice. LEAs in England all followed a general set of guidelines as they devolved money to schools. The guidelines addressed such issues as which functions should be handled centrally and which at the site and defined the key structural elements of the formula—age-weighted-pupil units, adjustments for additional education need, and so on. The statewide framework ensured that all LEAs followed the same set of guidelines and budgeted the dollars to schools using the same formula structures. But LEAs were also able to make numerous local decisions about the values of all the key formula parameters and so were able to tailor their specific formulas to the schools' needs and other contextual factors within the local communities. In this way, the statewide policy framework provided both common structure and local flexibility, a combination supported by all national and local school officials we interviewed.

Third, designing and implementing a school-based funding system brought a series of fiscal equity issues to the top of the education finance policy agenda. Such issues as funding differentials between primary and secondary schools, funding differentials across LEAs, different approaches to funding services for students with additional education needs, and the size and justification for price adjustments were raised in nearly all our interviews and had become dominant topics of school finance policy deliberations across the country. The issue of overall fiscal equity and the rationales for any special adjustments to the base amounts were heightened by the move to school-based financing in ways that few people predicted and probably fewer anticipated, a reality that emerged in Victoria, Australia, as well (Odden and Odden, 1996b). Put another way, fiscal inequities are likely to become even more problematic when a state moves to a school-based funding structure, and the result is renewed discussion of why disparities in financing schools exist and should be tolerated; how to reduce, if not eliminate, them; and how to improve all adjustments for different education needs or district or school circumstances such as facing higher prices in the education labor market.

Fourth, a specified approach for LEAs to determine how to formula-budget each school added both structure and fairness to the financing of grant-maintained schools, the English version of charter schools (see Appendix 5.1). GM schools did not "negotiate" their budgets with LEAs, as many charter schools do in the United States (Wells, 1996; see also Chapter Three). They received their funding according to the same formula as other LEA schools or according to a statewide formula created just for them. Put a different way, the state structured with some detail how the budget for GM schools would be calculated and required, as it did for LEA schools, that the budget be determined by an objective and public formula.

Fifth, the existence of GM schools highlights the problems of funding differences across schools or LEAs. Quasi-independent from the LEA, GM schools had difficulty understanding why some should be funded at higher or lower levels than others, and many therefore pushed to have all GM schools funded equally via some statewide formula. Again, fiscal inequities seem to be less and less justified and less and less rational as a country or state moves to a school-based funding system.

Sixth, school finance policy becomes much more public and "transparent" when a school-based education financing system is designed and implemented. Each LEA in England not only had to publish the formula it used to determine each school's budget but also had to publicly stipulate how much more it was weighting some students over others and what the total budget and budget per pupil was for each school. These realities had not been publicized before the reform. The process of making them public triggered substantial discussion about the differences and the values they reflected. In short, school-based financing leads to deeper and more widespread understanding of how education funds are distributed, the differences that are explicitly built into the policy structure, the values behind those distributional patterns, and subsequent pressures to eradicate inequities and strengthen any and all special adjustments.

Seventh, school-based financing led over time to a simpler formula structure that could be even more easily understood. In both Victoria (Caldwell and others, 1996) and in England, efforts were being made to reduce the number of factors in the various formulas. Many LEAs in England had used fifty to sixty factors in their initial formulas, in part to match the levels of historical funding in order to reduce gains and losses as they moved to a formula funding system. But over time, both LEAs and school officials began to develop formulas with fewer elements that distributed the funds in pretty much the same way. They also concluded that such simpler formulas were more easily understood and thus were preferred to more complex formulas with dozens of factors, however justified initially.

Eighth, the English experience shows that such a dramatic new approach to education financing can be implemented in a relatively short period of time. The initial legislation allowed for a five-year implementation phase. The bulk of the English school-based financing system was implemented well within that time span. Two elements required a longer implementation period: the percentage of the school budget that would be devolved to the site and the charging of the actual teacher salary in any particular school rather than the average salary.

As described earlier, England initially required that only 75 percent of the school budget be delegated to the site; the requirement in mid–1996 was 85 percent, and the average amount actually delegated has risen above that level. All told, it took about eight years to reach the 90 percent level of devolution.

Further, from the beginning, England charged each school for the actual teacher salaries rather than average amounts. And although LEAs were allowed a five-year transition to assist schools in meeting their budgets, most LEAs actually needed six to eight years to fully implement the new salary strategy.

Ninth, implementing school-based financing should be accompanied by substantial training of headteachers and others at the school who will be administering the fiscal system. England provided very little of this type of training, a shortcoming identified by nearly everyone interviewed at the LEA and school levels. By contrast, Victoria mounted a massive training program for both school principals and the school secretaries who ran the computers on which the school financial data were compiled, which facilitated implementation in nearly every school (Odden and Odden, 1996b).

Tenth, under LMS, schools spent educational revenues differently. Headteachers gave numerous examples of contrasts between traditional LEA spending decisions and school spending decisions made regarding their school and educational programs. This indicates that there may be important differences in how money is spent on education, depending on whether the decision is made at the central, LEA, or school level. Put differently, site-based financing is a stimulus to resource reallocation.

Finally, we believe England invested too little in the computer infrastructure needed for a school-based financing system. Most secondary schools we visited hired administrative staff, including accountants, to administer the school's new financial responsibilities, a finding corroborated by other studies of the English reforms (Levacic, 1995; Thomas and Martin, 1996). However, the English primary schools we visited generally assumed their additional financial responsibilities with existing staff by having the school secretary take on data input.

Regardless of whether the school hired additional staff, we found numerous examples of data systems that were not linked or consistent throughout the LEA. Consequently, the reporting requirements between the school and the LEA required extensive paperwork on the part of both entities, thereby increasing the workload rather than realizing efficiencies thanks to the technology. As a result, a significant extra portion of the money devolved to schools was spent on administration and not instruction.

By contrast, Victoria accompanied the shift to school-based financing with a sophisticated school-based computerized information system. This system provides not only school finance information but also data on student attendance and performance. The system will eventually be networked statewide; that should reduce inefficiencies in reporting and provide a rich data source for assessing school progress. Despite the implementation of this sophisticated information system, few schools in Australia hired additional staff to run it. Instead, school secretaries were given additional training and, in most schools studied, salary bonuses as well (Odden and Odden, 1996b) for assuming that task.

Based on these lessons and the overall findings, we conclude that the English approach to school-based financing could easily be adapted to the U.S. context. States could use current funding systems as the template for a statewide structure that could guide how local school districts would devolve money to sites, similar to the Budgetary Framework in England. States could identify functions or expenditure areas to be retained at the district level and let districts decide on which other functions or areas would be retained. States could write formulas for calculating the amounts each school would receive. One formula would be created for the base amount of per-pupil funding and others for differences based on student characteristics (level of schooling, additional educational need). Such a system would also help rationalize charter school funding (Bierlein and Fulton, 1996; Wells, 1996).

These changes would represent major departures from how education is currently funded in the United States. Nevertheless, the English experience with LMS shows that such dramatic change in education financing can be designed and implemented quickly and effectively and is almost immediately hailed and supported by both district and school leaders.

Importantly, however, although England's system for school-based financing has many commendable features and was part of a broader national education reform, the link was not always clear between school-based financing and schools using the money more effectively *to support student achievement*. Unfortunately, there is minimal evidence—based on our research and that of others (see Levacic, 1995, and Thomas and Martin, 1996)—that headteachers and LEA officials focus on the connection between resource allocation and student performance. This lack of connection does not, however, detract from the care with which England designed its school-based financing system but reinforces the attention required to ensure that districts and states in the United States pursue a decentralization financing strategy that is part of a larger standards-based education reform strategy that focuses schools on the primary agenda of improving student achievement and holds schools accountable for student performance.

PART THREE

RECOMMENDATIONS

CHAPTER SIX

A BETTER FINANCING FRAMEWORK

In 1993–94, all states reported that they were implementing some form of site-based management, and fully 56 percent of all schools reported they had some form of school-based decision making body (National Center for Education Statistics, 1996d), the proportion ranging from 22 percent in Nebraska to 86 percent in West Virginia. But very little budgetary authority accompanied this decision-making authority. Although most states and districts argue that they already decentralize funding to sites, nearly all retain staff funding decision making at the district level, and few, if any, actually provide a total budget number to the school site. Since personnel expenditures account for more than 85 percent of the district education budget and since capital and some other functions are also retained at the district or state level, the result in most cases is that only a small proportion of funding is actually sent to the school site, giving schools inconsequential budget authority. In short, the rhetoric about school-based decision making and financing blurs the financial reality (Wohlstetter and Odden, 1992).

This aversion to decentralizing education finance permeates most states' education reform strategies. No state, even of the several that have endorsed strong school-based management, has proposed either that the bulk of education funds be budgeted to the school site in a lump sum or has described how such a new education finance structure would work.

But the finance side of standards- and school-based education reform should not remain an ignored, underdeveloped, or poorly designed policy element. As

Chapter Two argued, the lack of school authority over the budget is beginning to emerge as one of the key obstacles to effective school restructuring, and school-based financing is a critical element of effective school decentralization. School sites need authority over the vast bulk of their budget (including personnel) if they are to change the ineffective use of current education dollars (see Chapter One) to more effective uses in a variety of high-performance school designs (see Chapter Seven).

The 1996 education proposals of Minnesota Governor Arne Carlson sought to address the financial weakness of that state's standards-based education reform strategies. Coupled with requiring each district to identify a performance agreement with each school, the proposals required that if the district or school decided on site-based management, the district had to provide the school site with a lump-sum budget that included the funds not only for instruction and administration but also for many other school or potential school functions.

This chapter draws on a paper written for that state to suggest how such a school-based financing system could be structured. It describes the key elements of the overall structure, the rationale for functions that should or could be retained at the district level, the district process for devolving budgetary and functional authority to schools, how the formula for determining each school's budget should be designed, and typical issues that emerge when a school-based financing system is implemented.

Overall Structure of a School-Based Financing System

In a school-based financing system, the state requires that school districts provide the bulk of education resources from all government sources—local, state, and federal—to each individual school in a lump sum. This could be simply mandated by the state, but no state or nation in the world has yet enacted a school-based financing system without also creating an overall policy framework within which this major change in education financing is implemented.

The following recommendations draw from the experience in developing school-based financing systems in England (Chapter Five) and in Victoria, Australia (Chapter Four) and the strong points of charter school financing in the United States. Of course, the first task for the state is to decide whether it will simply allow each local school district to devise its own system for budgeting dollars to the school, without any structure or guidelines from the state. Unfortunately, this has been the approach taken for the funding of many states' charter school programs. But the result has been confusion and inequity, and this is not the recommended approach for constructing a school-based financing system (Bierlein and Fulton, 1996; Wells, 1996). We strongly recommend that states construct an overall school-based financing framework within which each district would design its specific system, as England has done. The proposed framework covers funds from the capital budget, the general fund, and the categorical program fund operating budgets.

Our proposed structure would not be exactly the same for each school district. Most states have school districts that are very diverse. Most are quite small, with enrollments under twenty-five hundred students and three or fewer school sites. Indeed, states could choose to exempt small districts from the school-based financing requirement. That is also a policy choice that should be seriously considered.

But even if states exempted their smallest and lowest-enrollment districts from a school-based financing policy, the remaining districts would still be quite diverse. No single school-based financing formula would work for each district or each school within a district. The framework we propose here would allow each district to follow a common procedure and address common issues but would allow districts to make different decisions as they make finance policy around these issues. In short, we describe a framework that outlines how each district would construct a school-based financing system, allowing districts of various types to make specific policy decisions that tailor their school-based funding policies to the needs, expertise, and context of their community and their schools.

The proposed framework would require districts to construct their school-based financing system in five steps:

1. Identifying new district roles and responsibilities in a decentralized system
2. Specifying the core district functions and their budget levels and calling the remaining funds the "potential school budget"
3. Determining the proportion of the potential school budget that would be devolved to sites in a lump sum and how that percentage would increase over time
4. Structuring the formula each district must develop to calculate the actual school budget for each school site
5. Describing the general type of program budget each school site would be required to develop with its lump-sum budget allocation

Steps 1 and 2 do not require that a district moving to a school-based reform strategy strip away all district roles and responsibilities. Indeed, the assumption in education that school-based management eviscerates the role of the central office is simply wrong. When a district or any large system adopts a decentralization strategy to improve system results, the district or center must redesign the entire system, including new roles and responsibilities for the center (see Chapter Eight).

The purpose of step 1 is to identify these new roles and responsibilities to ensure that a sufficient level of resources is retained at the district level for the new district activities.

After reaching a new understanding of the roles and responsibilities of the district, the next step in developing a school-based budget is to make specific decisions about the core educational functions that should or could be provided by the district and to set their funding amounts. The goal is to be as parsimonious as possible in delineating such functions but to be clear that certain core responsibilities and functions are best provided by the district, even in a decentralized, site-managed education system. This step entails decisions about which functions might be more effectively and efficiently provided by the district in a centralized or decentralized system and is one of the major tasks in setting up a school-based financing system.

The type of thoughtful analysis proposed for this step is more complex than simply requiring that some arbitrary percentage of the operating or capital budget be devolved to the school site. Although the percentage approach has been considered in the past and is being used in many state charter school funding policies, it is imprecise and arbitrary, it does not allow each district to tailor some specifics to the local context, and it is unlikely to lead to a sound and justifiable system. Shifting to a school-based reform strategy creates a series of new and important functions for the district, each of which is crucial to making a decentralization strategy successful and each of which needs a specific budget. In addition, some functions are best performed by the district with or without a decentralization strategy, including those of the superintendent's office and of the district school board.

In short, in addition to identifying the general roles and responsibilities of the district in a decentralized system, the critical next step involves identifying in specific terms the myriad of functions that are provided in local school systems and specifying which of those functions should or could remain as core district functions and the levels of funding that would support those functions.

The remaining funds would be termed the potential school budget (PSB). A simplistic approach would require that all monies at this step should be devolved to schools, but we do not recommend that approach. First, the goal of the preceding step was to identify a small list of core district functions. As a result, there might be many additional functions that could rationally be retained at the district level. One purpose of the strategy proposed for *this* step is to allow districts flexibility in retaining such functions, which would vary by district and even district type. Second, sending 100 percent of the PSB to each site could force an overly hasty implementation of school-based financing. Requiring at this step that only a portion of the funds be devolved to the schools would allow a state and its local districts to phase in a school-based financing system, allowing for a smoother transition to a decentralized school-based management and financing structure.

Thus step 3 would specify the minimum proportion of the PSB that the state would require districts to transfer to school sites as their actual school budget (ASB). We recommend that it be a fairly large percentage and that the percentage increase over time. The percentage devolved must be more than sufficient to finance core instruction and school administration functions. Further, by allowing districts to retain some additional funds at this level, the proposed framework will also require districts to identify which additional functions they would retain and the revenue amounts that would support them. By requiring that an increasing percentage be devolved to schools over time, the proposed system signals that districts will need to devolve more and more functions over time.

But by requiring at this step that only a portion—albeit a large portion—of funds be devolved to school sites, the proposed framework allows districts to differ in the types of functions they retain at the district level. Furthermore, this provision allows districts to tailor their specific school-based funding policy to the needs of the community and its schools. We would expect that there would be significant differences in the decisions that city, suburban, and rural districts of various sizes make about these functions. By structuring the proposed framework in this way, one overall state policy framework can be used while allowing for differences between districts in the school-based financing structure.

It was at this step that England required districts to provide 100 percent of the PSB to their version of charter schools, called grant-maintained schools. A state could make a similar requirement for its charter school financing. This would ensure that charter schools would receive funding for both the site functions they administer and the district-type functions they must administer because they are semiautonomous entities. In addition, by providing charter schools with 100 percent of the PSB, this requirement would ensure that charter schools received not only their fair share of state and federal categorical dollars but also their fair share of local referendum levy dollars. Whether or not states take this route to charter school financing in the future, the proposed school-based financing framework could be used as a vehicle to finance not only district-affiliated schools but also charter schools.

Step 4 would specify how districts would construct the formula for determining each school's budget. This step would identify the degree to which the formula would need to be based on pupil units, the definition of those pupil units, the weights that could be provided for grade-level differences, the weights that could be provided for extra student needs, and other relevant but objective factors. This step would also stipulate whether variables other than pupil-related factors could be used to determine the school budget, such as the size of the physical plant or of the school grounds.

Finally, step 5 could require that sites create program budgets and specify a minimum number of budget program categories that must be included. The state could also require that site-managed schools clearly link their budget to their school improvement plan.

Figure 6.1 identifies the major elements of the proposed school-based financing framework. Recall that the state school-based financing framework should cover revenues from the major funds and budget categories, including the capital budget (capital expenditure fund, building construction fund, debt redemption fund), the general fund, special-purposes budgets for student-related categorical program services, the pupil transportation fund, food services, and the community services fund. We shall provide details of these elements and discuss the rationales for each.

District Roles and Responsibilities in a Decentralized System

In a decentralized education system, many of the traditional district roles are shed, but new district roles must be assumed. As mentioned, the notion that a site-based system eliminates the need for central system leadership and management is incorrect. An effective decentralized system is not one in which the center makes no decisions and schools make all the decisions; rather, an effective decentralized system is one in which schools are given the responsibility to accomplish system goals, largely because teaching and learning occur in classrooms and schools, and schools are given much more authority and autonomy to determine how they will meet those goals. An effective decentralized system is also one in which numerous traditional roles and responsibilities of the district—recruiting and selecting teachers, developing curriculum, providing professional development related to instruction, determining how students are grouped in school, even the structure of the school day and week—are no longer lodged at the district level but are delegated to the site. But to make such a system work and to succeed in teaching more students to higher standards, the district must design a decentralized system and assume new roles and responsibilities.

Chapter Eight provides examples of the key responsibilities, roles, and functions of the school district for an education system that devolves the accomplishment of key system goals to the school site. Districts must first orchestrate a process to create the awareness that high levels of results are required, that significant change is likely required to produce those results, and that the school board and district management have decided that a decentralized school-based management

FIGURE 6.1. SCHOOL-BASED FINANCING FRAMEWORK: NEW DISTRICT ROLES AND RESPONSIBILITIES IN A DECENTRALIZED SYSTEM.

Core District Functions

Mandatory district functions
Optional district functions

Potential School Budget

Minimum portion devolved to schools
  Year 1: 75 percent
  Years 2–8: 2 percent more each year, so by year 8, 89 percent is
    devolved to sites

List of functions retained at the district

Actual School Budget

85 percent minimum budgeted to school on a weighted
    per-pupil basis

Weights
  Education level: elementary, middle, high
  Student need: low-income, disabled, limited-English-proficient,
    gifted and talented, other

Other factors for budgeting the remaining maximum of 15 percent
  Characteristics of buildings and lands
  School size in terms of number of pupils
  Provisions for the severely disabled or other categories of
    additional educational needs
  Other measurable factors

---

approach is most likely to produce those desired levels of results. Districts then need to develop curriculum content standards, student performance standards, and an assessment system to measure student results, aligned with state standards and assessments.

Districts must also create the conditions that allow schools to work toward their performance targets. This entails designing procedures for devolving budget and personnel authority to sites. The budget element of this redesign responsibility is addressed later in this chapter. Districts further need to create a school-based information system; organize a comprehensive professional development strategy that has specific and different (though complementary) roles for systemwide professional development, particularly for principals and teacher leaders; and design and administer an accountability system that includes rewards and sanctions. The accountability structure should include an approach to performance-based reviews of principals and schools, with intervention strategies for schools that consistently fail to improve.

Districts must also provide site-specific training for high-performance designs, which schools may select to help them reach their performance targets. To boost performance, schools need to create or adopt a whole-school vision, centered on a high-standards curriculum and instructional program, that will produce the desired results. Several high-performance school designs currently exist, including those provided by the New American Schools (Stringfield, Ross, and Smith, 1996), the Coalition of Essential Schools, Accelerated Schools, Learner Centered Schools, the Edison Project, and several other school reform networks.

Core District Functions

The purpose of step 2 is to identify a small set of core district functions—those that each district *must* retain at the central office and those that each district *could* retain. Each of the suggested functions has strong rationales for being performed by the district rather than the site, be they new roles essential to making a decentralization strategy work, legal responsibilities, or tasks performed more efficiently by the district.

We have identified nine mandatory district functions and six optional district functions that seem applicable to nearly all school districts (see Figure 6.2). By allowing discretion over even this relatively short list of potential core district functions, the framework signals that districts should devolve as much of the functional responsibility and the accompanying revenues as possible to schools but allows for district flexibility in making most final decisions. The framework does not include any minimums or maximums on the amount of money that each district budgets for each function. The framework simply identifies a set of functions that must be retained by the district and a set of functions that could be retained by the district and then requires each district to identify which optional functions they will retain and the amounts of money that will be budgeted for each district function.

Mandatory District Functions

We recommend that states *require* districts to retain nine functions at the central office level. Several of these functions need only small budgets, and several reflect important new roles that districts must assume to make decentralization successful.

FIGURE 6.2. CORE DISTRICT FUNCTIONS.

Mandatory Functions

1. Building construction
2. Technology infrastructure, capital expenditure
3. Capital financing
4. Board of education
5. Office of the superintendent
6. Information services, quality benchmarks
7. Accountability system
8. Individual education plans for disabled students
9. Monitoring of federal and state categorical programs

Optional Functions

1. Transportation to and from school
2. Food services
3. Legal services
4. Insurance and workers' compensation
5. Districtwide education initiatives
6. Federal program services not devolved

Building Construction. Capital expenditures for school buildings have been retained at the central level in nearly every education system that has developed a school-based management and financing policy. Building new schools and rehabilitating old schools is an expensive task and requires analysis of where capital facilities need to be placed in order to provide easy access to schools. Usually school sites are chosen with the concentrations of children in an area and transportation costs in mind. Capital expenditures are also "bulky," in that they are large when they are necessary, but they might be required only every ten to twenty years for any individual school. Capital expenditures often demand access to the capital markets if the expenditures are financed by bonds; districts rather than schools have better and more efficient access to such markets. For these and other reasons, capital expenditures should remain a district responsibility.

Retaining decisions for building construction at the district level also means that the district will retain decision-making authority over where school buildings are placed and when existing schools will be refurbished. To make this system fair, district planning should include the needs of both charter schools and district schools. If over the same time period a state determines, as England has (see Chapter Five), that it is difficult for districts to be fair to both types of schools, a separate state agency could be created to administer the capital expenditure function for charter schools. But in both cases, the capital expenditure function is retained at the center and not delegated to school sites.

This recommendation does not prevent schools from building or refurbishing classrooms using their own budgetary resources. The recommendation to retain capital expenditures at the center simply recognizes that the major decisions for locating, building new schools, and refurbishing old ones should be a central and not a site responsibility.

This recommendation also does not imply that schools can use their facilities only for their own educational programs. Schools should be allowed to rent or lease their buildings for other purposes, for community use after school or during the weekends, for day care and preschool programs, or for purposes consistent with laws pertaining to the use of public facilities. Further, schools should be allowed to retain the revenues from those lease or rental agreements.

Technology Purchases and Support and Other Capital Expenditures. Technology purchases and support are a component of capital expenditures, but because technology has become so important in today's world, we list it as a separate function. Research shows that schools need to select and install computer equipment and software that are appropriate for their instructional program; thus the district function refers largely to the costs associated with developing a technology infrastructure for the school district. The infrastructure would include the following elements: a districtwide local area network (LAN) linking all school sites; the computer servers for this network that could be used for both instructional and business operations, including the information system (to be described shortly); the electronic wiring or rewiring that schools require to become technologically equipped; and asbestos removal, if necessary. This is a function that is short-term and, if budgeted, should have a zero budget within five years. This function also separates the district role in technology costs (creating the electronic infrastructure) from the school role (determining the technology needed for the school's program) in how that technology will be incorporated into the school's curriculum and instructional program.

This budget area also covers all other expenses for equipment, vehicles, and other capital needs.

Capital Financing. Capital financing, or debt redemption, must remain a central responsibility. First of all, many districts are already responsible for servicing bonds that have been issued in the past. They need to set aside sufficient budget sums to pay those costs. Further, districts will continue to have to build new schools, refurbish old ones, and set up the needed technology infrastructure, financing these expenses by floating bonds. Districts must then set aside revenues to service those bonds over their full term. In short, districts should retain both the responsibility for debt redemption and the revenues for those expenditures.

Board of Education. No state is proposing any type of radical school district re-organization, such as elimination or even reconstitution of school boards. One of the strengths of school-based financing is that it can be implemented within the current board and district structure; indeed, it could be argued that the existence of many districts and boards enhances the ability of a state to implement decentralization strategies by tailoring specific designs to local contexts. Although decentralization will likely change some of the roles and responsibilities of school boards and central offices, school boards will continue to exist and will continue to play important policy and decision-making roles. Therefore, as today, this function should be retained at the district level, financed by a specific budgeted amount.

Office of the Superintendent. In addition to the board function, the office of the superintendent must also be included as a core district function with a specific budget.

However, this function should be limited to the office of the superintendent only. It should not include any other district offices, such as those for curriculum and instruction, categorical programs, business and administration, personnel administration, or professional development. Each of these other offices and their functions should be addressed separately and independently.

The superintendent's office can vary in size and staffing, but it should encompass only the superintendent and his or her direct roles and functions. The superintendent's office could include a policy function and a public relations and communication function, but it would not include any operational functional tasks.

Information Services and Quality Benchmarks. This is suggested as a new core district function; it is now an often weakly implemented function embedded within general administration support. It would have two specific emphases. First, it would have the responsibility for creating and administering an automated *school*-based information system that would include all of the following:

1. Financial data, such as revenues, expenditures, and expenditures relative to budget
2. An electronic purchasing and invoicing system
3. Data on student achievement, including longitudinal data, and data that could be disaggregated by subject area, by topic within subject area, and by characteristics of students
4. An instructional management system that teachers could use to monitor individual student performance relative to performance standards
5. Descriptions of best practices, for example, curriculum programs or units, instructional strategies, professional development strategies, and whole-school

high-performance designs such as those from the New American Schools, the Edison Project, and other school reform networks (Education Commission of the States, 1997)
6. A personnel records system for teaching, professional, and classified staff

This system should, in the medium term, be an on-line, interactive, relational database, easily usable by every school site in the state.

The system should incorporate and build on any state's current management information systems. But changes in how these systems are used as well as in state-required data reporting are needed to produce accurate school-level financial, student, and teacher information (Cohen, 1997; Farland, 1997). First, districts and schools need to code all appropriate expenditures to school sites or administrative units. This means that the state must develop a *common* mechanism for districts to allocate all central office expenditures on behalf of schools (for example, operations and maintenance) to the appropriate school sites. Second, districts and schools need training to code all expenditures in comparable ways. Third, states would need to require reporting by school site or administrative unit. Fourth, the entire system needs to be automated statewide, most efficiently through the World Wide Web, and not just lodged in various large district and regional computer systems. Fifth, teacher data would also need to be fully automated and incorporated into the overall relational data set. Finally, longitudinal student data would need to be included.

The second focus of the information and best-practices function would be for the district to provide quality benchmarks for various curriculum programs and units, instructional strategies, professional development programs and opportunities, and whole-school high-performance designs that it puts on the information system. This district function should be conceived so as to help school sites select effective school design, curriculum, and professional development strategies but not to preempt school decision making on these issues.

Accountability System. This also is suggested as a separately identified district function. Creating and administering an accountability system is a critical district function under site-based management. It entails the following tasks:

1. Developing curriculum content and student performance standards consistent with state standards
2. Selecting and administering a testing system that would be used for public accountability purposes, creating the school performance agreement (see item 4), and aligning it with the state testing system

3. Creating a database of results for each school
4. Negotiating a set of specific, annual performance improvement targets for each school—the school performance agreement
5. Designing awards that would be provided to schools for meeting or exceeding performance improvement targets, including, for example, a new compensation system that provides base pay increases for skills and competencies rather than education units and years of experience, and school-based performance awards that could be used either for salary bonuses or school improvement purposes (Odden and Kelley, 1997)
6. Creating sanctions that could be used for schools that consistently fail to meet performance targets or whose performance consistently drops

Although the specific nature of each district's accountability system could vary, the state could require that it include at least these six components. But for the purpose of the finance system, this important district function would need to be recognized and funded in the budget development process.

Individual Education Plans for Disabled Students. Under current federal law, the development of an individual education plan (IEP) for disabled students is the responsibility of each school district. There is no reason to change the placement of this responsibility. A school-based financing system can operate with this assessment and program development function technically remaining with the district, since in nearly all instances, both site professionals and parents will be involved. Further, this responsibility has remained at the district level in England for the past eight years and has worked quite well.

Monitoring of Federal and State Categorical Programs. The final required district function, largely a legal requirement of federal and state categorical programs, is to administer the monitoring function for state and federal categorical programs, such as Title I, special education, programs for limited-English-proficient students, gifted and talented students, and desegregation. This function, often part of instructional administration, should be minimal and should focus on conducting compliance monitoring that focuses only on state and federal requirements, leaving as much discretion as possible to the site for designing and implementing programs. If not restructured by the state, the district should seek to monitor categorical programs in the most efficient way by consolidating monitoring activities for all or nearly all categorical programs into one process that is conducted at each site at only one point in time during the year or over some multiyear time period.

Optional District Functions

We also recommend that six additional functions be identified as optional district functions. Most observers would probably agree that these functions are better provided centrally than by each individual school, but in some cases the function could be devolved to the site.

Transportation to and from School. This would generally involve expenditures from the pupil transportation fund. In nearly all cases, transportation to and from school is more efficiently provided by a central authority, in this case, the school district. Devolving responsibility for organizing and administering transportation to and from school would preclude most schools from taking advantage of the economies that districts can offer by operating a transportation system for a larger geographical area. Further, a districtwide transportation system is also best designed to help transporting students who choose to attend a school different from the one within whose attendance boundary they reside.

In geographically small districts, where there is little need for transportation to and from school, transportation responsibilities could be devolved to school sites. That is why this function is identified as an optional district function. But the vast majority of districts can probably provide transportation services more efficiently from a districtwide perspective. Most districts would retain transportation for disabled students at the district level.

This function does not include transportation required at the school level for school trips and other types of school-initiated excursions. These funds and the arrangements for transportation services, which could include purchase of the service from the district transportation office, should be made a site responsibility.

It should be noted that in the most recent state charter school laws, transportation to and from school is often specifically identified as a function that would be provided by the district. Although we generally agree with that, we recommend that the option be provided to allow districts, under the right conditions, to devolve these functions to sites.

Food Services. Meals and other food services, both for students eligible for free or reduced-price lunches and for students who purchase their meals, can often be provided more efficiently by districts. Districts can negotiate lower prices by purchasing food in larger quantities. Districts might also be able to negotiate better prices with companies if they decide to outsource the food services function to a private firm.

However, school meals are not known for their high quality. Further, many districts operate their own food services program even though they lack quality management expertise for this activity. Many schools in Victoria, Australia, where the education system was decentralized four years ago, lost money when they ran their own food services but made money when they turned the function over to a private contractor (Odden and Odden, 1996b). There are anecdotal examples of similar practices in schools in the United States, particularly charter schools. For example, the Vaughn Street Charter School in Los Angeles claimed to have saved tens of thousands of dollars the first year it operated its own food program, outside of the district program, by adopting the management techniques recommended by a food services consultant.

In short, although food services and school meals can often be provided most efficiently to all schools by the district, scenarios can be constructed that would have schools providing better and cheaper meals. Thus this function is recommended as an optional district function.

Similar to transportation, most recent state charter school laws identify food services as a function that would be provided by the district. Again, although we generally agree with that trend, we recommend that districts be given the option, under the right conditions, to devolve this function to sites.

Legal Services. Superintendents and school boards will continue to be legally responsible for school districts' compliance with laws affecting public sector entities, as well as with laws, regulations, and court orders specifically pertaining to public schools. But in an era of changing school contexts including site-managed schools, charter schools and even contract schools, school boards could begin to offer free or fee-based legal assistance to schools. As the degree of decentralization increases and schools become more independent organizations (as they are in England and Victoria), they will need legal advice and representation on contracts, labor law, and liability.

Further, the laws pertaining to individual schools are evolving rapidly as charter and contract schools—privately managed but publicly accountable—are established. For the foreseeable future, schools will face uncertainties about their legal rights and obligations. Central offices will likely need to offer legal advice and occasional representation for at least the short to medium term until the legal responsibilities of districts and schools are resolved. The volume of legal work to be done would also depend on whether state and federal laws affecting school districts can be simplified.

Insurance and Workers' Compensation. This function covers both liability insurance for teachers, administrators, and school council members and comprehensive insurance for fire, theft, vandalism, or other damage to school property. In most cases, districts should be able to negotiate more cost-effective insurance rates for all their schools, as compared to having each school negotiate individually. An insurance company could lower the price to a district because the insurance package would be larger and the risk for any one school would be spread over a larger number of schools. Thus it is probably wise to have insurance remain a district function.

However, in certain instances, it would be to the advantage of schools to negotiate their own insurance coverage. First, specific insurance needs vary by school site; a districtwide contract would require each school to have essentially the same insurance package. Second, individual schools, through their own efforts, could possibly qualify for a lower insurance rate. For example, vandalism and theft could be generally high in urban districts, warranting high rates. But a school in a high-crime neighborhood that created a program of community involvement that dramatically reduce vandalism and theft should be allowed to enjoy the financial benefits of its efforts through lower insurance costs.

For these reasons, we recommend that districts be given the option of devolving insurance responsibility to sites. Of course, an intermediate strategy would be for the district to negotiate prices and to devolve insurance funds to each school site, allowing each site to purchase the insurance package it desires.

The argument for workers' compensation is generally the same: that such costs could be lower if provided on a districtwide basis, by spreading risk over all schools. But individual schools could reduce the need for workers' compensation, and there are many examples across the country of individual schools actually doing so. This, too, is a function that districts could choose to retain or devolve, depending on the context and perhaps the desires of the different schools.

Districtwide Education Initiatives. This is a proposed new function. England allows districts to retain a maximum proportion of their total budget for districtwide education initiatives. Some districts with low reading scores have created a districtwide literacy initiative; others have started science initiatives to enhance the science program across the district. Today, many districts set up technology initiatives or even professional development initiatives. Such districtwide initiatives tend to be tightly focused programs planned for the short to medium term. We recommend that the option for districts to create some type of districtwide educational initiative be included in the funding structure, on condition that such initiatives be limited to a maximum of 2 percent of the district's overall budget.

Federal Program Services Not Devolved. There are some federal and perhaps even state categorical program service responsibilities that cannot legally be devolved to schools. In addition, for those that can, particularly under the federal law that allows districts to consolidate Title I, Eisenhower, bilingual education, and several other programs at the school level, states must seek permission for schools to merge such funds to provide more coherent services at the site level. Currently, funds and services under the federal Individuals with Disabilities Education Act are not part of the aforementioned consolidation program but could be consolidated as long as IEPs were modified to support services provided in a more inclusive and coherent school environment. But this budget category would cover all remaining federal and state categorical programs that cannot be devolved to school sites.

The Potential School Budget

The potential school budget (PSB) would equal the total amounts from all funds, minus the amounts budgeted in the fifteen categories of core district functions. But the PSB would not be completely budgeted to the school site. The actual school budget (ASB) would be less than the PSB and would be determined by two additional steps: setting the minimum proportion of the PSB that would be devolved to schools and designing the formula that would determine each school's actual budget.

Setting the Minimum Proportion of the Potential School Budget Devolved to the Site

As we just said, we do not recommend that a school receive 100 percent of its PSB. The proposed school-based financing framework is designed to allow each district considerable flexibility in constructing the system that would best meet its needs and those of the schools in that district.

Rather than proposing that all of the PSB be devolved to school sites, we recommend that the state mandate the minimum proportion that each district must devolve to school sites. This approach allows districts to retain additional functions at the center and provides for a somewhat slower-paced implementation of school-based financial responsibilities.

There is no perfect minimum percentage. The percentage must be large enough to cover the bulk of the school's regular instruction, vocational education, special education, community education, instructional support, pupil support services, operations and maintenance, school administration, and related employee benefits, thereby allowing the school discretion over a large part of the budget so that it can reallocate resources as dictated by the needs of its higher-performing vision.

We recommend that states follow the process successfully implemented in England and set the minimum percentage initially at 75 percent. We also suggest that states increase this minimum percentage by 2 percentage points for each of the next seven years, which would mean that over an eight-year implementation period, districts would need to devolve a minimum 89 percent of the PSB to each site.

Potential Additional Functions Retained by the District

In deciding what proportion of the PSB the district would provide as the ASB, the district would need simultaneously to determine what additional functions it would retain at the district level. The state should therefore require each district to identify both the functions it decides to retain and the amounts budgeted for them. This requirement would make public the decisions that different districts make in terms of the types of functions they decide to devolve to schools over time. Figure 6.3 identifies the most likely services that would be retained, but arguments to retain or to devolve can be advanced for each of them.

Business Support Services. Given the powers and capabilities provided by today's computer technologies, it would be wise for districts—indeed, for the state—to create a computer software system that could automate the processing elements of business services: purchasing, invoicing, maintaining personnel records, pay-

FIGURE 6.3. FUNCTIONS THAT MIGHT BE RETAINED BY THE DISTRICT WITHIN THE POTENTIAL SCHOOL BUDGET.

1. Business support services: financial, accounting, payroll
2. Business support services: personnel records and administration
3. Business support services: purchasing, invoicing, auditing
4. Instructional administration of categorical programs
5. Mobile specialist staff
6. Substitute teachers
7. Services for the severely disabled
8. Community services
9. Instructional support for curriculum development and supervision
10. Instructional support for professional development for administrators and leaders
11. Instructional support for professional development for teachers
12. Instructional support for technological media
13. Pupil support services: counseling, psychologists, social workers, attendance
14. Pupil support services: health services, nurses
15. Major facilities renovation
16. Minor facilities renovation
17. School operations costs
18. School maintenance costs
19. Salary transition
20. Extracurricular activities and sports

roll, and so on. This still leaves many elements of the business office, such as negotiating contracts and purchasing in bulk, that could remain a central office function. Conversely, many schools often believe for a variety of reasons—timeliness, quality, choice—that they can purchase materials more inexpensively on their own. Thus aside from creating and operating the information system and the processing functions that accompany it, reasonable arguments could be made either to devolve or to retain central office business functions.

Instructional Administration of Categorical Programs. Districts will legally retain the responsibility for monitoring categorical program implementation, but they do not have to retain any role in categorical program implementation, such as working on program quality or even writing proposals for or reports about the district's or school's categorical programs. Other than providing categorical funds to schools as part of the formula for distributing the PSB, the district role in categorical program administration has a weaker rationale and, just as with the role for curriculum supervision, could well be a function fully devolved to schools over a relatively short time frame.

Mobile Specialist Staff. These costs are expended within the regular instruction budget. Many districts provide art, music, physical education, and even librarian staff to schools on a part-time basis; often, these staff travel from school to school to provide their specialist services. The dollars for these staff, and the functions they perform, could simply become part of the school-based funding formula, or the staff could be retained at the district level and the services could be provided to schools under the authority of the central office.

Substitute Teachers. Many observers might argue that substitute teacher costs, generally part of the regular instruction budget, should be borne by the district, especially the need for long-term substitutes. But again, most places that have implemented a decentralized education system have quickly devolved the responsibility for substitute teachers and the revenue streams to support them to the school sites. In England, districts often purchase insurance to protect themselves against the need for long-term substitutes. Districts can negotiate the insurance rates for such coverage, devolve the funds to schools, and encourage schools to purchase the insurance. Further, when schools have the responsibility for providing substitute teachers, they often become quite clever in providing it, and the need for substitute teachers is generally reduced. Schools that are successful in reducing the money spent on substitute teachers and have control over that revenue stream have thus created for themselves a new revenue source that they can allocate toward more pressing school priorities.

Services for the Severely Disabled. Although the district would retain the financial responsibility for the services required by all disabled students, including severely disabled students, it could devise a variety of structures for providing the services. Indeed, districts could develop special programs in selected schools to serve these students or provide these services through other special mechanisms. In both Victoria and England, districts have adopted the full range of possibilities for this function and the revenues supporting it—full retention at the center, partial devolution to schools, or full devolution to schools. Each state should determine the type of service provision for severely disabled students that best meets its districts' contexts and needs.

Community Services. Both schools and districts provide services that are expended in the community services budget area. The funds for the school portion, ordinarily the bulk of these expenditures, should be sent to schools, but the funds for district-provided community services activities, such as adult education, perhaps, could be retained at the central office.

Instructional Support for Curriculum Development and Supervision. Districts have an important role to play in creating clear and high-quality curriculum and student performance standards. But their role in actually developing curriculum units or other curriculum elements is less clear. A school-based reform strategy, particularly one that involves each school implementing its version of a high-performance vision with a high-standards curriculum at its core, assumes that schools have the concomitant responsibility to decide on the specific instructional and curriculum approaches that they will use. This was a finding of a five-year study of school restructuring (Newmann and Wehlage, 1995) and is a key feature of each high-performance school design of the New American Schools (New American Schools, 1995; Stringfield, Ross, and Smith, 1996). To be sure, districts could provide ideas, advice, and even materials to schools, but they could also simply devolve those tasks to schools. Thus some or all of this function could be retained, or some or all of it could be devolved to school sites.

Because schools have more curriculum responsibility in a school-based reform strategy and can adopt different strategies for their curriculum approach, the rationale for a district role in curriculum *supervision* is called even more strongly into question. This function could well be retained at the district in the early years of a decentralization strategy and then devolved to schools over a fairly short time period.

Instructional Support for Professional Development. In most districts, the bulk of professional development is controlled by the district. But as we argue in Chapter Eight, there are clear divisions in professional development roles and responsibilities in a school-based managed system. There are appropriate central office roles (such as training principals and leaders in management and financial skills), and there are roles that should be under the control of the school (such as training in specific instructional strategies). Further, schools should be given the authority to purchase the professional development they need from any appropriate source—say, experts from a design team, if a school is implementing a high-performance design from one of the national school reform networks. Schools could also purchase training from the central office if the central professional development unit provided desired training programs on a fee-for-service basis. These are some of the reasons why neither the professional development function nor professional development financing should be predetermined by the state as a district or school activity. Decisions about how this function should be handled could vary quite dramatically across districts, reflecting differences in district size, geographical location, and education improvement strategy selected.

Instructional Support for Technological Media. Many districts believe that it is a district responsibility not only to create the technology infrastructure to support school use of computer technologies but also to purchase computers, printers, video equipment, software, and other computer-based courseware for each school. Yet the research is fairly strong in concluding that schools should choose their own computers and software to increase the probability that it will be appropriately linked to the school's instructional program and actually used by teachers. Again, this is a function that could remain at the district or could be decentralized to school sites, depending on the desires of different districts in the state.

Specifically identifying a budget category for the purchase and support of technological media underscores the importance of computer operations for the schools of the future. We recommend that this become a standard budget line item in both district and school budgets. Whether a district or a site functional responsibility, the education system will need to invest in computer technologies, software, upgrades for each, and maintenance of the overall system on an annual basis for many years into the future. The budget system should be structured to identify the degree to which this need will receive resource attention.

Pupil Support Services. We recommend that the budgets for counselors, social workers, psychologists, nurses, and other individuals and services be decentralized to schools. Some school districts provide these services on a formula basis; under this structure, the professionals are considered site staff and are managed at the site. In other districts, these staffing positions remain central office positions, and the individuals in those positions provide services to schools on an hourly or daily basis; under this approach, the individuals are considered central office staff and are usually managed by the central office. In many high-performance school designs, these functional responsibilities are integrated into broader teacher roles, and the funds used to support these positions are used for other purposes (Odden, 1997b). Thus districts could make many different decisions about these staffing positions and how these functions could be provided in a site-managed system.

Districts might also want to distinguish between counselors, social workers, and psychologists as a group and health service providers such as nurses as a separate group for determining the locus of funding for these services.

Facilities Renovation. The conventional wisdom would retain facilities repair at the district level. But here, too, the practice in places that have adopted a school-based financing policy tends to be devolution of this function to school sites. To be sure, the responsibility for completely renovating a school in significant disrepair should remain with the district. But short of that drastic scenario, arguments could be made for devolving both major and minor facilities repair or allowing districts to determine how much of this function could be devolved. For example, many districts in England devolve facilities repair or enhancements under a certain monetary limit; others fix up all buildings in the short term and then completely devolve future facilities repairs to the schools. Further, many school sites invest considerable funds in upgrading the school building, including adding classrooms. Thus both major and minor facilities repair are functions that could be addressed at either the site or the district level, and the decision should be left to each local district.

School Operations and Maintenance Costs. These are the costs for electricity, heating, telephones, cleaning, and other necessities to operate and maintain school buildings. Most districts manage these operations from the central office, although operations staff are generally located at school sites. However, districts often do not keep school-specific records for utility costs, so they do not know the actual costs for each building. Further, if a building requires less than the average operations and maintenance services and thus spends below the average, districts rarely return the saved funds to schools and allow them to use the funds for other purposes.

Although it takes some new expertise to manage these site operations and maintenance activities, they can be taught and learned in a relatively short time. The practice in Edmonton, Victoria, and England has been to devolve these functions and the revenues supporting them to schools sites, and that is our recommendation as well. Nevertheless, we place this function among the potentially retained functions, allowing each district to decide for itself to what degree and how quickly it will devolve this function to the school sites.

Salary Transition. A critically important issue in designing and implementing a school-based financing system involves expensing staff salaries. The question is whether to charge schools for the actual salary of each person in a school or the district average salary for the position that each individual holds. The fact is that individual teacher salaries differ depending on years of experience and the number of education units the teacher has earned. Further, the average mix of years of experience and education units varies quite dramatically across schools, and these differences lead to differences in resources provided to schools. When most districts resource schools by a staffing formula, giving schools with equivalent students the same number of staff, they actually provide more dollars to schools whose staff have above-average years of experience and education units and fewer dollars to schools with less senior and less educated staff.

Each state will need to decide whether to continue this inequitable distribution of resources by charging each school for the average rather than the actual teacher salary or to redress this imbalance by beginning to charge the actual teacher salary. The latter strategy would reflect a policy of more fairly distributing resources, but it would need to be phased in over a multiyear period to let schools with above-average salaries manage their staff costs to their more equal per-pupil budget. The fact that some sites might choose to "save" money by hiring lower-priced, less experienced teachers reinforces the need to have a strong accountability system that provides rewards and sanctions based on results to help ensure that schools select the strategies that produce the largest positive effects on system results and the school performance agreement.

This recommendation reflects others' experience. Although Edmonton, Canada, and Victoria, Australia, have charged the average teacher salary, they are reconsidering this policy. England has from the beginning charged schools the actual teacher salary but provided for transition to this policy. England thought it would take five years to switch over, but it took seven. In the United States, Los Angeles is under a court decree to charge each school for the actual salary; the court allowed the district seven years to transition from its previous system of resourcing schools via a staffing formula to resourcing via a per-pupil formula and requiring each school to manage its salary costs within its standard per-pupil base budget.

We recommend that states adopt a policy of having each district charge schools actual teacher salary costs and allowing them to transition into this system over a seven-year period. This budget category simply includes the funds districts would need to augment the budgets of schools with above-average salary costs;

it should shrink to a relatively small amount within three or four years and should phase to zero by the end of the seventh year.

We also recommend that the employee benefits charges, now often included as a component of a separate expenditure item called "fixed charges," be tracked to individual staff and that charges reflect actual salaries and benefits for each individual. Compensation costs are the sum of salary and benefits and should not be completely separated but should follow each individual and be charged in tandem.

Extracurricular Activities and Sports. This is a complicated function, generally included in the regular instruction budget. Some educators might be concerned that if these dollars are devolved to schools, some schools might decide to deemphasize competitive sports. But most team sports are school-specific, so it would make sense to give the budget for this activity to each site. Although the state could mandate how this function should be handled, it would make better sense to let each community and thus each school district debate and discuss this issue and decide which portion, if not all, would be retained by the district and which portion, if not all, would be decentralized to the school site.

Summary

There could well be other types of functions that districts would decide to retain and finance with the proportion of the PSB that they control. But the ones we have just discussed are the most important categories that are likely to be retained, based on the experiences of other places that have implemented a school-based budgeting system. Further, if states adopt a policy of requiring 75 percent devolution initially and ultimately 89 percent over a seven-year period, districts would have to devolve more and more functions, and their supporting revenues, over that implementation period. Since most states have literally hundreds of diverse districts, each with different community desires and different district and school contexts, the proposed framework would permit each district to choose which functions and services to retain or to devolve and would require that a maximum of 11 percent of the PSB be retained after the seven-year phase-in period.

The Actual School Budget

The actual school budget is the amount of money actually budgeted to school sites in a lump sum. We will first discuss the major types of functions that would accompany the school budget and then describe how districts determine each site's actual school budget.

Functions Devolved to School Sites

The list of functions to be included in the PSB may seem lengthy, but it will ultimately reflect only a small portion of the overall district budget. The bulk of the budget should be devolved to schools, and the largest two functions—instruction and school administration—actually comprise, on average, significantly more than 65 percent of the education budget in most districts. Thus the number of functions identified should not necessarily be cause for alarm, since many of them reflect only small dollar amounts. Nevertheless, it is useful to have an understanding of the types of functions and services that most likely would be devolved to schools in most districts. Figure 6.4 is one such listing. It can be considered typical but should not be construed as inflexible or exhaustive.

These are merely the functions that have the highest probability of being devolved to school sites. Certainly the first three—school administration, regular instruction, and categorical program instruction—would very likely be devolved in most districts. Most districts would probably devolve the other functions in the list as well. But the strength of the proposed framework is that all of the specific decisions would be made by each district, within the constraints proposed—determining the mandatory and optional core district functions, devolving a minimum but high proportion of the PSB to the site, and specifying which additional functions would be retained at the district and the revenues supporting those functions. The flexibility allows the state school-based financing framework to structure the process of devolution for all districts while allowing each district considerable autonomy to tailor the specifics to its unique community context.

FIGURE 6.4. FUNCTIONS DEVOLVING TO SCHOOL SITES.

1. School administration
2. Regular instruction (regular classroom teaching staff)
3. Categorical program teaching (vocational education, compensatory education/Title I, special education for the mildly to moderately disabled, bilingual education, desegregation, gifted and talented, and so on)
4. Instructional aides from both the general fund and other funds
5. Community services
6. Curriculum development and supervision and teacher supervision
7. Instructional materials (textbooks, workbooks, paper, supplies, and the like)
8. Professional development
9. Technology (computers, software, printers, video equipment, and so on)
10. Guidance counselors, social workers, and psychologists
11. Clerical and other administrative staff
12. Staff travel
13. Transportation for school activities
14. School improvement planning and implementation

Calculating the Actual School Budget

After districts have determined the proportion of the PSB that they will distribute to school sites, they still need a process, mechanism, and formula for determining each school's specific dollar amount. States should also structure this step for each district. We recommend that each district use a formula for calculating the ASB for each site and also recommend that states prescribe the structure of the formula and the factors that it should include.

First, we recommend that states require each district to budget a minimum of 85 percent of the ASB to schools through a weighted pupil formula. Districts should be able to set weights for pupils according to school level (elementary, middle, or high school) and special school programs based on educational need (for low-income, limited-English, and mildly disabled students, for the gifted and talented, for students pursuing vocational education, and so on). The remaining funds could be provided to schools on the basis of a variety of different but measurable factors such as number of students, building or campus size, historical utilities costs, other special circumstances and conditions, or even, for very small schools, a lump sum to each school to cover the basic costs of a principal.

This approach requires that the bulk of school dollars be determined on the basis of a weighted student count but again allows districts discretion to consider the unique needs and requirements of their schools, which could vary dramatically. Districts know very well that no single formula is sufficient to ensure that each school has the funds it needs, particularly very small schools. By providing districts the authority to budget a percentage of site funds on a basis other than the number of weighted students, states would allow each district to address the unique and sometimes idiosyncratic needs of particular schools.

Example of a School Formula

The proposed framework provides districts wide freedom in designing the specific formula they would use to calculate each school's budget. Districts should be encouraged to construct as simple a formula as possible while still providing an equitable amount to each school site. In places around the world that have moved to a school-based financing structure, districts have initially tended to create quite complex formulas, often using multiple formulas even for small portions of the budget. Over time, they learn that simpler formulas can produce nearly the same distribution of revenues, and they begin to redesign their formulas according to these simpler structures.

Figure 6.5 is an example of a simple yet comprehensive school formula. The proposed grade-level weights reflect those currently used in many states: 1.0

FIGURE 6.5. SAMPLE SCHOOL BUDGETING FORMULA.

Lump Sum

$100,000 for elementary schools
$150,000 for middle schools
$200,000 for high schools

Base Allocation per Pupil and Pupil Weights

Base allocation: $3,500
1.0 for grades K, 3–5
1.2 for grades 1 and 2
1.2 for grades 6–8
1.3 for grades 9–12

Extra Weights for Special Needs

0.4 for compensatory education
1.3 for all categories of disabled students
0.2 for students with limited English proficiency

Special Factors

Square footage of buildings or land
Unique school needs
Special programs for the severely disabled

for each student in kindergarten or grades 3–5, 1.2 for each student in grades 1–2 or grades 6–8, and 1.3 for each student in grades 9–12.

For a K–5 elementary school with 420 students (about 70 students in each grade), 50 percent of them low-income and 10 percent disabled, the budget would be as follows:

$100,000 + \$3,500[140(1.2) + 280(1.0) + 420(0.50)(0.4) + 420(0.10)(1.3)] + unique factors

$= \$100,000 + \$3,500(168.0 + 280.0 + 84.0 + 54.6) + \text{unique factors}$

$= \$100,000 + \$3,500(586.6) + \text{unique factors}$

$= \$100,000 + \$2,053,100 + \text{unique factors}$

$= \$2,153,100 + \text{unique factors}$

In short, this formula shows that the school would receive a lump sum of about $2.15 million plus any budgets for unique factors.

Of course, this is just an example. Formulas could be more or less elaborate, and the weights and base allocation amounts could differ from one district to another. The weights and base allocation levels would also be constrained by the size of the total budget, the functions and associated revenues that are retained at the district, and the size of the ASB.

Budget Requirements

The state school-based financing framework should require each district to develop and make public its specific responses to the requirements. Further, the state should require each district to provide an annual budget and expenditure report for all specified functions, both for the district and for each school. Note in the combined list of functions in Figure 6.6 that school sites could have expenditures in all functional categories below the nine identified as mandatory district functions. Such annual fiscal reporting would provide detailed information on both school-level and district-level spending and the amounts spent at each level on different functions.

Figure 6.6 brings together the lists of functions identified in Figures 6.2, 6.3, and 6.4. It shows the full range of decisions districts must make in determining the total amount of money that would be devolved to schools, the likely functions that would be devolved to schools in that process, and both district and site expenditures by function.

Additional Issues for a School-Based Financing Structure

People will raise many issues about how to implement a school-based financing system, such as how quickly to implement such a program, what issues or problems are most likely to arise, and whether any elements are more important than others. Here we briefly address some of the most salient implementation concerns.

First, the proposed framework could be used in any state for implementation in the next subsequent school year, with schools receiving 75 percent of the PSB. Experience in Edmonton, Victoria, and England (Thompson and Lakin, 1997) suggests that school-based financing can be implemented quickly and that schools can handle their new responsibilities in a relatively short time period. Indeed, the experience in England, the only country in the world to adopt a school-based financing structure that is administered through local school districts, suggests that once started, schools want a quick (two-year) implementation period. The approach of phasing in budget decentralization function by function, starting with the small categories of supplies and materials, turns out to be more confusing than helpful (Thompson and Lakin, 1997). On the contrary, England

FIGURE 6.6. DISTRICT AND SITE FUNCTIONS AND THEIR BUDGETS.

Core District Functions

Mandatory Functions	District Budget	Site Budget
1. Building construction		
2. Technology infrastructure, capital expenditure		
3. Capital financing		
4. Board of education		
5. Office of the superintendent		
6. Information services, quality benchmarks		
7. Accountability system		
8. Individual education plans for disabled students		
9. Monitoring of federal and state categorical programs		

Optional Functions

1. Transportation to and from school	
2. Food services	
3. Legal services	
4. Insurance and workers' compensation	
5. Districtwide education initiatives	
6. Federal program services not devolved	

Functions Retained Within the Potential School Budget

	District Budget	Site Budget
1. Business support services: financial, accounting, payroll		
2. Business support services: personnel records and administration		
3. Business support services: purchasing, invoicing, auditing		
4. Instructional administration of categorical programs		
5. Mobile specialist staff		
6. Substitute teachers		
7. Services for the severely disabled		
8. Community services		
9. Instructional support for curriculum development and supervision		

FIGURE 6.6. (continued)

Functions Retained Within the Potential School Budget

	District Budget	Site Budget
10. Instructional support for professional development for administrators and leaders		
11. Instructional support for professional development for teachers		
12. Instructional support for technological media		
13. Pupil support services: counseling, psychologists, social workers, attendance		
14. Pupil support services: health services, nurses		
15. Major facilities renovation		
16. Minor facilities renovation		
17. School operations costs		
18. School maintenance costs		
19. Salary transition		
20. Extracurricular activities and sports		

School Functions

	Site Budget
1. School administration	
2. Regular instruction (regular classroom teaching staff)	
3. Categorical program teaching (vocational education, compensatory education/Title I, special education for the mildly to moderately disabled, bilingual education, desegregation, gifted and talented, and so on)	
4. Instructional aides from both the general fund and other funds	
5. Community services	
6. Curriculum development and supervision and teacher supervision	
7. Instructional materials (textbooks, workbooks, paper, supplies, and the like)	
8. Professional development	
9. Technology (computers, software, printers, video equipment, and so on)	
10. Guidance counselors, social workers, and psychologists	
11. Clerical and other administrative staff	
12. Staff travel	
13. Transportation for school activities	
14. School improvement planning and implementation	

found that decentralizing budgets to high schools in the first year and then to elementary schools in the second worked quite well.

Second, although our recommendation for charging actual teacher salaries and benefits might be somewhat controversial, we do recommend a gradual phase-in of the practice over a period of eight years. The experience in England shows that this is an adequate time span. It would be harmful to certain schools and students to move immediately to charging actual teacher salaries and benefits, but it would be unfair not to move to this policy eventually.

Third, developing an interactive school-based financial information system is crucial. The technology for doing so is straightforward and available—Coopers and Lybrand offers districts a software package that could accomplish this goal, and the Seattle school districts (http://sps.gspa.washington.edu/sps/) use the Internet for this task. Without such a computerized information system, schools will have to pay administrative and clerical staff, increasing spending on administration—the exact opposite of one intended purpose of decentralization. At the time a bill that requires school-based financing becomes law, the state education department should set up a task force and give it no more than three months to find or develop a system that will allow computers in principals' offices to track school budgets and expenditures.

Fourth, to maximize the opportunity for school-based management to raise student achievement to higher levels, the state will need to launch a training program for principals and for teachers who will handle leadership functions within schools. Principals will need training in the following areas:

- Program budget development
- Implementing and monitoring a whole-school budget
- Financial analysis and understanding of the state and district accounting system to ensure that all sites and districts list expenditures in the correct expenditure category
- Personnel administration
- Creating a team-based, collegial school organization
- Encouraging more teachers to assume instructional leadership roles
- Orchestrating a process for the school to adopt a higher-performing vision, including possible participation in national school reform networks
- The elements of whole-school change and managing a whole-school change process
- Facilitative leadership skills (skills to help decision-making teams make good decisions)

In addition to curriculum, instruction, and other training for the specific program strategies that schools decide to implement, teachers will need training in the following areas:

- Program budget development
- Running decision-making teams, including setting agendas, leading the group to decision making, following through on decisions, and monitoring implementation
- Collegial teamworking skills

Districts will need training in how to design and implement a decentralized education system. Chapter Eight elaborates on the new roles and responsibilities of the district, but some statewide training on the general issues, as well as how to develop some of the proposed mechanisms, would be wise for the state to orchestrate.

Fifth, another issue that might emerge and cause controversy as districts make public their own school-based financing framework is differential funding by level of school—elementary, middle, and high school. Indeed, this practice was one of the most controversial issues in England and in Victoria when they adopted explicit school-based funding policies. The public strongly questioned the larger funding differentials for high schools, which are greater in these two places than in the United States. Nevertheless, districts should be prepared for public debate about differential funding, particularly once current practices become public. In other words, districts should have sound, substantive, and justifiable reasons for the weights they use in formulas to determine funding for each school site.

Sixth, if experience in other places is a guide, the shift to a school-based financing system tends to reinvigorate debate about disparities in education funding across schools and districts. After a school-based financing system is implemented, schools with the same numbers and types of students will compare budgets across districts and raise anew the question of why budgets should vary when student characteristics are the same and school sites have no independent taxing authority. Put another way, as states move to a school-based financing system, it should expect new pressures to provide more equal funding across schools and districts.

Finally, a system of school-based budgeting and accounting for expenditures will provide a statewide database on school level expenditures (Farland, 1997). The new data would inform states as to how much is spent on elementary, middle, and high school students, how that varies across the state, and whether it is related to student achievement results. School-level spending data will dramatically expand the financial information base in any state and thus will make it easier to answer more complicated education policy questions—including education productivity questions—in the future.

CHAPTER SEVEN

REALLOCATING EDUCATION DOLLARS TO IMPROVE RESULTS

I n this chapter, we address in detail how sites can reallocate education dollars for school designs created to teach students to higher standards. Once schools are provided a lump-sum budget along with the authority to use dollars differently, they must exercise that authority. This chapter provides numerous examples of possible new spending practices in the context of financing higher-performance school strategies. We analyze some current strategies for using education dollars better; the possibilities discussed are not exhaustive. Our hope is that as more schools and school districts meet the challenge of using education dollars more productively, many additional ways will be discovered.

To be sure, more money is probably needed to improve student achievement by 200 percent, the goal of the national education reform movement. But there are many ways to boost current levels of achievement by using extant school resources more productively. As explained in Chapter One, schools are labor-intensive, and without change, they will have a difficult time raising results without more money. Envisioning how education dollars can be used more effectively requires identifying better ways to use teachers and other professional resources in schools. This chapter identifies several school restructuring and redesign strategies being implemented across the country that use teacher resources differently

---

This chapter draws from Odden (1997b, 1997c).

and improve results, thereby improving the productivity of currently budgeted education dollars.

Again, the point is not to deny that more money may be needed to improve education results by 100 to 200 percent—to raise the percentage of students scoring at or above proficiency from 25 to 50 or even 75 percent. Rather it is to show that there are ways to use current resources better and that schools can begin the process of increasing student achievement with the funds already in the education system. More money may be needed to improve results, but the following examples show that the education system can begin to substantially improve student achievement with the dollars currently in the system.

Examples from School Restructuring

Karen Hawley Miles and Linda Darling-Hammond (1997) recently completed a Consortium for Policy Research in Education study of five schools across the country that adopted or created a new school vision and reallocated the resources they had to the needs of their new design. All schools were in urban districts serving large numbers of low-income and, in some cases, handicapped students. They studied three elementary and two high schools. Three of the schools were "new starts," brand-new schools; the other two restructured themselves. All schools experienced large increases in student achievement and other desired results such as higher attendance and graduation rates and greater student engagement.

To varying degrees, the schools implemented five different resource reallocation strategies. They increased the number of regular classroom teachers, thereby devoting more of their budget to the core education service, teaching a classroom of students. They also provided varied class sizes for different subjects, grouped students differently from the age-grade groups of today, expanded common teacher planning time, and increased teacher professional development. The consequently enhanced instructional program resulted in higher levels of student performance.

None of the schools studied was given resources beyond those provided through normal district budgeting; these schools were staffed with the same total number of professional positions and resourced the same as all other schools in the district with similar numbers and characteristics of students. But these schools used their professional teaching resources differently. They all expanded the number of "regular" teachers. Two of the schools "traded" administrative positions for more teachers and then involved more teachers in the management of the school. Most of the schools converted the bulk of their "specialist" teacher positions, largely funded with categorical program dollars, to "regular" teacher positions, which allowed them to lower actual class sizes. Unlike Boston, for example, which had regular classroom teachers with class sizes of twenty-eight students supported by many specialist teachers outside of the regular classroom, these schools traded the specialist positions for more classroom teachers and lowered class sizes across the board. Two schools, however, slightly increased class sizes (still in the mid–twenties range) in order to release dollars to finance the professional reading tutors they needed for the Success for All reading program they adopted.

All schools had different class sizes for different subject areas. These schools provided the lowest class sizes—sometimes as low as eight students—for reading and language arts. In the Success for All schools, all teachers taught reading, including the reading tutors and sometimes even the librarians; this allowed them to reduce class size to around fifteen for reading. Other schools had some large "lecture" classes that were supplemented by smaller discussion groups and individual student advising. These schools required everyone in the school to teach at some point, thus providing quite small class sizes, and then required less than half the staff to teach larger classes at other times, thus freeing those not teaching for other activities, including both common planning and professional development.

Most of the schools also grouped students differently from the traditional age grouping seen in most schools. Several schools put students of two or three different ages in the same classroom and had the same teachers work with those students over a two- to three-year period. This permitted teachers to build a relationship and develop rapport with students at a much deeper level, resulting in a more "personalized" classroom atmosphere and eliminating the need for an extended adjustment period at the start of each year when teachers must get to know a new class of students.

In addition, the high schools created block schedules with longer class periods, which let them reduce the daily teacher-student load from over 150 to less than 60 in one case. This also granted teachers time to get to know a smaller number of students on a deeper level and thus provide a more individualized instructional program. The high schools also assigned small groups of students to each teacher for ongoing advising and counseling, yet another strategy that enhanced the personal, caring nature of the school environment, which research shows helps improve achievement (Bryk, Lee, and Holland, 1993; Newmann and Associates, 1996).

All schools gave teachers more planning time or rescheduled planning time so that teams of teachers could work together. Nearly all schools already provide planning and preparation time. Too often, however, schools do not schedule this time for all members of a teacher team at the same time during the day. Thus one way to expand common teacher planning time is to schedule all teachers in a team for the same planning period during the normal school day. These schools tapped this simple, cost-free way to expand joint planning. But they also used the flexibility provided by their different class sizes for joint planning. Both during times when students were in larger classes and, in the case of one high school, during times when students were out of the school working on community service projects, the schools scheduled common teacher planning time. In this way, each school was able to arrange for more common planning time for their faculty by using both money and time differently.

Finally, all schools expanded professional development. Although the additional professional development for the teachers in these schools was an important new way of using their resources, none of these schools expanded professional development to the level of $50,000 a year for a school of five hundred, which, as we will see later in this chapter, is about the level required for major school restructuring.

Because these schools traded specialist positions for regular classroom teachers, including many specialist teachers for students with mild disabilities such as the learning-disabled, each school had specific strategies for instructing low-achieving or learning-disabled students within the regular classroom or as part of the core features of the school design. For example, the Success for All reading program tutored all students, including disabled students, not reading at grade level. A school that mainstreamed all special education students trained the entire faculty in the expertise to instruct students in this more inclusive environment. To make the school approach to this service provision for the disabled legal, each handicapped student's individual education program was modified, with parental consent, to be aligned with the instructional strategies of the school. The achievement data showed that these special-needs students also improved their performance, a result often not achieved by the pull-out, resource room specialists typically required by individualized education programs (Allington and Johnston, 1989).

Schools implemented their restructuring and resource reallocation strategies over a number of years. In no case were teachers moved precipitously; many teachers, however, assumed new roles, with training sometimes accompanying those new roles. Miles and Darling-Hammond (1997) noted that school implementation processes would have been assisted if the schools had had more authority over recruiting and selecting staff committed to the vision they were deploying, one of the nine key elements of effective school-based management discussed in Chapter One.

In short, without any additional resources, these schools accomplished all of the following:

- Reduced class sizes
- Created even lower class sizes for reading

- Reduced daily student-teacher contact numbers
- Personalized the teaching and learning environment
- Provided common planning time
- Expanded professional development

Although all schools faced obstacles and challenges in implementing these different resource use strategies, they nevertheless made substantial progress and engaged in substantive resource reallocation. They also improved educational results for students, including student achievement in core academic subjects. In short, all five schools improved the productivity of their existing educational dollars through programmatic, organizational, and resource restructuring.

High-Performance School Designs

Despite the fact that three of the five Miles and Darling-Hammond schools created their own designs, developing an effective whole-school design is a complicated and daunting task that not all schools can successfully accomplish. Today, school faculties should not feel that they have to construct their own higher-performance school vision. During the 1990s, many efforts have been made to involve the best education talent in the country in devising higher-performance school designs. Several national school reform networks now offer whole-school education designs created to produce higher levels of student achievement. In fact, most designs were constructed with the goal of teaching the vast majority of students to new high achievement standards (Education Commission of the States, 1997). Organizations such as New American Schools (NAS), which offers seven school designs (Stringfield, Ross, and Smith, 1996); Core Knowledge Schools (Hirsch, 1996); Accelerated Schools (Finnan, St. John, McCarthy, and Slovacek, 1996); the Coalition of Essential Schools (Sizer, 1996); the School Developmental Program (Comer, Haynes, Joyner, and Ben-Avie, 1996); and the Edison Project (1994) now provide whole-school high-performance designs and the technical assistance to implement them. We will discuss the NAS and Edison school designs in greater detail because their cost structures are quite clearly delineated.

New American Schools

New American Schools offers seven different school designs to teach students to higher achievement levels (New American Schools, 1995; Stringfield, Ross, and Smith, 1996). The core element of each design is a high-standards curriculum program, with content standards in at least mathematics, science, reading and language arts, and social studies; the Modern Red Schoolhouse design includes art and music standards as well. Some of the designs require a different teaching and learning structure than the typical school, including multiage or multiyear student groupings (as in the Expeditionary Learning–Outward Bound and National Alliance programs); other designs (such as Audrey Cohen College) function with structures more like current schools. Some designs have substantial computer technologies, particularly Co-NECT and the Modern Red Schoolhouse. Although all work well in poverty environments, ATLAS and Roots and Wings draw on programs designed specifically for students in urban schools in high-poverty communities.

We should note that these and other characteristics of NAS designs reflect our conclusions in Chapter One regarding effective school-based management, particularly those requiring a primary focus on a rigorous curriculum and instructional program and the involvement of teachers in school management, especially of the instructional program. This chapter will show how the costs of these NAS designs represent seven different ways of restructuring for higher educational productivity. The curriculum and programmatic features of each NAS design are described more fully in Stringfield, Ross, and Smith (1996) and at the NAS World Wide Web site (http://www.naschools.org/home.htm).

Research shows that NAS designs are producing improvements in student performance—both educational achievement in the core subjects and other desired results, such as better attendance, more engagement in academic work, and greater satisfaction with school (Comer, 1993–94; New American Schools, 1996; Fashola and Slavin, 1997; Slavin, Madden, Dolan, and Wasik, 1996; Slavin and others, 1996). Schools and districts need to remain hard-nosed about the results and track over time the degree to which designs boost student learning. Early results show that NAS designs improve student achievement and, because they can generally be funded with extant resources, demonstrate how higher levels of valued educational results can be produced at current levels of school funding.

Three important characteristics of the NAS designs need to be underscored:

1. Each design has a strong standards-oriented curriculum at its core, which the school is supposed to adopt. The curriculum itself does not carry a cost; the costs are the components each design requires, in addition to the core staffing, to have the curriculum taught in the school. Because this chapter focuses so heavily on the components and cost issues, it is important to remember that the focus of each NAS strategy is a high-quality standards-based curriculum program.
2. Each design is intended to be a whole-school design; it should not be thought of as an add-on, a program "on top of" what a school already has. It needs to

be understood as a new and complete schoolwide program, to be financed with general fund and categorical program dollars in the school.

3. Most designs require a different grouping of students and the high involvement of teachers in managing the school.

These design elements, reflecting strategies for providing instructional services and for managing a school, differentiate NAS designs from typical schools across the country.

Each NAS design begins with fairly skeletal core staffing for a school—one principal and twenty teachers for a school of five hundred students (making the class size twenty-five, the rough average in many schools before implementing NAS designs). That is significantly less staffing than exists in most schools across the country. Let's take a look at the additional components required by each NAS design; the costs, shown in Table 7.1, reflect 1996–97 prices.

ATLAS requires (1) a half-time instructional facilitator; (2) a school liaison team that addresses health and family issues and is composed of various combinations of family liaison, guidance counselor, psychologist, social worker, educational specialist, and nurse; (3) $4,000 for instructional materials; (4) limited technology, including a computer with Internet and e-mail connections; (5) $28,000 of design team–based professional development; and (6) a weeklong summer institute for the entire staff that costs $15,000 for teacher stipends. The low figure in the total cost range in Table 7.1 is for a school with 50 percent of its students from low-income families and a half-time health team; the high figure is for a full-time health team in a high-poverty school.

Audrey Cohen College requires (1) a full-time staff resource specialist, (2) $7,900 for instructional materials and student trip costs, (3) $36,700 of materials and design team–based professional development, and (4) a weeklong summer institute for the entire staff that costs $15,000 for stipends.

Co-NECT requires (1) a full-time technology coordinator and instructional facilitator; (2) substantial computer technologies, best phased in over a number of years at a cost of about $125,000 per year; (3) $53,500 of design team–based professional development; and (4) a weeklong summer institute and other activities that cost $14,000 for stipends, substitutes, and staff travel.

Expeditionary Learning–Outward Bound (ELOB) requires (1) an instructional facilitator (the high-end cost figure in Table 7.1 is for one full-time professional; ELOB is finding, however, that this function is best filled by several individuals in the school, working together as a team. In some schools, these individuals work on the extra tasks for no extra money; in others, they are provided extra release time, which is a cost item), (2) funds for instructional materials and trips (the rope course costs are one-time expenditures for the initial purchase of the items),

TABLE 7.1. 1996–97 FIRST-YEAR COSTS FOR NEW AMERICAN SCHOOLS DESIGNS (DOLLARS).

NAS Design	Design Team Assistance	Design Team Materials	Design Team Costs	Operating Costs Above Core	Total Costs
ATLAS	$28,000	$4,000	$32,000	$150,000–$250,000	$182,000–$282,000
Audrey Cohen College	36,700	7,900	44,600	70,000	114,600[a]
Co-NECT	53,500	—	53,500	189,000	242,500
Expeditionary Learning–Outward Bound	71,000	13,280	84,280	30,000–80,000	114,280–164,280
Modern Red Schoolhouse	70,000	5,000	75,000	279,000[b]	354,000
National Alliance	37,000[b]	8,000	45,000[c]	61,600	82,600[c]
Roots and Wings	18,000	26,000	44,000	180,000–305,000	224,000–349,000

Note: Costs indicated do *not* include core funding for a principal and regular classroom teachers.

[a]Plus one-time district license fee of $7,000.

[b]Includes one art and one music teacher.

[c]Plus $24,000 district-paid participation fee.

Source: Odden, 1997a.

(3) $71,000 in design team–based professional development, and (4) a weeklong summer institute for the entire staff that costs $15,000 for stipends.

Modern Red Schoolhouse requires (1) a full-time technology coordinator (half time in year 1); (2) one art and one music teacher; (3) substantial computer technologies, phased in over many years at an annual cost of $125,000; (4) $70,000 in design team–based professional development, including a weeklong summer institute for the entire staff and other training experiences.

National Alliance requires (1) a school leadership team for each of five key task areas: standards and assessment, the learning environment, public engagement, community services, and high-performance management; (2) $8,000 for materials on teaching students to standards and use of the New Standards assessments; (3) participation in a national conference on standards-based teaching and leadership; and (4) work through the district for ongoing professional development and training at a cost of $37,000 annually, $24,000 of which is a district-paid participation fee.

Roots and Wings requires (1) a full-time instructional facilitator for a school with 100 percent of students from low-income families or a half-time instructional facilitator for a school with 50 percent low-income students, (2) a half-time family liaison, (3) four tutors for a school with 100 percent of students from low-income families or two for a school with 50 percent low-income students, (4) $26,000 in instructional materials, and (5) $18,000 in design team–based professional development.

The cost data in Table 7.1 are based on several assumptions. First, several of the specific items of each design are grouped into major categories; the descriptive literature for each NAS design (http://www.naschools.org/home.htm) needs to be read carefully for schools to grasp the general nature of each design and the specific components and strategies each requires (Odden, 1997a; Stringfield, Ross, and Smith, 1996). Second, for the purposes of national comparison, the table assumes that the average cost of a teacher is $50,000, including salary and benefits. Third, the data represent the first-year costs for each NAS design, although most designs are implemented over a three-to-six-year period. Some designs cost more in the first year and taper off in the final years; other designs cost more in the middle years of implementation. But none of the design costs vary dramatically over the first three years of implementation, so the figures in the table provide a good estimate of the components and core costs that need to be financed. Fourth, the data reflect the additional components and their average extra costs for a school of five hundred students; obviously, resource levels and costs will be higher for schools with more students and lower for schools with fewer students. Each school will have to determine how its specific costs will vary, depending on actual enrollment and actual salary costs.

The annual costs consist of two parts: (1) "out of pocket" expenses paid to design teams for materials and the expert technical assistance each school needs during the three to four years it takes to implement the design, and (2) operating costs for running the design. The design team costs range from \$32,000 to \$84,280, averaging about \$45,000. However, the designs include more than technical assistance and materials: each design has a set of components in addition to teachers that must be funded, such as the health team for ATLAS, technology for Co-NECT and Modern Red Schoolhouse, and tutors for Roots and Wings. Each design also requires a schoolwide instructional facilitator, staffed as one individual or as a team of teachers. Schools and districts would need to finance both the design team costs and the operational costs in order to restructure into each full design.

An interesting cost element in these seven programs is the substantial professional development included. This important expenditure is not found in many traditional schools, although training and capacity development is identified by many as a key ingredient for implementing standards-based reforms (Goertz, Floden, and O'Day, 1995) and is a key element of successful school restructuring (see Chapter One). For many designs, professional development costs around \$50,000 in design-based technical assistance and training and about \$15,000 for teacher stipends, mainly for summer institutes. Assuming that schools (as compared to districts) spend \$6,000 per pupil on average, a 2.1 percent school set-aside would provide the dollars for ongoing training the average NAS design requires. Districts and schools would need to budget such a percentage of their dollars for ongoing professional development even after the NAS designs are completely implemented because teachers continually need to upgrade and expand their professional competencies, and new knowledge, strategies, programs, and skills will always have to be mastered.

The total cost for each NAS design is the sum of the cost of the design team, out-of-pocket expenses, and operational costs. The total ranges from just over \$80,000 (plus district-paid participation fees) to \$354,000. For example, a school of five hundred students would need between \$82,600 and \$354,000 in current resources above the core of a principal and twenty teachers in order to restructure into an NAS design and fund all of the necessary costs.

The financial goal for the development of each NAS design was a cost structure that would enable a school with the national average level of resources per pupil to afford any NAS design. Schools would not need extra money to implement an NAS design—the idea was to have schools use current resources differently, reallocating them to reflect the cost structure of the selected NAS design.

Of course, the question is whether schools have the level of money required for NAS designs. To answer this question, we analyzed data from the 1993–94

Schools and Staffing Survey (National Center for Education Statistics, 1994). We used school-level data for elementary schools with four hundred to six hundred students (averaging around five hundred students), middle schools with nine hundred to eleven hundred students (averaging around one thousand), and high schools with fourteen hundred to sixteen hundred students (averaging around fifteen hundred). Table 7.2 shows the average staffing resources for the elementary, middle, and high schools of interest. In addition, the table indicates the dollar value associated with staffing, using the figure of $50,000 for each professional staff slot and $15,000 for each instructional aide.

Again, the data are provided for an average elementary school of about five hundred students, an average middle school of around a thousand students, and an average high school of approximately fifteen hundred students. The professional staffing resources in these schools reach into the millions of dollars (line 7); if the classified staff (secretaries, maintenance), operations, utilities, discretionary resources, and other funding were included, the totals would be even higher. Line 9 indicates the total dollar value of the staffing resources in these schools above those required for the core staffing for each design (one principal and twenty teachers for every five hundred students to provide class sizes of twenty-five students). The results show that the additional resources are more than sufficient to finance even the most expensive NAS designs. The figures in line 10 indicate the additional resources available for each group of five hundred students; these extra resources average about $650,000, whereas the most expensive NAS design requires only $375,000! In other words, the national average elementary, secondary, or high school could not only pick any NAS design and fully finance it but would also have nearly $300,000 in additional funding that could be used for several purposes: reducing class size below twenty-five students; adding music and art teachers, which also would help with more direct financing of preparation and planning time; retaining librarians and other student support personnel; or whatever a particular school deemed most important.

The data in Table 7.2 show quite clearly that NAS designs are affordable in the average school in America. To be sure, schools with resources below the average would have more difficulty financing a NAS design, and schools with resources above the average would have even more excess resources. But the information in Table 7.2 indicates that NAS designers met the goal of creating a higher-performing school design that could be implemented in the average American school with no additional funding.

The national figures suggesting that the average school in America has sufficient resources to finance an NAS design are also reflected in many of the schools in districts that began to implement NAS designs in 1995. Table 7.3 shows the staffing configuration for several schools in these districts. All schools have a

TABLE 7.2. SCHOOL RESOURCES IN NATIONAL AVERAGE ELEMENTARY, MIDDLE, AND HIGH SCHOOLS.

Component	Elementary School (grades K–5, 400–600 students)	Middle School (grades 6–8, 900–1,100 students)	High School (grades 9–12, 1,400–1,600 students)
Average enrollment	≈500	≈1,000	≈1,500
1. Principal	1.0	1.0	1.0
2. Assistant principals	0.0	2.0	3.0
3. Teachers	27.0	57.5	85.5
4. Librarians and media	1.5	2.0	3.0
5. Counselors and psychologists	2.5	4.0	6.0
6. Teacher aides	6.0	5.0	6.0
7. Total staff resources	$1,690,000	$3,400,000	$5,015,000
8. Total core resources	1 principal, 20 teachers $1,050,000	1 principal, 40 teachers $2,050,000	1 principal, 60 teachers $3,050,000
9. Total above core (line 7 minus line 8)	$640,000	$1,350,000	$1,965,000
10. Total above core per 500 students	$640,000	$675,000	$655,000

Source: Analysis of staffing data from National Center for Education Statistics, 1994.

principal, classroom teachers, and other professional resources. The table shows the number of regular classroom teachers and then the additional components and their dollar values—assistant principals, regular education, categorical program and pupil support specialists, and school-controlled professional development. Again, for discussion purposes, each professional staff member has been priced at a national average of $50,000 for salaries and benefits, and each teacher aide has been priced at $15,000.

The data reveal several facts about teacher and administrator resources in these schools. Again, millions of dollars are being spent in each of these schools (line 8), as is typical of most schools across the country. Second, the number of regular classroom teachers in the two urban schools produced large class sizes (over thirty-two and twenty-eight, respectively), larger than those desired by each design. Third, the number of teachers in the New England and midwestern schools provided low class sizes of twenty, lower than that required by the design; if necessary, these schools could use some of these teacher resources to finance their design. Fourth, each school has hundreds of thousands of dollars above the core funding necessary for a staff of regular classroom teachers and a principal. Indeed, these staff

TABLE 7.3. SCHOOL RESOURCES IN SELECTED NEW AMERICAN SCHOOLS JURISDICTIONS.

Component	Urban Middle School (1,050 students; 90% poverty)	Urban Elementary School (1,100 students; 95% poverty)	New England Elementary School (500 students; 15% poverty)	Midwestern Elementary School (500 students; 50% poverty)	Southern High School (1,000 students; 50% poverty)
1. Principal	1 $50,000	1 $50,000	1 $50,000	1 $50,000	1 $50,000
2. Assistant principals	2 $100,000	1 $50,000	1 $50,000	0	2 $100,000
3. Regular teachers	32 $1,600,000	39 $1,950,000	25 $1,250,000	25 $1,250,000	33 $1,650,000
4. Regular specialists	9 $450,000	11 $550,000	4 $200,000	3.4 $170,000	8 $400,000
5. Categorial specialists	10 teachers, 13 aides $695,000	2 teachers, 12 aides $280,000	0 teachers, 4 aides $60,000	6 teachers, 0 aides $300,000	6 teachers, 0 aides $300,000
6. Pupil support specialists	3 $150,000	2 $100,000	1 $50,000	1 $50,000	3 $150,000
7. Professional development	$80,000	$80,000	$10,000	—	—
8. Total resources	$3,125,000	$3,060,000	$1,670,000	$1,820,000	$2,650,000
9. Total for core staffing	1 principal, 42 teachers $2,150,000	1 principal, 44 teachers $2,250,000	1 principal, 20 teachers $1,050,000	1 principal, 20 teachers $1,050,000	1 principal, 40 teachers $2,050,000
10. Total above core staffing	$975,000	$810,000	$620,000	$770,000	$600,000
Total per 500 students	$464,000	$368,000	$620,000	$770,000	$300,000

are now used for many purposes, but these purposes are achieved by other strategies in most NAS designs.

Of course, the key question is whether the level of these resources is sufficient to finance the NAS designs. NAS designs use class sizes of about twenty-five, so the corresponding number of teachers—one for every twenty-five students—has been included in core costs. Recall that the total costs above the core for each NAS design is the sum of the cost of the design team, out-of-pocket expenses, and the operational costs, a total that ranges from just over $100,000 to $375,000. The data in Table 7.3 show that these dollar figures are less than or equal to the resources above the core that are already available in all but one of the schools in our example (line 10 in Table 7.3). In other words, these schools do not need more money to implement the designs. What they need is to reallocate current resources to design requirements over a three-to-five-year implementation period, and this reallocation will take effort and hard work. But they do not require more money to engage in this implementation process. These schools even have sufficient resources above the core to hire more regular classroom teachers to reduce class sizes to twenty-five; they can not only lower class sizes but also fund a high-performance school design with their current resources.

To be sure, in the short run, restructuring and resource reallocation will be constrained by federal, state, and local rules, regulations, and contract provisions, which would need to be changed over the medium to long term. In fact, many districts and states are providing waivers for schools and districts implementing NAS designs.

To jump-start this restructuring and resource reallocation process, many districts involved in having their schools select and implement NAS designs are also providing up-front money during the first couple of years to fund the design team technical assistance costs. But even these costs can be slowly transferred to the school over time; on average, these costs can be covered if one professional position is not filled and traded for cash.

Sources of Funding for High-Performance School Designs. Both the national (Table 7.2) and the NAS (Table 7.3) school examples show in specific terms the arguments made in Chapter One about resources in schools and school uses of professional teacher resources. Traditional schools, New American Schools, and many other high-performance schools all have a principal and classroom teachers as the base of their staffing structure. But traditional schools have a staffing structure above this core that is different from NAS and other high-performance school designs.

As indicated in lines 4, 5, and 6 in Table 7.3, this additional staffing is in three categories: regular education specialists, categorical program specialists, and pupil support specialists. Each category has become a "regular" part of most school programs and is assumed as "necessary" or "expected" for running schools. These staff are not perceived as fat or organizational slack. They have been provided to schools for many years because they have been assumed to be critical to accomplishing school goals. The reality for schools that choose to implement an NAS design (or any other high-performance school design) is that they have these resources today, but few of them are part of any high-performance school design.

Regular education specialists are teachers who generally do not have a regular class of students, such as librarians, or who teach special classes, such as art, music, physical education, vocational education, or home economics. Many elementary schools have reading and writing specialists; some even have mathematics and science specialists. Numerous districts also provide teachers with instructional aides who are paid from the general fund budget. There might be other categories of regular education specialists in different district and school budgets.

Except for the Modern Red Schoolhouse design, which also has standards for art and music, none of these teacher resources are required in any NAS design. This does not mean that the NAS designs are not supportive of art, music, or other learning areas. No NAS design would find the inclusion of any of these teacher specialists in a school at odds with its design. Indeed, the design may include these subjects in ways that do not require a teacher specialist. However, NAS and most high-performance schools focus on mathematics, science, social studies, writing, and language arts. Specialists are simply not a core element of the design and thus would have a secondary priority for budget resources funded after the NAS components were resourced and if additional money were still available.

Although these specialist teachers are often used to provide "preparation time" for teachers, each NAS design, just like those in the Miles and Darling-Hammond (1997) schools, has numerous alternative ways to provide for common planning time for teachers that do not depend on a school's having these specialist teachers.

Nevertheless, many schools might want to retain art and music teachers. This adds only $100,000 to the cost of the school program (per group of five hundred students), is easily afforded by schools funded at the national average or above, acknowledges the value of both art and music to the instructional program, and makes providing preparation and planning time much easier.

The second category of resources generally not required by the NAS designs includes teachers and other components typically bought with categorical funds from such sources as federal Title I, state compensatory education, desegregation, and bilingual education funds and a portion of the learning disabilities component of the special education budget. Schools typically use these funds for three categories of services: (1) pull-out resource room specialists who teach remedial mathematics and remedial reading to small groups of five to eight students, (2) instructional assistants, and (3) basic-skills computer laboratories. Again, none of the NAS designs requires any of these components. Indeed, nearly all NAS designs explicitly urge schools to trade these resources for the components of the NAS design. (Of course, special services would need to be maintained for the severely disabled and other categories of disability that require separate pull-out services, but a large number of students in the learning disabilities category are often not best served by these strategies.)

The third category of components not generally found in NAS designs are pupil support specialists—guidance counselors, deans, social workers, psychologists, and nurses. These staff can comprise about 10 percent of the average school district budget but, except for ATLAS, are not core components of any NAS design, largely because the NAS designs have teachers working with a smaller number of students over more than one academic year and have moved the guidance and counseling function into teacher teams.

In short, there are three categories of resources typically found in schools across America—regular education specialists, categorical program remedial specialists, and pupil support specialists—that are not generally included as core components of NAS or other high-performance school designs.

Figure 7.1 shows how the approach to staffing and resourcing schools taken by NAS and other high-performance school designs differs from the approach typical of schools across the country. In addition to the core staffing of one principal and twenty teachers for a school of five hundred students (twenty-five students per classroom), districts usually hire a series of specialists—regular education specialists, categorical program specialists, and pupil support services specialists, with little or no money for training. The specialists are supposed to handle functions, duties, and student needs that are different from regular instruction.

To account for these functions, NAS designs expand teacher jobs to include instructional as well as other specialized tasks. They require an instructional facilitator (to help teachers continually improve the instructional program) and substantial investment in ongoing professional development, to develop new skills and competencies. These are key differences, with traditional schools representing a bureaucratic approach and NAS schools representing a high-performance approach to organization and management.

Indeed, the reduction of "specialists," the stronger emphasis on staff providing the core service of instruction (teachers, in education), the expansion of the job of the core service provider to include multiple functions, and the emphasis on ongoing training and professional development are characteristic of most evolving high-performance organizations (Lawler, 1986, 1992, 1996) and particularly high-involvement, high-performance schools (Darling-Hammond, 1996; National Commission on Teaching and America's Future, 1996). This is how organizations restructure and reorganize for higher performance using current or even reduced

FIGURE 7.1. STAFFING IN REGULAR VERSUS HIGH-PERFORMANCE SCHOOLS (PER 500 STUDENTS).

Core Funding *(Ideal class size: 25 students)* 1 principal 20 teachers	
Additional Resources in *Traditional Schools*	*Additional Resources for NAS or Other* *High-Performance School Designs*
Regular education specialists	Schoolwide instructional facilitator
Categorical program specialists	Teachers with multifunctional roles
Pupil support specialists	Professional development: $75,000
School-controlled professional development	Design-specific resources (tutors, health team, and so on)

resources. And that is also why compensation is revamped to a system based on skills and competencies, which typically allows the core service providers—teachers, in education—to earn higher salaries (Odden and Kelley, 1997).

Moreover, for these reasons, *efficiencies* is the wrong descriptor; *restructuring* and *reallocation* are the correct terms when discussing the financing of NAS school designs. New American Schools—and other high-performance schools—are staffed, structured, organized, and run differently from traditional schools. To implement an NAS design, a school needs to restructure itself, including the resources it purchases with its school budget.

Educators and policymakers will need to monitor the level of results produced by NAS and other high-performance school designs to ensure that student achievement rises when the designs are fully implemented. But as stated earlier, the first results are promising. NAS designs seem to be worth the effort it takes both to restructure programmatically and to reallocate existing resources.

Appendixes 7.1 through 7.7 provide examples in school districts around the country of how current resources can be reallocated to finance different NAS school designs.

Resource Reallocation: Approach with Care. Although resource reallocation is a possible route to financing various NAS school designs, it must be undertaken with care and must address two key issues. First, resource reallocation involves people and thus must be implemented carefully, fairly, and compassionately. Many specialists could be retrained to assume the roles of teacher, instructional facilitator, tutor, and other staff in the different designs. Schools should tap all possibilities for redeploying specialists to new teacher roles. Schools could implement resource reallocation via normal teacher attrition, choosing to leave open positions unfilled and to channel that money to other uses. Districts should also be encouraged to develop cooperative programs with local colleges and universities to help instructional assistants become trained as fully certified teachers.

Second, local, state, or federal rules, regulations, and requirements limit—in some cases severely limit—a school's ability to reallocate its specialist resources. The examples show that reallocation *could* provide the dollars needed for any NAS design. But each school, district, and state would have to assess the legal constraints that currently prevent sites from participating fully in this resource reallocation process and consider changing codes, providing waivers, or otherwise lifting the limitations on a school's ability to spend its dollars differently. For example, schools would have to change individual education plans for disabled students in order to provide services within the regular instructional program. State or local requirements for specific extra staffing, such as a guidance counselor in every elementary school, or for specific class sizes would have to be waived. Collective bargaining contracts requiring the same working conditions in each school would need to be altered to allow teachers in each school to create the conditions specified by the design. In the final analysis, schools can reallocate only to the extent allowed by the legal, regulatory, and political environment in which they exist.

In other words, the process of resource reallocation must be done thoughtfully, sensitively, and legally. It will undoubtedly take schools two to four years to complete the process, during which time rules, regulations, tradition, and even politics might have to change. But at the end of the process, schools will have created a new, higher-performing educational organization; will have implemented a high-quality, rigorous curriculum; and should have students achieving to much higher standards. Such results should make the restructuring and resource reallocation efforts worthwhile and rewarding.

The Edison Project

The Edison Project provides yet another example of a high-performance school design that can be financed with current dollars in the education system through resource reallocation. Edison is not only a high-performance design but also one infused with computer technologies. An Edison school of about five hundred students would feature multiage "houses" containing four teachers and at most 120 students, depending on overall funding; one tutor for each house; two art, two music, and two foreign language teachers; a library and media specialist; a community liaison; a technology coordinator; and a principal. In addition, each student is provided with a laptop computer to use at home, and each classroom is equipped with at least four computers. The mathematics program for elementary and middle schools is Chicago Math (Hirschhorn, 1993; Usiskin, 1986); the reading program is based on the Success for All program (Slavin and others, 1996). Reading is taught by all professionals in the school, so reading classes are small, averaging around fifteen students per class. Schools can select their own science and social studies programs, but Edison also provides options for these subject areas, which include the International Baccalaureate and advanced placement (AP) classes for the high school model. The school day runs for eight hours, the school year for eleven months. Teachers are paid at competitive rates (sometimes the district salary schedule) with supplements for the longer day and year. Each house is coordinated by a lead teacher who earns a salary supplement.

School structure and cost are the same for elementary, middle, and high school designs. The Edison School design can be financed in any district that spends just below the national average expenditure per pupil or more. To run an Edison school, the Edison Project receives the district average operating expenditures per pupil from state and local sources, plus appropriate categorical program dollars. Since districts typically spend more on high schools than on elementary schools, Edison funding entails a shifting of resources from high schools to elementary schools as well as resource reallocation within each of those schools. Third-party evaluations from the first year of implementation of the elementary model showed impressive results (Edison Project, 1996a, 1996b, 1996c, 1996d). Results from subsequent implementations, especially for middle and high schools that adopt the Edison School model, have not yet been reviewed.

The fact that Edison is offered by a for-profit organization has caused some controversy, even though Edison has yet to actually make a profit. Many observers believe that public school dollars should not find their way to private sector profits. But schools already purchase many items from profit-making firms: books, supplies, electricity, heating, transportation, food, and tutoring such as that provided by Sylvan Learning Centers. Implementing the Edison design would mean that they would buy core instructional services from a vendor as well. Since the Edison Project provides an ambitious design for instruction as well as modern technologies, all with currently available resources, districts might be wise to consider it even though the design is sponsored by a profit-making firm.

Finally, Edison schools often avoid many of the implementation obstacles to resource reallocation that other schools, such as those implementing an NAS design, may face, largely because Edison operates school sites under a contract with the school board or a charter, in the case of Edison charter schools, both of which give Edison the authority to install its design. In both cases, the contract or char-ter gives Edison more up-front authority to staff the school and use resources according to the Edison design, in exchange for accountability for student achieve-ment results.

Other Funding Strategies

Reallocating the entire school budget to the needs of a high-performance school de-sign is difficult but possible. Some schools have less onerous options—they need only reallocate their Title I funds. Other schools, particularly in low-spending districts, do not have sufficient funds above the core of a principal and regular classroom teach-ers and thus need new money to restructure themselves into a high-performance school. The following analysis elaborates these possibilities and realities.

Title I Funding

Ironically, many schools with high concentrations of students from low-income families may be in the most advantaged position for implementing an NAS, Edi-son, or other high-performance school design. For the 1996–97 academic year, schools with just 50 percent of students from low-income backgrounds could use Title I funds to implement schoolwide programs.

These new possibilities were created in part because Congress, the Clinton administration, and many analysts believed that the traditional pull-out programs of the past had not had the desired impact on student achievement and that more coherent schoolwide strategies could have more powerful effects. In fact, core com-ponents of three of the designs—the School Development portion of ATLAS and the Success for All portion of both Roots and Wings and the Edison School—began as schoolwide Title I programs; moreover, each has large positive impacts on student achievement (Comer, 1993–94; Slavin and others, 1996).

Another potential benefit for school implementation of more powerful, whole-school designs is to improve the probability that students in Title I schools are ex-posed to and learn to the higher standards of a more ambitious, thinking-oriented curriculum. For years, research has shown that most Title I programs provide intensive instruction in basic skills alone, thus denying eligible students the op-portunity to learn at much higher levels. The curriculum program in every NAS design has rigorous content standards and high student performance standards and thus avoids this shortcoming of too many district and school Title I programs.

Finally, both federal and state Title I staff are urging districts to have schools with 50 percent or more of their students from poverty backgrounds redirect their

Title I funds toward high-performance, schoolwide programs designed to teach all students to high standards. Indeed, many of the first jurisdictions implementing NAS designs have also encouraged Title I schools to shift their use of Title I funds away from pull-out remedial specialists, basic-skills computer labs, and instructional assistants to the needs of high-performance school designs.

Districts could speed up the more productive use of Title I funds by *requiring* schools to apply Title I funds toward high-performance school design costs. And in many cases, these funds would cover the cost of even the most expensive NAS design. For example, a five-hundred-student school with just 80 percent eligible for Title I funds receives $900 per Title I student in many districts and states; sometimes the school receives additional amounts in state compensatory funds. That is sufficient for both Roots and Wings and ATLAS (for schools with that level of poverty) and could finance any NAS design. If that school's Title I funding were dedicated to NAS, any design could be implemented with those funds alone. Further, if the school's population included just 50 percent of students from poverty households and received $700 for each Title I–eligible student, it would have $175,000, nearly the total needed for the Roots and Wings or ATLAS programs for that level of poverty and more than enough for either of two other NAS designs.

In sum, schools that are allowed to use Title I funds for schoolwide programs would be able to dedicate these to NAS, Edison, or other high-performance designs. In many cases, those dollars alone would be sufficient for the school to finance a powerful whole-school, high-performance design created to teach all its students—including its Title I students—to high academic standards.

New Money

States and districts should also consider raising or using new money to finance these and other high-performance school designs—both operating costs and design-based technical assistance. Indeed, this might be the only option for schools in districts spending substantially below the national average. Recall that Chapter One argued for solving the most egregious school financing disparities by raising the spending of all schools to either the state or the national median. With more money, they might decide to fix their physical plant and purchase other items normally found in average schools (Adams, 1994; Firestone, Goertz, Nagle, and Smelkinson, 1994; Picus, 1994). However, sooner or later they need to spend their substantial new money on the instructional program. High-performance school designs, such as those provided by NAS, Edison, and other national school reform networks, could be attractive options.

Each high-performance school design offers a particularly worthy use for such new money—much higher results for modestly increased costs. This has been a goal of state legislatures for many years—they want to know how much increased funding is needed to produce student achievement results. The NAS and Edison designs offer attractive options. The NAS extra costs range from $100,000 to $375,000, or $200 to $700 per child, which is well within the range of new money most schools in property-poor districts receive as part of a school finance reform program.

If school finance reform dollars were used to fund a high-performance school design, a state or a district could argue that an increase in education spending would result in a large increase in student achievement. Such an argument would likely have strong public and political appeal and provide additional support for the politically tough decisions required for school finance reform. Also, as shown earlier, it would avoid having schools spend the funds in traditional ways on specialist staff and then having to change this expenditure pattern when they decided to restructure themselves as a higher-performance school.

Given these arguments, it is now possible to make the links between equitable school funding and teaching to high standards much more explicit. Recall from Chapter One that improving school fiscal equity for districts in the bottom half of the distribution could be a reasonable goal today. But an even better strategy is to cost out a high-performance school design and ensure that each district or school receives sufficient funds for such a program. The analysis in this chapter has done this for many NAS designs and to some degree for the Edison Project. The Modern Red Schoolhouse program is a prototypical example, having both high content and performance standards and embedded modern technologies. It costs $1,050,000 for core staffing of one principal and twenty teachers for a school of five hundred students. That must be augmented by about $350,000 for the components of Modern Red Schoolhouse, bringing the total to about $1.4 million. As also suggested in this chapter, these cost figures might be somewhat low, providing insufficient time for teacher planning and training and no school librarian. Adding these costs would bring the total to about $1.6 million. But these costs cover only instruction, pupil support, and school site administration which, as Chapter One shows, account for about 75 percent of a school's expenditures. Adjusting the $1.6 million to a total expenditure would thus yield a figure of $2,133,333 for the national average cost of a high-performance school with an enrollment of five hundred students. That comes to about $4,270 per pupil, which, as Chapter One also shows, is quite close to the 1996–97 national median of basic education revenues per pupil for K–12 school districts. (Increasing the 1991–92 median of $4,166 by 4 percent to account for inflation gives a 1996–97 figure of $4,332.)

These figures suggest that bringing all schools up to the spending level of the national median would be sufficient for schools to finance any of a variety of high-performance school designs. This policy would affect the lowest-spending states, providing a substantively justified degree of horizontal equity. States with a median above the national median would need to use their higher state median to improve horizontal equity for the bottom half, and such a policy would also ensure more than sufficient resources for a high-performance school. Thus a national policy of benefit to all states would be to raise spending to the state or the national median, whichever is higher, and such a policy would allow all schools in America to finance one of several emerging school designs created to teach students to high standards (Education Commission of the States, 1997; Herman and Stringfield, 1997).

Using the same data set as in Chapter One, we estimate that the cost of this latter policy would have been $25.2 billion for the 1991–92 school year, which is 13.9 percent of estimated state plus local revenues per pupil. This total would represent $32.2 billion in 1996–97 dollars, or 156 percent of 1996–97 federal education revenues. Revenues would have been raised in 8,481 of the total number of school districts, or almost 58 percent of the nation's school districts. See Appendixes 7.8, 7.9, and 7.10 for the state effects.

Conclusion

Current education reform goals can be accomplished only by improving the productivity of the American educational system. This means that current education dollars have to produce higher student achievement results. Seen from inside the typical elementary, middle, or high school, rising to this challenge seems virtually impossible. But as we have shown, there are many ways to use professional teacher resources other than the ways they are used in the typical school. Several schools across the country have devised ways to make the curriculum program more rigorous, lower class size, provide more planning time for teachers, reduce daily student-teacher contacts in secondary schools, and provide intensive professional development to improve student achievement. Numerous high-performance school designs have also been created. The results so far show that these designs have been successful.

Reallocating resources currently used largely to pay specialists not included in the core staffing of one principal and twenty teachers per five hundred students is a route many schools could take to fund the costs of high-performance school designs. Title I schools and schools in high-spending districts would have the most flexibility for this type of resource reallocation. Schools in average-spending districts around the country would have a tougher resource reallocation challenge; they would have to trade in almost all of their teacher specialists above the core staffing. This would provide sufficient dollars to fund high-performance designs, but the process would be challenging. Schools in low-spending districts and states, however, would likely need more money, which would require school finance re-form focused on schools spending below the median. Such schools generally do not have resources above the core of a principal and regular classroom teachers. But again, each high-performance design would enhance their argument for more money—a specific amount of money would be identified, the way it would be spent would be clear, and schools could be reasonably sure that they would achieve higher levels of student performance.

Yes, more money might be needed to raise student achievement from today's level of only 25 percent performing at or above proficiency to 50 or even 75 percent at that level. But in most places, dramatic improvements can be made with current dollars. Schools and districts would do well to adopt these strategies to boost results and begin to enhance educational productivity. If the education sys-tem shows that it can raise performance at current funding levels, policymakers and taxpayers might be convinced that putting more money in public schools would be a sound investment.

CHAPTER EIGHT

NEW ROLES AND RESPONSIBILITIES FOR THE DISTRICT

The actions described in the preceding chapters represent major change for public schools. Implementing a real and comprehensive decentralized management strategy would completely alter the way the public education system is organized and managed. Budgeting dollars to schools in a lump sum and having schools decide how to use them would represent a major departure from current practice. Having schools use those resources in the different ways described in Chapter Seven would constitute additional change. In short, the proposals in this book call for major, fundamental changes in school curriculum, management, and funding operations and promise to be the most successful route to greater productivity in the nation's public schools and hence higher student achievement.

Such deep and fundamental change will not occur without active leadership and system redesign by central offices, superintendents, and school boards. Contrary to some popular understanding, districts remain important even when many management functions are decentralized to schools. In light of the goal set for schools at the beginning of Chapter One—to raise achievement so that 75 percent or more rather than just 25 percent of students meet high standards—a

---

This chapter draws heavily on Odden (1997a); it includes some ideas from Hill, Pierce, and Guthrie (1997).

change in the education management strategy is more than justified, as Chapter Two argued. However we do not advocate the abolition of the school district or school district central offices. Although the book has emphasized the school site, a switch to decentralized education management does not mean that the district is divested of all management responsibilities. Even under decentralization, the school system must be managed, and final responsibility for district and school results still remains with district leaders, the superintendent, and the school board.

Nevertheless, the nature of the central office, and many of its key responsibilities, changes when a district adopts a decentralization strategy. First, central office leaders must initiate a districtwide process in which all parties come to understand why they need to change from a bureaucratic, top-down system to a decentralized, bottom-up one. Second, the central office must design the mechanisms that provide schools with their key management authorities, including control over their budget. Third, the central office must identify and understand which functions should be decentralized to schools (such as personnel and curriculum), which functions should remain at the central office (such as capital construction), and which functions must be created or enhanced at the central office (such as school-based information and accountability structures). In short, central offices must redesign the district in a way that will support these changes.

In this chapter, we discuss the key district roles and responsibilities resulting from a decentralized management strategy. Functional detail is provided in Chapter Six; here we emphasize the more macro-level roles of the district under decentralized management.

An Overview of District Decentralization

The core idea of a decentralized district is that schools should not be regulated in detail by the district; district-school relationships should be based on school-specific performance agreements that stipulate the results schools are to produce, allowing each school to select the strategy—such as implementing a high-performance design offered by one of the national school reform networks—to produce those results. These agreements would be similar to agreements under which charter schools are supposed to operate, as well as contracts for many magnet and special-program schools—all of which provide schools with authority to design their own programs and select staff members who complement the school's instructional strategy, under the condition that they produce specified results. Such agreements have two parties: the local school board, which promises to waive certain rules to allow a school to provide a focused and distinctive instructional program (such as a whole-school design offered by a school reform network), and the school, which promises to produce student achievement results according to agreed performance targets, implement a clearly enunciated vision, follow civil rights requirements, and use public funds and assets responsibly.

Under this type of decentralized system, a key role for the local school board and central office staff is to write performance-based agreements with every one of the school sites in a district, each of which could be implementing a different high-performance school design if it so decided. Creating such agreements would entail negotiations between the school and the district on the magnitude of increased results that the school would commit to producing. The current school system would be transformed into a network of high-performing schools (Bryk and others, 1997). The core set of performance targets would be the primary factors for which each school would be held accountable by the district.

Within this vision of decentralization, each school would become an organization with its own staff, mission, and approach to instruction. The local public school board and central office would, in effect, become investors and portfolio managers, rewarding schools that met their performance targets, supporting the expansion or imitation of successful school designs, organizing new schools in place of failed ones, and terminating and reconstituting failed schools.

Before specifying and discussing all of the key elements of a district decentralization strategy, it is important to note again that decentralization alone will not improve schools. Chapter Two identified many studies that have shown that school decentralization, as an isolated initiative, rarely produces better student achievement results. Chapter Two outlined the many key elements that must be part of any effective decentralization strategy in education and argued that schools must then take the authorities provided in the decentralized management structure to upgrade the curriculum and instructional program through some form of schoolwide restructuring. All of these actions at both the district and the school level must be fully implemented and, when they are implemented, represent major change in the operation of school systems as we know them.

To implement such an education reform strategy, districts first need to play a leadership role in creating broad-based awareness at both the district and school levels of the need for such fundamental change in district and school management. Second, districts then have to develop a mission that emphasizes student achievement in the core academic subjects, bolstered by curriculum content standards, student performance standards, and tests of achievement to the standards. Third, districts must invest up front to initiate the decentralization, restructuring, and resource reallocation processes required for school-based restructuring around a higher-performing school vision. Fourth, districts must provide sites with the key conditions—the operating environment—necessary to implement a high-performance vision: power over the budget and personnel functions, a rich information system including financial data, a range of professional development, and a full-fledged accountability system with rewards and sanctions. Finally, districts have to understand the new roles for the board, superintendent, and central office staff in a decentralized system in which the center sets the direction and runs the accountability system, and schools, led by a new breed of principals, do the direct work to produce higher levels of student achievement (see also Hill, Pierce, and Guthrie, 1997, and Bryk and others, 1997).

Awareness of the Need for Fundamental Change

Teaching students to high standards cannot be done by superficially changing today's schools. In most instances, major school restructuring through whole-school, high-performance designs, such as those offered by the various national school reform networks (Education Commission of the States, 1997), will be needed. District leadership is crucial in helping schools and central office staff understand that higher levels of student achievement are needed, that the management strategy to produce those results is to devolve more authority and responsibility to schools, and that at the site level, fundamental whole-school restructuring is required to accomplish the new goals.

Helping schools and district staff recognize that there is a large gap between current levels of student achievement and the levels needed to enable all students to participate fully in the future economy and society is a first step in developing the understanding that major change is needed. One activity for raising this awareness is to work with the entire district community and the faculty of each school to analyze current and desired levels of achievement. This activity should also assess the performance of subgroups within the district and school—achievement differences between low- and high-income students, between majority and minority students, and (in mathematics and science) between boys and girls. The analysis should push beyond the numbers to identify key factors behind unacceptable levels of achievement. Often the main factor in elementary schools is that too many students are unable to read well. Another factor is a weak curriculum; for example, students tend not to write well unless writing is taught and students receive detailed feedback on their writing efforts. The goal of this joint analysis task is to ensure that all key professionals in the school—and the community, for that matter—understand current levels of achievement, their distance from desired levels, and some of the reasons for the gaps. This helps everyone understand the immensity of the task of reaching the desired levels of performance. The importance of this task cannot be underestimated; if schools and other district staff are convinced that major change is required to meet ambitious new goals, they will be better able to weather the challenges of decentralization, restructuring, and resource reallocation necessary to implement a successful school-based financing program.

For that reason, another aspect of this awareness building is to "make the case for decentralization." Since decentralization represents a new management strategy, district leaders need to convince staff that a decentralized management system would have a high probability of producing significant improvements in results. Reviewing the improved results of such a change in management in other organizations as well as in education could be part of this process.

A third aspect of this awareness building is helping schools learn about several ambitious schoolwide strategies that show promise for producing the desired student learning objectives. This could entail creating a descriptive catalogue of the various national school reform designs and networks (see Chapter Seven). Another tactic is to have school faculties visit schools that have implemented these designs, especially schools that have students with characteristics similar to theirs. Such trips not only expose faculties to powerful new whole-school designs but also let them see other teachers educating similar students to much higher levels of achievement. Districts can sponsor symposiums and "fairs" that allow teachers and administrators to learn about numerous high-performance school designs and to interact with the key members of those school design teams. These activities offer schools alternative visions of how they could accomplish the goal of teaching their students to higher levels.

The process of raising awareness of alternative educational strategies is necessary because the difficult job of school restructuring, including resource reallocation, is not a task that most districts or schools will spontaneously take on. Schools and their teachers must become convinced that there is a need for major change, that there are viable options for teaching students to higher standards, and that there will be significant consequences for not accomplishing this goal. Districts play a crucial role at the beginning of the restructuring process. Once convinced that the only viable way to high performance is through school-based restructuring and resource reallocation, schools can be expected to proceed with energy and commitment. Without such understanding, schools might drag their feet and never mount the drive needed to implement any higher-performance school strategy fully and successfully.

Mission, Standards, and Assessment

To guide, focus, and measure the results of such a change process, districts need to define the mission of the district, create rigorous curriculum content and student performance standards, and select a testing system to measure results. The mission statement should be simple and state that the primary goal of the district is to teach all students to high academic standards in the core academic areas, generally mathematics, science, language arts (including writing), and history or social studies. Such a mission does not preclude schools from accomplishing other desired results; indeed, the pedagogical strategies required to teach students to high standards produce many other desired student behaviors (Bruer, 1992). But the mission should signal that the top-priority goal is boosting student achievement in the basic academic subjects.

This mission needs to be supported by a set of curriculum content standards and student performance standards that indicate substantively what the district wants students to know and be able to do. In many states, district content and performance standards would be more specific versions of emerging state content and performance standards, and the more detailed standards and curriculum units for any school design would have to be adapted to the district's standards.

Finally, districts need to select a testing system that will provide baseline data of student performance and will indicate the progress over time that the district and each school is making in accomplishing both the district's overall goals and each school's performance targets (which would be written into the performance contract). Such a testing system should be criterion-referenced and benchmarked to specific standards of performance. The ideal would be to have the district testing system benchmarked at least to state performance standards, as well as to national performance standards, such as those in the National Assessment of Educational Progress (Musik, 1996).

This district role is critical both for focusing the school-based management effort and for measuring the degree to which each individual school and the district as a whole are making progress toward the ultimate goal of teaching students to high standards. As Summers and Johnson (1996) showed, all too often, districts deploy a school-based management strategy under the rationale of improving performance but rarely measure the results of that initiative or even adopt a system for doing so. Developing a mission that states that student achievement in the core academic subjects is the top priority of the district, creating content and performance standards that give specific meaning to that mission, and then deploying a system that measures results and can be used to set specific performance targets are indispensable district responsibilities behind a school-based management strategy that will produce the desired results. Although these are also part of a full-fledged accountability system (to be discussed further), they should be viewed as up-front district responsibilities that will guide the early steps of the decentralization and restructuring efforts and over time be used in the accountability system as well.

Funding One-Time Expenses

Yet another district responsibility for initiating the decentralization and restructuring process is to invest in several up-front one-time needs. Developing a broad-based information system, one that includes detail on student achievement, is one such need. Indeed, developing a comprehensive school-based computerized information system is an important district task, for it eliminates the need for schools to hire administrative staff to administer new responsibilities, particularly financial responsibilities.

A second need pertains to a technology infrastructure; technology-based school designs often require that the school be updated electrically and rewired for digital and voice communication. Many emerging school designs also require local school and districtwide area computer networks. Indeed, technology will pervade education in the twenty-first century, whatever the specific curriculum strategy adopted.

Third, high-performance designs require more collaborative work within schools, a new style of principal leadership, and the implementation of high-performance management. Although these types of skills should be part of ongoing training and specific aspects of them are often part of school design team assistance, district training in these areas becomes an important area for district investment and support. Districts should consider setting aside about 1 percent of their operating budget for ongoing professional development, for these skills are needed by leaders in all schools, regardless of specific school design and curriculum strategy.

Further, since few schools have the resources required to hire training teams from the many national high-performance school networks, districts initially need an additional source of funds to help some schools begin the ambitious training they need to effectively implement their selected school design. For this purpose, some districts set aside a pot of training money that would cover a site's first-year professional development costs for implementing a high-performance vision, as a way to "jump-start" school planning and implementation.

Fourth, some high-performance designs require new curriculum and instructional materials before previous costs for books and other items have been fully amortized. Schools selecting these designs will need some one-time funding to purchase such items.

In short, there are several areas that require district investment in creating an infrastructure for school restructuring toward high-performance designs. Although the ongoing operational costs, including those for technology, must ultimately be met by the site through resource reallocation, each district should assess the level and nature of the up-front investments for a variety of needs and budget for them so as to fully support the launch effort.

Districts should view this investment fund as a long-term obligation to continuously improve the education system and determine a budgeting strategy to ensure funds on an ongoing basis. Gradually setting aside a fixed percentage of the operating budget, say, 1 to 2 percent over time, would be a medium-term strategy to create this investment fund. Going through a mock budget-cutting exercise would be a way to provide these funds in the shorter term; the cut funds would be placed in the investment pool and used as catalyst money to launch districtwide improvement activities.

The Operating Environment for a Decentralized School System

A district's greatest task is to design a decentralized education system. Districts need to create the conditions that allow schools both to restructure around a higher-performance design or strategy and to reallocate their resources to the needs of the design or strategy. To create an effective decentralized school system, research shows that the district needs to decentralize four key resources: power, professional development, information, and an accountability system with clear rewards and sanctions.

Power

Power includes decision-making authority over the budget and personnel. The district must provide the school with a lump-sum budget and allow the school to spend the dollars in ways that support their whole-school high-performance design, as detailed in Chapter Six. Power also means providing the school with the authority to recruit, select, develop, and evaluate personnel.

Professional Development

Professional development includes the skills, knowledge, and competencies school professionals need to teach a high-standards curriculum and engage in school management and restructuring (Corcoran, 1995; Corcoran and Goertz, 1995; Darling-Hammond and McLaughlin, 1995; Little, 1993). But professional development is more than just developing new curriculum and pedagogical expertise, although that should be a core focus for new investments in professional development. Professional knowledge and skills are needed in at least four areas: (1) working together effectively in group or team settings; (2) developing new curriculum and peda-gogical expertise required to teach a high-standards instructional program; (3) counseling, parent outreach, and other roles now usually performed by non-teaching staff; and (4) managing the fiscal aspects of the school, including the expertise to reallocate resources to support whole-school designs (Odden and Wohlstetter, 1995; Wohlstetter, Mohrman, and Robertson, 1996). The importance of professional development cannot be understated; insufficient attention to the development of needed skills and expertise can doom an otherwise well designed decentralization strategy.

Districts also need to determine how investments in ongoing training will be financed. A straightforward way to fund such training would be to require budget set-asides at both the district and site levels, totaling about 3 percent of the oper-ating budget. A portion of this (say, one-third) could be retained by the district to train administrators and principals in decentralized management techniques and to train teachers in leadership skills that will be needed to engage in deci-sion making at the site level. Districts can also train site staff in the business, man-agement, and financial skills required for school-based budgeting.

The major portion of the professional development budget should be financed with a school set-aside. A goal should be to have the school amount be at least $50,000 to $75,000 a year for a school of five hundred students; a minimum amount in the short term would be $25,000. Schools need this money to purchase external technical assistance and training (see Chapter Seven), often provided by the expert team that created the school design.

Information and Best Practices

In a typical district, most information stays at the central office. But if sites are to make sound decisions, particularly if they are provided the power, responsi-bility, autonomy, and accountability for producing results, they must have access to a wide array of information.

First, sites need to learn about a wide variety of high-performance school de-signs. Compiling a list of such designs and making sure all schools know about them is a key district responsibility. There are perhaps two dozen such designs at this writ-ing, the best known being provided by the New American Schools, Accelerated Schools, Edison Schools, Paideia Schools, E. D. Hirsch Core Knowledge Schools, and Learner-Centered Schools (Education Commission of the States, 1997).

Sites also need data and information in numerous areas to manage the school: district and site revenues, costs of school staff and materials, "best practices" (pro-grams and strategies with proven effectiveness), parent and student satisfaction data, benchmarks with other schools, and data on the local community. Sites could also manage the official personnel information about their staff. Further, sites could use curriculum data, including an instructional management program that allows teachers to track student performance relative to curriculum content and student performance standards.

The entire information package should be organized into a relational data system and placed on an interactive computer network with link-ups at each school site. Developing such an automated information system is one way to reduce administrative staff at both the site and the central office and thus free up money for required investments in the whole-school design implementation process. This is an important district responsibility, for as Chapter One argued, information must be decentralized to school sites when schools are empowered to make key strategic and managerial decisions.

To be most effective, schools should actively share their information with the major stakeholders in the school community. Providing instant computer access to the information base is one information-sharing strategy. Having a network of teacher teams "managing" the operations and instructional program of the school, a strategy embodied in most high-performance designs, is another strategy. These teams need such information to accomplish their goals. In current school systems, most of the information is retained in the central office; in a decentralized system, the information must be made available to and then be used by all professional staff at each school site.

Accountability, Rewards, and Sanctions

Decentralization works best when it is coupled with a comprehensive and focused accountability system that includes at least four elements: (1) clear and measurable educational goals, centered on student achievement in core curriculum content areas; (2) measures that indicate the current status of student performance, changes over time, and annual or biennial improvement targets for each school; (3) a reporting system that periodically informs the public, the school system, parents, and students of a school's success in accomplishing results and degrees of improvement; and (4) an array of both rewards and sanctions, which are consequences tied to changes in schoolwide performance over time. Implementing a sound accountability structure can be controversial, but accountability is an important element in creating and sustaining not just high-performance schools but a high-performance education system.

First, a high-performance decentralized district should have a well-developed "instructional guidance" system that focuses a school on the teaching and learning program. The core elements of an instructional guidance system would include high-quality curriculum content standards, ambitious student performance standards, and a test or assessment system that would produce measures of performance relative to the standards. Each school's specific curriculum design needs to be aligned with the district's own content and performance standards, meeting or exceeding those standards. Indeed, standards and testing are indispensable in a high-performance organization. Since districts in states with state testing programs should inevitably have their students perform well on those tests, districts may need to augment with performance-based assessments any state testing program that focuses too heavily on just basic skills.

Districts would use results from these assessments in developing the performance agreement with each of its schools. Each school should have long-term, five-year goals and annual performance targets that would allow the school to meet its goals over the length of the district-school agreement. The district-school agreement should be clear about the core performance targets for which each school will be held accountable. Each year the district should make public detailed performance reports for each school, identifying which targets were met and which were not.

Rewards and sanctions should also be part of the accountability system. Rewards generally mean teacher compensation (Conley and Odden, 1995; Firestone, 1994; Kelley and Odden, 1995; Mohrman, Mohrman, and Odden, 1996; Odden, 1996; Odden and Conley, 1992; Odden and Kelley, 1997). The organizing principle of teacher compensation could shift from seniority to knowledge and skills. A pay-for-knowledge-and-skill salary structure would reward teachers and other school staff for developing the expertise needed to accomplish school goals. Such a system would have to specify the knowledge areas that would qualify for pay increments and have a way for assessing whether individual teachers had the knowledge and skills identified. Knowledge and skills could be related to an increasing depth of content and instructional skills in a subject area (or two subject areas, especially for schools having a multidisciplinary curriculum program); curriculum development, staff development, and student counseling; and management skills for developing and monitoring school budgets, running decision-making teams, and monitoring a school's strategic plan with respect to an indicator system providing data on various measures of the school's performance. These areas of expertise, it should be noted, would also be the focus of the professional development program. Such a new salary structure could also include a pay increment for certification from the National Board for Professional Teaching Standards (Odden and Kelley, 1997).

A second component of pay could include performance bonuses, allocated on a schoolwide basis and provided for value-added improvements in student performance, as discussed in Chapter Two.

Sanctions will also be needed. As also discussed in Chapter Two, a full-fledged accountability structure would be accompanied by a phased-in intervention and reconstitution program for schools that consistently fail to meet performance targets. Although there is no one best way to design such a program, districts cannot allow low-achieving schools to continue forever. A system first needs to provide assistance; if such assistance does not produce improved performance, some sort of reconstitution will be required, whereby the school leadership and portions of the faculty are changed.

Facilitative Principal Leadership

Another role for districts is to recruit and train principals in facilitative leadership skills. Principals of restructuring schools will need a wide array of new and different skills than principals in traditionally organized and managed school systems. Principals using facilitative leadership will manage a large-scale school change process in which others (teachers) make key decisions, provide opportunities for teachers to engage in curriculum and instructional leadership, help teachers create a culture of shared decision making, and serve as brokers of information, knowledge, and resources between their faculty and the community (Murphy and Louis, 1994; Odden and Wohlstetter, 1995; Wohlstetter, Mohrman, and Robertson, 1996). Producing this type of site leader usually requires both a substantial principal professional development strategy and new recruitment strategies that employ different standards for selecting and hiring principals.

Summary

In sum, the district needs to do more than just let schools select and implement higher-performance designs. Districts must restructure the entire system to create an operating environment that provides schools with the needed time, authorities, resources, professional knowledge, information, best practices, leaders, and rewards and sanctions required for whole-school restructuring. Another key district role is setting the standards that each school must meet. Without creating this type of operating environment, schools will be ill equipped to engage in the wide-ranging change that is necessary to implement and finance schools that produce marked improvements in student achievement results.

Changed Orientation for the School District

Executing the tasks required for a decentralized district puts the central office, school boards, and district in a new context: the central office exists primarily for the purpose of performing public functions to free schools to produce results, ensuring that there are enough effective schools to permit every student to attend one, setting performance targets for schools, authorizing schools to receive public funds, assessing the performance and productivity of schools, holding schools accountable for results, and helping students whose schools have failed to find alternatives. However, schools will still need assistance, technical advice, staff training, and some business-oriented services, although the financial services should be provided through technology.

The Superintendent

With the school board functioning as an education portfolio manager offering schools a variety of whole-school designs and routinely closing and replacing the lowest-performing schools, the superintendent becomes the chief executive officer of a highly diversified organization—a network of high-performing schools, if you will. Playing this role, the superintendent is heavily engaged in long-range planning and analysis of the match between the community's needs and the mixture of schools it provides. Superintendents no longer have direct responsibility for the day-to-day management of schools or for the management of a functionally organized central office. Such superintendents supervise a central office staff responsible for such functions as negotiating agreements with schools and new school providers, advising the school board on whether to approve proposed agreements, writing checks to schools on the basis of their enrollments, keeping computerized school-based financial accounts, helping schools become savvy consumers of staff development and other services related to instructional improvement (such as the national school reform networks) by providing costs of different providers and information on other school experiences with different vendors, managing a lottery-based student admissions process for schools that are oversubscribed, and publishing unbiased information about all schools' programs and performance.

Central Office Administrative Staff

Central office staff roles also change dramatically and the number of staff decreases, but the central office must not disappear altogether. In a decentralized system, schools do not simply operate on their own. The system needs to be managed, and the management tasks are complex and challenging. But managing a decentralized system of more autonomous schools requires central office staff to engage in new roles and activities. In particular, the central office administrative structure as we know it will no longer exist. As Chapter Six suggested, central offices would no longer employ large numbers of staff development, curriculum, or supervisory specialists. They would, however, employ people responsible for helping schools gain access to independent sources of help in many of these areas.

The main instruction-related functions of the central office would be to create curriculum content and student performance standards and to develop and administer a testing system to monitor student, school, and system performance. It would also maintain a school-based information system to support the superintendent's long-range planning activities, allocate dollars to schools largely through a per-pupil formula, provide automated financial services, and collect and disseminate information on schools and school performance. Finally, central office staff would sponsor parent information centers, intended to inform parents about what is happening in schools and educate them regarding the school choice process.

District leaders will need to take considerable initiative in orienting central office staff to these new roles. That task will not be easy; central office staff will have to shift from decision-making roles to activities that help others—those at schools—make good decisions. Some but not all central office staff can make this transition to a customer service role.

This orientation task also includes the teacher union. Although many districts have found teacher unions to be quite supportive of schools that aspire to higher-performance visions and of the freedoms schools need to implement them, many union contract provisions, particularly those focused on work conditions, inhibit the requisite restructuring. Over time, the district and the union will need to rewrite union contracts to exempt schools from contract provisions that are obstacles to design implementation.

Conclusion

To create an operating environment conducive to restructuring using a whole-school, high-performance design, districts must also restructure themselves. They must convert the district to one that supports a school-based decentralization strategy and raise awareness that major and fundamental changes are needed to reach the goals of teaching more students to high standards. They have to invest in up-front actions that jump-start the restructuring and decentralization process. The district has to develop curriculum content and student performance standards and administer a testing system that provides data on how well students, schools, and the system are performing. They need to negotiate performance targets with each school to identify the kinds of improvements required. Districts must also give schools power over their budget and personnel functions, create a school-based information system, invest widely in professional development, and implement an accountability system with clear rewards and sanctions. And they must orient the school board, the superintendent, the central office staff, and even the union to new roles and functions that support site-based management, restructuring, and accountability.

These are substantial, challenging, complicated, and critically important roles and functions. As we stated at the beginning of this chapter, school districts do not wither away when they adopt a decentralized management strategy. They redesign themselves and redesign the district to provide the operating environment necessary to support schools as they strive to produce the major improvements in student achievement that the system desires.

CHAPTER NINE

SUMMARY: PUTTING MONEY WHERE IT MATTERS MOST

School-based funding, the budgeting of a significant portion of education financing to the school site, has been the primary focus of this book. We firmly believe that the only way to meet the current education reform goal of teaching students to much higher standards is to improve the productivity of the education system; having schools determine the best use of the dollars in the system is a core element of improved productivity. The only way schools can rise to this challenge is for them to be given their budget in a lump sum. In short, we have concluded that school-based financing is a key to improved school performance and should therefore be the next important step in the evolution of school funding within the states and nationally.

Throughout the book, we have tried to convey the logical consistency of school-based financing with current education reforms in the United States. After all, from the finance side of the education system, school-based funding is consistent with standards-based reform initiatives that set clear directions and goals (standards and assessments) at the top (state or district level) and give schools the responsibility and—most important—the authority for meeting student performance objectives. Ensuring that schools have considerable control over the resources necessary for meeting students' academic needs is crucial to holding schools accountable for educational performance.

In trying to conceptualize how to finance schools for higher performance, we first stepped back and assessed the current condition of education financing in the United States. We showed that contrary to popular opinion, the education system has amassed considerable financial resources throughout the twentieth century, with gains between 25 and 75 percent in real per-pupil terms each decade during the first nine decades of the twentieth century. However, we also showed that the education dollar is neither distributed fairly nor spent effectively. Based on analyses of district-level data, we identified large disparities (thousands of dollars per pupil) in education funding within and across states and quantified those disparities using traditional and new equity statistics. Our review of the vast resources available for the education enterprise revealed a system where some students, by accident of place of residence, get more and others get less, regardless of their individual educational needs—the very antithesis of the goal of deploying resources so that all students can achieve to high and rigorous standards.

A key reason for such funding disparities has been local district control of education, including substantial local fiscal control. Of course, the compromise between freedom and equality has long been a source of public policy tension in the United States, and this is no less true when applied to educational opportunity and financing. Disparities in education funding are seen as problematic by some and a reflection of public freedom to choose by others. Although we do not advocate a system that eliminates a local school district's freedom to choose a more expensive educational program for its students, we reject a system whereby freedom is suppressed due to a school district's inability to obtain sufficient resources. Thus we proposed several strategies for reducing the most egregious funding disparities, focusing on the lowest-funded districts in and among all states.

In keeping with current state-controlled education finance policy, the first alternative operates state by state to solve the dilemma of unequal and inadequate school funding. Using cost-adjusted per-pupil local and state general funding (thus excluding state categorical and federal funding), this equalization strategy brings all of the lowest-funded districts up to the median funding level in each state. The median was selected both because it provides substantial equity for the bottom half and because research in two midwestern states found that the median was a sufficient amount to teach students to a state achievement standard. Combining the cost estimates from all states, this would require only a 4.5 percent increase in nationwide revenues for education—$10.9 billion—but would affect a whopping 37 percent of all districts across the nation. Thus a fairly modest increase in funding could positively affect more than a third of the country's school districts, eliminate all of the "savage" fiscal inequalities in the country, and provide an adequate amount of funding in most states.

The second alternative extends across state boundaries and addresses the educational system as a nation. Again using cost-adjusted per-pupil local and state general funding, this equalization strategy brings all of the nation's lowest-funded districts up to the *national* median. Understandably, this plan is more expensive—$21.2 billion in 1996–97 dollars—but even so, it reflects a relatively small (8.7 percent) increase in funding and affects almost 33 percent of all school districts across the United States. This alternative has the highest impact for states, largely in the South and West, where funding for education is relatively low. And by focusing on these states, the federal government would address the systemwide need for improving educational opportunity and results *nationally.*

For either alternative, the federal government could play an important role in ameliorating inequities in education funding, especially for the lowest-spending districts.

However, simply rectifying the most flagrant school financing inequities will not "fix" the educational productivity quandary. Yes, a modest amount of additional money is needed for about a third of the nation's school districts so that they have a sufficient level of resources. Nevertheless, merely throwing more money at the problem won't fix it.

That is why we devoted most of the book to improving the use of education resources. Cognizant that accomplishing the reform goal of teaching all students to high standards requires a doubling or tripling of current education results, we concluded that a new management strategy was required to accompany the standard setting, measurement of results, and accountability that are part of standards- and school-based reform. The new management approach would be a performance-based, decentralized system in which schools would be granted substantial authority and autonomy to accomplish results within a context in which the state and districts set goals, standards, and directions and administer a true accountability system. From research in both education and other settings, we have shown that providing budget authority to the site responsible for producing results—schools in the case of education—is a key element of this new management strategy.

For the majority of states and districts, school-based financing will require a totally different budgeting system—sending dollars to schools in a lump sum rather than in the form of district-determined resources such as teachers, teacher specialists, instructional aides, and other human and physical capital. Thus we discussed how school-based financing has been implemented in other places, drawing on charter school legislation in the United States and experiences in the state of Victoria, Australia, and in England, both of which implemented a comprehensive form of school-based financing in the 1990s.

U.S. charter school laws vary widely in breadth and depth—especially in financial terms. Some states do not even address finances as a charter school issue, and those that do have produced a motley set of policies that often force the school to negotiate with the district over the amount of funding it will receive. States addressing the financing side of charter schools have also inevitably bumped up against equity concerns: should the charter receive the district average per-pupil funding or a state-determined amount? The former method ensures that the charter school has the same funding per pupil as other schools in the district, thus presumably giving the charter at least an equal local footing. The latter ensures that all charters are comparable throughout the state, even charters in low-spending districts. Nevertheless, U.S. charter school funding policies have not yet developed sufficient good practices on which to found a more extensive school-based financing program.

Although funding equity is an important issue that must ultimately be discussed, jumping straight to this aspect of charter school financing may be putting the cart before the horse. Instead, we have concluded that states constructing or revamping charter school finances should conduct a thoughtful analysis of the appropriate functional roles and responsibilities of schools and districts. Such an analysis would identify the essential functions that make sense at the district level (such as goal setting, accountability, capital construction, and diagnostic and ongoing special education services) and those more appropriately handled at the school level (such as instruction and site administration). This analysis should be the cornerstone of *any* American version of decentralization and school-based financing, regardless of whether the discussion is about charter schools or the entire education system. To help in this type of analysis, we studied the experiences of Victoria, Australia, and England.

Victoria and England both created and implemented a school-based financing system for education in the first half of the 1990s. For Victoria, an Australian state without school districts, the model is a state-to-school funding system. For England, the model is a state (national central government)-to-district-to-school funding system. Both Victoria and England determined which roles and responsibilities should be centrally retained, which should definitely be decentralized to the site, and which could be either and thus be devolved more slowly over time. Their respective lists are not the same but have substantial overlaps; however, they both established these lists as an integral part of their approach to school-based funding. Both systems also produced information on how a pupil-weighted formula could be used to budget the bulk of the funds to the school site.

Moreover, both experiences with school-based financing point to the conclusion that such a system can be implemented fairly smoothly and fairly quickly. In addition, school staff like their increased budget authority, even though it inevitably involves more work and a steep learning curve. Finally, schools promptly use their increased budget authority to make different spending decisions regarding resource use. In other words, when schools are given a lump-sum budget and told to achieve specified results, education resources are prioritized differently, more in line with the specific school reform strategy, student needs, and the school community context. Time and again, we found that schools were able to achieve cost savings that had previously eluded districts using the same budget.

Our proposed system of school-based financing for education in the United States takes from the best of Victoria's and England's experiences. Following England's lead, this system would include a state-defined school-based financing framework to guide each district in creating its school-based financing policy. The framework identifies functions that would be retained by districts, those that would be devolved to schools, and those that could be devolved at district discretion. We propose a system that would over several years devolve 75 percent of both the operating and capital budget totals to school sites. The framework also includes a structure for the weighted per-pupil funding formula, within which districts would create their own specific formula parameters. Such a system would be what the Australians call "transparent" because the methods would be clearly defined and public at all points (state, district, and school). Making a system more transparent may also rouse informed debate regarding equity, especially between schools in a given district and between elementary, middle, and high schools; in contrast, current funding systems in the United States (like those in Victoria and England before their recent changes) obfuscate this issue, however unintentionally.

Strategic aspects of such a framework would include identifying new and continuing (core) district roles and responsibilities, determining the proportion of funding that should be allocated to schools in a lump sum, structuring guidelines for districts to calculate school budgeting formulas, and providing direction for school programs that ensures rigorous curricula, standards, and assessments for meeting high academic performance objectives. Chapter Six provides a more detailed discussion of this framework.

But when the schools receive their money, their challenge is to use that money more wisely to produce higher levels of student performance. In Chapter Seven, we discussed how this could occur. We drew heavily from schoolwide programs that focus on improving student achievement. Thus we continued to emphasize the *school* as the vehicle for change in improving student achievement. Certainly there is abundant literature on how students learn and, subsequently, what pedagogical technologies are most effective in improving student achievement. However, most of these technologies focus only on the classroom and often on subgroups or even one-on-one interaction between teacher and student in the classroom. Instead, our work attempts to support this classroom-by-classroom change by identifying structural and organizational change in education that focuses effort at the schoolwide level. To accomplish this, we referenced the several public whole-school, high-performance designs currently being implemented across the nation, including New American Schools (NAS) and the Edison Project. The schoolwide designs represented by these efforts reflect best practices in curriculum and teaching strategies and advance the structural and organizational change necessary to ensure *schoolwide* implementation of effective teaching, strong curriculum, high levels of student achievement, and accountability systems. We provide cost estimates for eight of these model whole-school designs, which a continually increasing body of evidence shows produce much higher levels of student results.

Our next task was to determine the costs of these programs and whether typical schools in America could afford them. Chapter Seven focused on those costs above core staffing of one principal and twenty teachers. We then showed that this level of resources was already available in elementary, middle, and high schools. Working from a nationally representative sample of schools from the Schools and Staffing Surveys, we quantified current average staffing allocations for elementary, middle, and high schools. Comparing these results with various alternatives from NAS and the Edison Project, we found that the schoolwide designs can be funded within current average resource levels.

Chapter Seven also took the cost of one of the designs, the Modern Red Schoolhouse, and showed that it approximates the median per-pupil spending in the nation. Thus the chapter provides an approach for combining the equity goal of Chapter One with the productivity and adequacy goals of the remainder of the book. Specifically, Chapter Seven suggests that if education spending in all states were raised to the higher of the state or the national median, fiscal equity would be attained for the bottom half of all students in the country and all schools would be provided with sufficient revenues to implement a high-performance, whole-school design.

Chapter Seven also stated that whether new or current resources are involved, schools implementing higher-performance designs would need to engage in a reengineering, restructuring, and resource reallocation process, substantially changing the way current dollars are spent and the staffing structure of schools. Instead of numerous out-of-regular-classroom specialists and instructional aides, high-performance schools put most instructional resources into regular classroom teachers, with smaller classes and broader roles—including roles in school management. More money is spent for ongoing training, each group of five hundred students has an instructional facilitator, and many designs gradually purchase and incorporate computer technologies into both the instructional program and instructional management systems.

Finally, we delineated the changed roles and responsibilities for school boards, superintendents, and central office staff in a decentralized, school-managed education system.

Our book is explicitly about education finance and school-based financing, but it is implicitly about the entire education system. In fact, understanding how school finances must be constructed to support strong educational programs in the schools is imperative to understanding the theme of the book. No longer can we afford to perpetuate the current disjuncture between education finance and education programming and management. By doing so, we lose valuable time and effort in meeting the needs of students. This book attempts to bridge the gap between funding and school performance, not by advocating massive increases in education funding, but by making education finance a part of standards-based reforms. For schools to attain the lofty goals of excellence in education as construed in standards-based reforms—teaching students to high standards—we propose that the following elements be combined: modest increases in funding for low-spending districts; allocation mechanisms designed to provide lump-sum budgets to schools; an educational enterprise that is structured with school-level budget authority and flexibility for school leaders and staff to see the cause-and-effect relationship between resource use and student performance; and an overall system that sets high and rigorous standards, measures results, and holds schools accountable for results. Only by combining these important elements can school-based financing make a difference in improving student achievement.

APPENDIXES

APPENDIX 1.1. DESCRIPTION OF THE DATA USED
FOR FISCAL EQUITY ANALYSIS.

For this study, we conducted a district-level fiscal equity analysis of all states and the District of Columbia. To that end, we used school year 1991–92 district-level data from the Common Core of Data (CCD), a database assembled by the National Center for Education Statistics (NCES), within the U.S. Department of Education. This particular school year was chosen because it is the most recent year available with data from a national set of districts. Data for the CCD were submitted by individual state education agencies and then edited by the U.S. Department of Education. This editing process is a means of standardizing the format of the data collected from the states. For example, some states submit data that is not consistent with national financial accounting standards, and in these cases, the U.S. Department of Education works with the individual states to clarify definitions and categories so that the data can be made consistent with the department's accounting format.

Cleaning the Data

One of our first steps in cleaning the financial data provided by the CCD was to examine high- and low-end outliers spanning the range of revenues per pupil.

We called individual departments of education to discover the explanation for these outliers.

Using the CCD, we examined state funding for regular school districts with students in kindergarten through grade 12, excluding administrative districts and districts serving unique student populations, such as vocational or special education schools. (Specifically, we excluded districts with agency codes 3 through 7 and school district codes 4 through 7.) It was also necessary to exclude districts with incorrect or incomplete revenue or demographic data. Of the 16,661 districts in the United States included in the CCD, we excluded 1,950 districts, for a total of 14,711 districts with 41,601,008 students. This represents 99.05 percent of the 42,000,343 students in the fifty states and the District of Columbia.

A Caveat Regarding California

California provided the NCES with 1991–92 district-level revenue and expenditure data in a nonstandard format. Consequently, the NCES and the Census Bureau manipulated the data to fit their standardized reporting procedures. The NCES and the Census Bureau believe their resulting data are accurate and comparable to those of the other states; the California Department of Education, however, challenges the assumptions made by the NCES in manipulating the data. For consistency, we used the NCES data for California.

Chambers Index and Cost Adjustment

Following the cleaning of the data, the individual states were merged with the Chambers Cost of Education Index, and each district was assigned a particular cost of education index (CEI); any district that had not been included in the Chambers Index was given a value of 1. Each district was then assigned a cost adjustment index, calculated as the district's CEI divided by the mean CEI of the state. In this way, the districts in each state were normed to 1. Each district's revenue data were then adjusted using the cost adjustment index. For example, a district's revenue per pupil following the cost adjustment would be its revenue per pupil divided by its cost adjustment index.

Equity Statistics

Descriptive statistics were then generated using these adjusted data, and McLoone and Verstegen indexes were also generated.

All districts in a state that fell below the median were artificially raised to the median, and the dollar amount needed to raise all low-spending districts to the median was calculated. (For these districts, the McLoone Index was not generated because in each case it equaled 1, and the Verstegen Index was not generated because it would have the same value as that generated using actual numbers.)

After each individual state's data file was run, the adjusted data from all states were combined into a national data file, and the equity statistics were generated.

Definitions

The first two terms are used in our own analysis; the others are defined as used by the NCES.

State general plus local revenues per pupil: The total of general formula assistance and total revenue from local sources divided by the number of students in the district.

Total revenues per pupil: Total revenues from all sources (local, state, and federal) divided by the number of students in the district.

Total revenue from local sources: "Taxes . . . [for] which the agency has the power to levy and set the rate. The following categories will be applicable to a relatively small number of districts: General sales or gross receipts tax; Individual and corporate net income taxes; and all other taxes. State taxes and state property tax relief payments are reported in Revenue from State Sources."

Total revenue from state sources: "All restricted and unrestricted payments made direct by the State government to local education agencies. These payments include but are not limited to foundation or basic support, transportation, pupil-targeted programs (special, gifted, vocational, and adult education), textbook funds, capital outlay, debt service payments on local school debt, property tax relief payments, child nutrition matching payments, employee benefit payments, and loans to local education agencies."

Total revenue from federal sources: All funds received from the federal government.

General formula assistance: "Revenue from general non-categorical state assistance programs such as foundation, minimum or basic formula support, principal apportionment, equalization, flat or block grants, and state public school fund distributions. Also includes state revenue dedicated from major state taxes, such as income and sales taxes. Includes all state payments made directly to the local education agency. Excludes state payments made on behalf of the local education agency."

APPENDIX 1.2. FISCAL EQUITY STATISTICS FOR STATE GENERAL PLUS LOCAL REVENUES PER PUPIL FOR HIGH SCHOOL DISTRICTS, 1991–92, BY STATE.

State	Mean ($)	Median ($)	Coefficient of Variation	Federal Range Ratio	McLoone Index	Verstegen Index
Alaska						
Arizona	$5,687	$5,074	0.19	0.65	0.961	1.225
Arkansas						
California	4,436	4,148	0.19	0.78	0.931	1.202
Colorado						
Connecticut	9,709	9,796	0.09	0.33	0.944	1.037
Delaware	5,629	n/a	n/a	n/a	n/a	n/a
District of Columbia						
Florida						
Georgia						
Hawaii						
Idaho						
Illinois	7,408	7,245	0.29	1.56	0.787	1.245
Indiana						
Iowa	7,989	8,959	0.19	0.42	0.843	1.000
Kansas						
Kentucky						
Louisiana						
Maine	6,099	5,970	0.10	0.30	0.971	1.070
Maryland						
Massachusetts	5,888	5,031	0.46	2.00	0.869	1.355
Michigan						
Minnesota	6,390	6,361	0.18	0.77	0.880	1.129
Mississippi	3,081	3,101	0.24	0.84	0.855	1.107
Missouri						
Montana	6,565	5,773	0.34	1.33	0.896	1.326
Nebraska	7,386	6,588	0.30	1.52	0.931	1.309

State						
Nevada						
New Hampshire	8,226	8,403	0.14	0.52	0.921	1.046
New Jersey	9,597	9,606	0.19	0.68	0.850	1.149
New Mexico						
New York	9,530	9,720	0.05	0.10	0.965	1.013
North Carolina						
North Dakota	6,550	7,274	0.23	0.54	0.796	1.064
Ohio						
Oklahoma						
Oregon	5,491	5,185	0.21	0.61	0.949	1.121
Pennsylvania						
Rhode Island						
South Carolina						
South Dakota						
Tennessee						
Texas						
Utah						
Vermont	6,316	5,942	0.19	0.78	0.898	1.207
Virginia						
Washington						
West Virginia						
Wisconsin	6,715	6,702	0.14	0.51	0.913	1.111
Wyoming						

Note: High school districts are districts, usually small, consisting of only a high school or a few high schools. A blank row means that the state (or the District of Columbia) does not have any high school districts.

n/a = not applicable.

Source: Analysis of U.S. Bureau of the Census, 1992.

APPENDIX 1.3. FISCAL EQUITY STATISTICS FOR STATE GENERAL PLUS LOCAL REVENUES PER PUPIL FOR ELEMENTARY DISTRICTS, 1991–92, BY STATE.

State	Mean ($)	Median ($)	Coefficient of Variation	Federal Range Ratio	McLoone Index	Verstegen Index
Alabama						
Alaska						
Arizona	$4,250	$3,898	0.27	0.93	0.931	1.246
Arkansas	3,539	n/a	n/a	n/a	n/a	n/a
California	3,509	3,254	0.29	0.99	0.931	1.226
Colorado	13,649	n/a	n/a	n/a	n/a	n/a
Connecticut	10,686	10,331	0.27	1.33	0.822	1.243
Delaware						
District of Columbia						
Florida						
Georgia	4,610	4,160	0.19	0.70	0.968	1.193
Hawaii						
Idaho	3,899	3,450	0.36	1.74	0.962	1.218
Illinois	4,349	4,031	0.30	1.41	0.830	1.330
Indiana	7,031	n/a	n/a	n/a	n/a	n/a
Iowa	5,735	5,602	0.29	1.84	0.817	1.229
Kansas						
Kentucky	3,397	3,225	0.14	0.35	0.957	1.111
Louisiana						
Maine	6,332	6,183	0.25	1.27	0.853	1.193
Maryland						
Massachusetts	7,468	6,943	0.37	1.57	0.809	1.344
Michigan	5,363	5,342	0.28	0.67	0.914	1.132
Minnesota	5,288	4,504	0.41	1.93	0.862	1.478
Mississippi						
Missouri	3,708	3,289	0.30	1.14	0.889	1.362
Montana	3,958	3,764	0.24	0.71	0.931	1.178
Nebraska	4,508	4,048	0.37	1.79	0.838	1.389

State					
Nevada	8,665	n/a	n/a	n/a	n/a	n/a
New Hampshire	7,510	7,272	0.27	1.67	0.840	1.221
New Jersey	7,513	7,123	0.27	1.14	0.847	1.264
New Mexico						
New York	9,016	6,977	0.52	2.32	0.895	1.683
North Carolina						
North Dakota	5,103	4,437	0.43	2.52	0.844	1.446
Ohio	21,841	n/a	n/a	n/a	n/a	n/a
Oklahoma	4,018	3,808	0.27	0.76	0.892	1.219
Oregon	4,428	3,964	0.32	1.19	0.951	1.284
Pennsylvania	9,382	8,754	0.13	0.20	1.000	1.072
Rhode Island	6,566	6,332	0.23	0.68	0.925	1.145
South Carolina						
South Dakota	4,969	3,296	0.59	2.53	0.983	1.572
Tennessee	2,458	2,466	0.15	0.54	0.883	1.109
Texas	4,768	3,822	0.58	1.79	0.834	1.634
Utah						
Vermont	8,440	8,325	0.23	0.92	0.844	1.182
Virginia	4,927	4,847	0.03	0.04	1.000	1.106
Washington	4,930	4,549	0.35	1.01	0.904	1.261
West Virginia						
Wisconsin	5,223	5,270	0.16	0.66	0.882	1.114
Wyoming	7,577	7,718	0.03	0.04	0.982	1.000

Note: Elementary districts are school districts consisting only of elementary schools. A blank row means that the state (or the District of Columbia) does not have any elementary districts.

n/a = not applicable.

Source: Analysis of U.S. Bureau of the Census, 1992.

APPENDIX 1.4. FISCAL EQUITY STATISTICS FOR TOTAL REVENUES PER PUPIL FOR K–12 DISTRICTS, 1991–92, BY STATE.

State	Mean ($)	Median ($)	Coefficient of Variation	Federal Range Ratio	McLoone Index	Verstegen Index
Alabama	$3,690	$3,602	0.14	0.51	0.931	1.059
Alaska	8,916	7,458	0.36	1.50	0.929	1.239
Arizona	4,917	4,703	0.19	0.68	0.947	1.083
Arkansas	3,855	3,740	0.15	0.52	0.939	1.061
California	4,950	4,835	0.15	0.44	0.908	1.070
Colorado	5,305	5,099	0.18	0.45	0.939	1.071
Connecticut	8,044	7,948	0.12	0.43	0.921	1.052
Delaware	6,000	5,820	0.08	0.32	0.967	1.050
District of Columbia	8,801	n/a	n/a	n/a	n/a	n/a
Florida	5,964	5,914	0.09	0.29	0.951	1.034
Georgia	4,659	4,462	0.15	0.55	0.930	1.080
Hawaii	5,704	n/a	n/a	n/a	n/a	n/a
Idaho	3,801	3,633	0.15	0.49	0.931	1.081
Illinois	4,772	4,856	0.15	0.45	0.871	1.047
Indiana	5,246	5,130	0.14	0.44	0.924	1.061
Iowa	5,043	4,970	0.11	0.41	0.935	1.047
Kansas	5,178	4,863	0.20	0.75	0.928	1.101
Kentucky	4,171	4,189	0.09	0.33	0.917	1.037
Louisiana	4,397	4,485	0.11	0.36	0.910	1.027
Maine	5,389	5,270	0.14	0.45	0.915	1.066
Maryland	6,343	6,137	0.12	0.43	0.939	1.065
Massachusetts	6,081	5,748	0.19	0.68	0.913	1.102
Michigan	5,598	5,512	0.19	0.83	0.874	1.079
Minnesota	5,862	5,754	0.15	0.50	0.912	1.063
Mississippi	3,360	3,345	0.12	0.47	0.907	1.052
Missouri	4,216	3,748	0.40	1.42	0.879	1.189
Montana	4,606	4,165	0.30	0.87	0.934	1.148
Nebraska	5,418	5,246	0.20	0.75	0.902	1.093

State					
Nevada	3,813	3,710	0.22	0.72	0.930	1.090
New Hampshire	5,703	5,454	0.17	0.69	0.909	1.092
New Jersey	9,280	9,159	0.12	0.47	0.917	1.055
New Mexico	4,321	3,995	0.19	0.64	0.974	1.097
New York	8,215	7,844	0.20	0.64	0.897	1.099
North Carolina	4,782	4,640	0.12	0.46	0.944	1.059
North Dakota	4,452	4,175	0.24	0.83	0.899	1.117
Ohio	4,986	4,721	0.22	0.70	0.898	1.107
Oklahoma	3,800	3,624	0.19	0.72	0.920	1.092
Oregon	5,442	5,202	0.14	0.53	0.931	1.081
Pennsylvania	6,401	6,324	0.13	0.53	0.908	1.058
Rhode Island	6,248	6,094	0.13	0.46	0.939	1.056
South Carolina	4,509	4,411	0.10	0.32	0.940	1.053
South Dakota	4,256	4,075	0.22	0.89	0.888	1.100
Tennessee	3,693	3,656	0.17	0.61	0.873	1.075
Texas	4,725	4,553	0.18	0.60	0.927	1.075
Utah	3,418	3,163	0.19	0.41	0.966	1.101
Vermont	6,357	6,277	0.15	0.65	0.896	1.066
Virginia	4,987	4,829	0.17	0.66	0.896	1.085
Washington	5,613	5,534	0.14	0.39	0.930	1.049
West Virginia	4,954	4,856	0.09	0.29	0.954	1.044
Wisconsin	6,114	6,109	0.11	0.41	0.921	1.040
Wyoming	6,226	5,595	0.30	0.73	0.937	1.145

Note: n/a = not applicable.

Source: Analysis of U.S. Bureau of the Census, 1992.

APPENDIX 1.5. FISCAL EQUITY STATISTICS FOR TOTAL REVENUES PER PUPIL FOR HIGH SCHOOL DISTRICTS, 1991–92, BY STATE.

State	Mean ($)	Median ($)	Coefficient of Variation	Federal Range Ratio	McLoone Index	Verstegen Index
Alabama						
Alaska						
Arizona	$6,120	$5,281	0.21	0.66	0.972	1.175
Arkansas						
California	5,531	5,307	0.18	0.81	0.901	1.092
Colorado						
Connecticut	10,802	10,732	0.09	0.44	0.956	1.037
Delaware	6,719	n/a	n/a	n/a	n/a	n/a
District of Columbia						
Florida						
Georgia						
Hawaii						
Idaho						
Illinois	7,880	7,681	0.27	1.46	0.808	1.123
Indiana						
Iowa	8,683	9,724	0.20	0.43	0.781	1.003
Kansas						
Kentucky						
Louisiana						
Maine	6,668	6,521	0.09	0.36	0.973	1.046
Maryland						
Massachusetts	7,485	6,244	0.39	1.50	0.955	1.233
Michigan						
Minnesota	7,869	7,762	0.18	1.03	0.900	1.066
Mississippi	3,899	3,803	0.18	0.56	0.928	1.067
Missouri						
Montana	7,337	6,576	0.37	1.72	0.856	1.189
Nebraska	8,043	7,168	0.31	1.58	0.918	1.175

State						
Nevada						
New Hampshire	8,834	8,517	0.19	0.79	0.912	1.099
New Jersey	12,038	11,838	0.16	0.65	0.879	1.077
New Mexico	10,204	10,420	0.05	0.10	0.945	1.010
New York						
North Carolina	7,651	8,366	0.18	0.43	0.780	1.029
North Dakota						
Ohio						
Oklahoma						
Oregon	5,984	5,540	0.21	0.72	0.966	1.114
Pennsylvania						
Rhode Island						
South Carolina						
South Dakota						
Tennessee						
Texas						
Utah						
Vermont	6,738	6,923	0.21	0.90	0.813	1.067
Virginia						
Washington						
West Virginia						
Wisconsin	7,986	7,835	0.19	0.75	0.869	1.100
Wyoming						

Note: High school districts are districts, usually small, consisting of only a high school or a few high schools. A blank row means that the state (or the District of Columbia) does not have any high school districts.

n/a = not applicable.

Source: Analysis of U.S. Bureau of the Census, 1992.

APPENDIX 1.6. FISCAL EQUITY STATISTICS FOR TOTAL REVENUES PER PUPIL FOR ELEMENTARY DISTRICTS, 1991–92, BY STATE.

State	Mean ($)	Median ($)	Coefficient of Variation	Federal Range Ratio	McLoone Index	Verstegen Index
Alabama						
Alaska						
Arizona	$4,786	$4,506	0.29	1.10	0.891	1.118
Arkansas	4,702	n/a	n/a	n/a	n/a	n/a
California	4,722	4,429	0.28	0.79	0.916	1.109
Colorado	14,842	n/a	n/a	n/a	n/a	n/a
Connecticut	12,210	11,269	0.21	0.93	0.903	1.133
Delaware						
District of Columbia						
Florida						
Georgia	6,847	6,695	0.18	0.74	0.896	1.076
Hawaii						
Idaho	5,433	4,891	0.38	1.83	0.902	1.201
Illinois	4,827	4,541	0.27	1.13	0.844	1.142
Indiana	7,767	n/a	n/a	n/a	n/a	n/a
Iowa	6,347	6,067	0.29	1.75	0.836	1.131
Kansas						
Kentucky	4,203	3,979	0.16	0.43	0.943	1.096
Louisiana						
Maine	7,364	6,970	0.29	1.43	0.855	1.129
Maryland						
Massachusetts	8,084	7,869	0.34	1.49	0.786	1.135
Michigan	5,803	5,673	0.28	0.93	0.894	1.106
Minnesota	6,686	5,571	0.42	2.03	0.883	1.259
Mississippi						
Missouri	4,997	4,768	0.26	1.07	0.853	1.122
Montana	4,546	4,166	0.27	0.85	0.940	1.121
Nebraska	5,194	4,873	0.36	1.67	0.810	1.161

State						
Nevada	9,208	n/a	n/a	n/a	n/a	n/a
New Hampshire	7,803	7,520	0.27	1.69	0.842	1.117
New Jersey	9,749	9,076	0.26	1.06	0.875	1.137
New Mexico						
New York	9,580	7,513	0.51	2.18	0.880	1.348
North Carolina						
North Dakota	6,608	5,194	0.61	3.48	0.875	1.338
Ohio	22,925	n/a	n/a	n/a	n/a	n/a
Oklahoma	4,764	4,496	0.30	1.13	0.850	1.137
Oregon	4,906	4,400	0.30	0.97	0.951	1.143
Pennsylvania	11,528	10,756	0.13	0.20	1.000	1.084
Rhode Island	7,309	7,121	0.21	0.60	0.869	1.100
South Carolina						
South Dakota	10,131	11,296	0.27	2.60	0.774	1.019
Tennessee	3,401	3,520	0.10	0.38	0.890	1.022
Texas	6,270	5,504	0.42	1.18	0.867	1.211
Utah						
Vermont	9,232	9,068	0.23	0.91	0.845	1.096
Virginia	6,207	6,165	0.01	0.02	1.000	1.000
Washington	6,323	5,815	0.33	1.12	0.880	1.158
West Virginia						
Wisconsin	6,284	5,971	0.23	1.01	0.882	1.111
Wyoming	13,376	12,649	0.08	0.12	1.000	1.058

Note: Elementary districts are school districts consisting only of elementary schools. A blank row means that the state (or the District of Columbia) does not have any elementary districts.

n/a = not applicable.

Source: Analysis of U.S. Bureau of the Census, 1992.

APPENDIX 1.7. COSTS OF RAISING DISTRICTS TO THE STATE MEDIAN OF STATE GENERAL PLUS LOCAL REVENUES PER PUPIL FOR K–12 DISTRICTS, 1991–92, BY STATE.

State	Total Revenues ($)	Additional Revenues to Raise to Median ($)	Increase in Total Revenues (percent)	Total Number of Districts	Number of Districts with Revenues Increased	Proportion of Districts with Revenues Increased (percent)
Alabama	$1,536,315,909	$83,034,240	5.40%	129	67	52%
Alaska	811,616,820	34,893,056	4.30	53	5	9
Arizona	1,822,384,196	40,915,136	2.25	86	34	40
Arkansas	1,424,045,676	28,796,480	2.02	317	100	32
California	12,707,531,422	373,219,328	2.94	284	102	36
Colorado	2,984,144,400	104,375,424	3.50	175	43	25
Connecticut	3,120,066,178	115,536,768	3.70	113	43	38
Delaware	491,043,877	21,621,440	4.40	15	11	73
District of Columbia	709,519,018	0	n/a	1	n/a	n/a
Florida	7,988,085,461	253,835,008	3.18	67	43	64
Georgia	4,839,118,977	201,268,992	4.16	176	124	70
Hawaii	996,756,888	0	n/a	1	n/a	n/a
Idaho	639,611,878	21,514,112	3.36	103	27	26
Illinois	4,801,895,969	204,011,264	4.25	420	261	62
Indiana	4,530,823,302	183,031,552	4.04	292	143	49
Iowa	2,244,407,778	59,824,000	2.67	376	80	21
Kansas	2,083,977,400	107,441,984	5.16	304	52	17
Kentucky	2,214,491,892	58,743,168	2.65	172	76	44
Louisiana	2,900,364,937	109,584,384	3.78	66	33	50
Maine	923,085,438	42,389,536	4.59	113	46	41
Maryland	3,733,704,384	209,912,320	5.62	24	12	50
Massachusetts	4,116,787,252	302,529,280	7.35	210	97	46
Michigan	8,719,138,155	358,689,792	4.11	523	294	56
Minnesota	3,760,113,377	148,834,432	3.96	346	161	47
Mississippi	1,379,333,748	52,473,728	3.80	149	76	51
Missouri	2,727,317,705	183,226,752	6.72	451	254	56
Montana	23,492,185	1,491,182	6.35	16	6	38

Nebraska	1,267,829,654	44,881,536	3.54	277	36	13
Nevada	755,312,249	25,916,352	3.43	16	2	13
New Hampshire	782,404,945	30,773,568	3.93	68	24	35
New Jersey	5,868,613,513	303,160,832	5.17	209	72	34
New Mexico	1,128,419,263	39,785,984	3.53	88	21	24
New York	19,253,109,394	987,601,408	5.13	653	92	14
North Carolina	4,102,812,488	168,296,064	4.10	132	63	48
North Dakota	451,162,970	21,713,584	4.81	200	31	16
Ohio	8,193,221,277	453,361,664	5.53	609	349	57
Oklahoma	1,968,373,951	60,230,848	3.06	436	89	20
Oregon	2,186,008,616	101,288,768	4.63	155	72	46
Pennsylvania	9,454,561,641	467,535,616	4.95	498	307	62
Rhode Island	836,253,928	35,686,016	4.27	33	14	42
South Carolina	1,853,524,836	102,069,696	5.51	91	55	60
South Dakota	486,474,856	29,049,520	5.97	165	38	23
Tennessee	2,387,890,256	190,813,824	7.99	123	95	77
Texas	12,954,235,579	681,691,648	5.26	972	232	24
Utah	1,058,591,348	31,765,344	3.00	40	7	18
Vermont	206,588,732	9,883,800	4.78	38	19	50
Virginia	4,474,135,096	223,753,472	5.00	131	77	59
Washington	3,986,464,013	156,925,952	3.94	247	101	41
West Virginia	1,224,823,685	22,187,200	1.81	55	23	42
Wisconsin	4,094,962,223	123,850,752	3.02	369	85	23
Wyoming	599,257,613	20,261,504	3.38	47	10	21
United States	173,804,206,345	7,633,678,310	4.39	10,634	4,104	38.59

Note: n/a = not applicable.

Source: Analysis of U.S. Bureau of the Census, 1992.

APPENDIX 1.8. COSTS OF RAISING DISTRICTS TO THE STATE MEDIAN OF STATE GENERAL PLUS LOCAL REVENUES PER PUPIL FOR HIGH SCHOOL DISTRICTS, 1991–92, BY STATE.

State	Total Revenues ($)	Additional Revenues to Raise to Median ($)	Increase in Total Revenues (percent)	Total Number of Districts	Number of Districts with Revenues Increased	Proportion of Districts with Revenues Increased (percent)
Alabama						
Alaska	$334,189,594	$5,930,240	1.77%	16	5	31%
Arizona						
Arkansas	1,838,796,912	57,721,728	3.14	102	22	22
California						
Colorado	60,616,287	1,797,766	2.97	7	4	57
Connecticut	3,377,240	n/a	n/a	1	n/a	n/a
Delaware						
District of Columbia						
Florida						
Georgia						
Hawaii						
Idaho	1,585,711,007	150,127,616	9.47	109	69	63
Illinois						
Indiana	4,758,165	515,977	10.84	3	2	67
Iowa						
Kansas						
Kentucky						
Louisiana	12,062,690	243,513	2.02	5	3	60
Maine						
Maryland	51,271,352	2,803,656	5.47	6	2	33
Massachusetts						
Michigan	18,272,258	1,083,293	5.93	11	6	55
Minnesota	5,875,574	456,574	7.77	4	2	50
Mississippi						
Missouri	292,556,754	12,815,816	4.38	162	27	17
Montana	32,030,183	1,037,482	3.24	21	7	33
Nebraska						

State						
Nevada						
New Hampshire	21,782,318	1,119,854	5.14	5	3	60
New Jersey	767,068,884	55,381,568	7.22	49	18	37
New Mexico	139,924,061	3,748,648	2.68	3	2	67
New York						
North Carolina						
North Dakota	2,474,612	319,548	12.91	4	2	50
Ohio						
Oklahoma						
Oregon	115,722,325	3,078,032	2.66	21	7	33
Pennsylvania						
Rhode Island						
South Carolina						
South Dakota						
Tennessee						
Texas						
Utah						
Vermont	97,993,642	4,520,152	4.61	20	9	45
Virginia						
Washington						
West Virginia						
Wisconsin	60,186,897	3,206,992	5.33	10	6	60
Wyoming						
United States	5,444,670,754	305,908,455	5.62	559	196	35.06

Note: High school districts are districts, usually small, consisting of only a high school or a few high schools. A blank row means that the state (or the District of Columbia) does not have any high school districts.

n/a = not applicable.

Source: Analysis of U.S. Bureau of the Census, 1992.

APPENDIX 1.9. COSTS OF RAISING DISTRICTS TO THE STATE MEDIAN OF STATE GENERAL PLUS LOCAL REVENUES PER PUPIL FOR ELEMENTARY DISTRICTS, 1991–92, BY STATE.

State	Total Revenues ($)	Additional Revenues to Raise to Median ($)	Increase in Total Revenues (percent)	Total Number of Districts	Number of Districts with Revenues Increased	Proportion of Districts with Revenues Increased (percent)
Alabama						
Alaska						
Arizona	$841,810,869	$26,027,360	3.09%	110	20	18%
Arkansas	499,000	0	n/a	1	n/a	n/a
California	3,893,976,745	122,072,576	3.13	601	127	21
Colorado	600,576	0	n/a	1	n/a	n/a
Connecticut	251,202,853	20,594,872	8.20	45	20	44
Delaware						
District of Columbia						
Florida						
Georgia	10,529,901	156,727	1.49	7	3	43
Hawaii						
Idaho	3,185,193	73,665	2.31	8	2	25
Illinois	2,171,111,739	160,618,816	7.40	411	236	57
Indiana	1,919,357	0	n/a	1	n/a	n/a
Iowa	67,449,844	5,604,590	8.31	46	17	37
Kansas						
Kentucky	4,151,638	102,936	2.48	4	2	50
Louisiana						
Maine	175,958,247	11,803,016	6.71	109	45	41
Maryland						
Massachusetts	512,948,260	43,115,840	8.41	99	43	43
Michigan	29,547,814	1,855,424	6.28	35	13	37
Minnesota	73,114,333	4,141,176	5.66	57	20	35
Mississippi						
Missouri	46,191,979	2,216,936	4.80	88	26	30
Montana	438,622,262	15,428,096	3.52	344	88	26
Nebraska	63,316,149	4,313,690	6.81	436	155	36

State						
Nevada	1,282,492	0	n/a	1	n/a	n/a
New Hampshire	210,847,250	15,265,976	7.24	85	29	34
New Jersey	1,629,761,440	111,599,936	6.85	296	101	34
New Mexico						
New York	228,594,474	9,516,400	4.16	44	7	16
North Carolina						
North Dakota	17,746,177	1,129,258	6.36	54	18	33
Ohio	87,365	0	n/a	1	n/a	n/a
Oklahoma	84,477,208	4,145,232	4.91	133	44	33
Oregon	187,485,997	4,118,136	2.20	114	27	24
Pennsylvania	6,266,889	0	n/a	2	1	50
Rhode Island	14,733,012	668,707	4.54	4	2	50
South Carolina						
South Dakota	5,893,416	45,212	0.77	9	2	22
Tennessee	36,640,265	2,054,991	5.61	12	9	75
Texas	86,075,654	5,407,642	6.28	78	78	8
Utah						
Vermont	397,117,590	28,667,376	7.22	183	70	38
Virginia	6,503,280	0	n/a	2	1	50
Washington	46,256,945	1,958,810	4.23	49	17	35
West Virginia						
Wisconsin	112,516,618	7,044,924	6.26	46	20	43
Wyoming	4,761,952	86,666	1.82	2	2	100
United States	11,663,183,783	609,834,985	5.07	3,518	1,173	33.34

Note: Elementary districts are school districts consisting only of elementary schools. A blank row means that the state (or the District of Columbia) does not have any elementary districts.

n/a = not applicable.

Source: Analysis of U.S. Bureau of the Census, 1992.

APPENDIX 1.10. COSTS OF RAISING DISTRICTS TO THE NATIONAL MEDIAN OF STATE GENERAL PLUS LOCAL REVENUES PER PUPIL FOR K–12 DISTRICTS, 1991–92, BY STATE.

State	Cost of Raising Students in Low-Spending Districts to Median ($)	Total Number of Districts	Total Number of Districts Raised to Median	Proportion of Districts Raised to Median (percent)	Total Number of Students	Total Number of Students Raised to Median	Proportion of Students Raised to Median (percent)
Alabama	$1,399,271,552	129	127	98%	725,695	717,667	99%
Alaska	1,299,921	53	2	4	117,359	1,133	1
Arizona	22,264,576	86	22	26	404,239	65,356	16
Arkansas	222,683,392	317	249	79	433,152	384,622	89
California	3,528,073,216	284	234	82	3,479,022	3,382,703	97
Colorado	9,224,096	175	6	3	592,763	47,542	8
Connecticut		113	0		436,371	0	0
Delaware	3,689,970	15	1	7	97,386	6,392	7
District of Columbia		1	n/a	n/a	80,618	0	0
Florida	425,418,752	67	44	66	1,929,239	1,154,894	60
Georgia	244,136,960	176	127	72	1,175,439	616,088	52
Hawaii		1	n/a	n/a	174,747	0	0
Idaho	263,585,216	103	84	82	223,734	216,752	97
Illinois	532,504,064	420	333	79	1,172,849	1,024,519	87
Indiana	39,913,856	292	21	7	951,333	80,356	8
Iowa		376	0		480,048	0	0
Kansas	24,713,600	304	18	6	437,034	83,524	19
Kentucky	238,722,304	172	158	92	632,906	490,910	78
Louisiana	164,165,120	66	35	53	759,465	415,281	55
Maine	3,687,400	113	6	5	183,513	13,985	8
Maryland	107,898,240	24	7	29	736,238	180,726	25
Massachusetts	202,067,456	210	76	36	741,941	311,964	42
Michigan	62,282,176	523	108	21	1,614,541	219,695	14
Minnesota	23,077,288	346	20	6	745,075	23,767	3
Mississippi	558,920,960	149	147	99	499,227	495,629	99
Missouri	797,050,752	451	410	91	810,250	689,486	85

Montana	2,602,626	16	8	50	5,619	4,780	85
Nebraska	4,737,428	277	8	3	260,533	13,712	5
Nevada	142,117,952	16	5	31	211,662	189,920	90
New Hampshire	3,728,768	68	5	7	142,065	20,154	14
New Jersey		209	0		812,757	0	0
New Mexico	143,204,480	88	34	39	308,667	276,864	90
New York		653	0		2,576,912	0	0
North Carolina	397,485,312	132	95	72	1,082,886	825,024	76
North Dakota	25,203,040	200	30	15	114,566	50,609	44
Ohio	380,269,824	609	308	51	1,769,015	780,337	44
Oklahoma	297,075,840	436	242	56	564,651	503,050	89
Oregon	12,916,704	155	18	12	435,448	38,372	9
Pennsylvania	15,665,568	498	25	5	1,662,596	66,751	4
Rhode Island	2,037,334	33	0		139,222	0	0
South Carolina	682,721,280	91	88	97	625,839	606,372	97
South Dakota	40,847,680	165	44	27	127,660	70,085	55
Tennessee	1,015,458,304	123	117	95	816,581	786,059	96
Texas	1,948,707,840	972	453	47	3,447,453	2,694,240	78
Utah	836,827,328	40	34	85	456,545	448,385	98
Vermont		38	0		34,813	0	0
Virginia	322,720,512	131	90	69	1,016,628	603,220	59
Washington	111,035,136	247	83	34	860,341	342,678	40
West Virginia	38,710,080	55	28	51	320,249	182,948	57
Wisconsin	1,101,594	369	3	1	784,866	4,969	1
Wyoming		47	0		100,263	0	0
United States	15,299,825,497	10,634	3,953	37	38,312,021	19,131,520	50

Note: n/a = not applicable.

Source: Analysis of U.S. Bureau of the Census, 1992.

229

APPENDIX 1.11. COSTS OF RAISING DISTRICTS TO THE NATIONAL MEDIAN OF STATE GENERAL PLUS LOCAL REVENUES PER PUPIL FOR HIGH SCHOOL DISTRICTS, 1991–92, BY STATE.

State	Cost of Raising Students in Low-Spending Districts to Median ($)	Total Number of Districts	Total Number of Districts Raised to Median	Proportion of Districts Raised to Median (percent)	Total Number of Students	Total Number of Students Raised to Median	Proportion of Students Raised to Median (percent)
Alabama							
Alaska							
Arizona	$5,247,816	16	3	19%	57,725	9,325	16%
Arkansas							
California	467,703,040	102	83	81	401,527	363,611	91
Colorado							
Connecticut		7	0		6,058		
Delaware		1	0		600		
District of Columbia							
Florida							
Georgia							
Hawaii							
Idaho							
Illinois	22,730,912	109	33	30	193,797	37,029	19
Indiana		3	0		531		
Iowa							
Kansas							
Kentucky							
Louisiana		5	0		1,938		
Maine							
Maryland							
Massachusetts	6,541,592	6	3	50	8,231	6,061	74
Michigan							
Minnesota		11	0		2,690		
Mississippi	3,511,598	4	4	100	1,759	1,759	100
Missouri							
Montana	669,254	162	3	2	46,608	1,521	4

State					
Nebraska	21	0			4,196
Nevada	5	0			
New Hampshire	49	0			2,512
New Jersey		0			74,157
New Mexico	3				
New York		0			14,289
North Carolina					
North Dakota	4				329
Ohio					
Oklahoma	21	5	1,760,366	20,515	21
Oregon		24		4,325	
Pennsylvania					
Rhode Island					
South Carolina					
South Dakota					
Tennessee					
Texas					
Utah					
Vermont	20	13	823,172	14,800	1,860	13
Virginia		2			
Washington					
West Virginia	10	0			8,485
Wisconsin					
Wyoming					
United States	559	136	24	508,987,750	856,757	425,491	50

Note: High school districts are districts, usually small, consisting of only a high school or a few high schools. A blank row means that the state (or the District of Columbia) does not have any high school districts.

Source: Analysis of U.S. Bureau of the Census, 1992.

APPENDIX 1.12. COSTS OF RAISING DISTRICTS TO THE NATIONAL MEDIAN OF STATE GENERAL PLUS LOCAL REVENUES PER PUPIL FOR ELEMENTARY DISTRICTS, 1991–92, BY STATE.

State	Cost of Raising Students in Low-Spending Districts to Median ($)	Total Number of Districts	Total Number of Districts Raised to Median	Proportion of Districts Raised to Median (percent)	Total Number of Students	Total Number of Students Raised to Median	Proportion of Students Raised to Median (percent)
Alabama							
Alaska							
Arizona	$6,444,536	110	6	5%	191,965	33,050	17%
Arkansas	4,753	1	1	100	141	141	100
California	634,809,088	601	394	66	1,075,054	945,694	88
Colorado		1	0		44		
Connecticut		45	0		21,580		
Delaware							
District of Columbia							
Florida							
Georgia		7	0	0	2,250		
Hawaii							
Idaho	40,887	8	1	13	798	223	28
Illinois	83,979,200	411	190	46	462,253	190,705	41
Indiana		1	0		273		
Iowa	71,516	46	1	2	10,784	289	3
Kansas							
Kentucky	103,895	4	1	25	1,192	333	28
Louisiana							
Maine	193,286	109	2	2	25,923	471	2
Maryland							
Massachusetts	874,980	99	7	7	62,915	1,707	3
Michigan	17,977	35	2	6	5,164	84	2
Minnesota	554,328	57	4	7	13,044	1,289	10
Mississippi							
Missouri	3,000,572	88	29	33	11,859	6,397	54

State							
Montana	1,627,848	344	17	5	106,930	5,727	5
Nebraska	857,734	436	60	14	13,087	2,273	17
Nevada		1	0		148		
New Hampshire		85	0		26,044		
New Jersey	2,461,368	296	1	<1	202,081	1,805	1
New Mexico							
New York		44	0	0	24,300		
North Carolina							
North Dakota	9,076	54	2	4	3,256	67	2
Ohio		1	0		4		
Oklahoma	693,506	133	10	8	19,991	2,460	12
Oregon	496,307	114	9	8	41,412	2,233	
Pennsylvania		2	0		668		
Rhode Island		4	0		2,142		
South Carolina							
South Dakota	75,426	9	1	11	1,177	109	9
Tennessee	12,391,216	12	12	100	14,071	14,071	100
Texas	2,607,408	78	1	1	16,918	6,140	36
Utah							
Vermont		183	0		43,656		
Virginia		2	0		1,320		
Washington	157,964	49	3	6	8,986	376	4
West Virginia							
Wisconsin		46	0		20,193		
Wyoming		2	0		617		
United States	751,472,870	3,518	754	21	2,432,240	1,215,644	50

Note: Elementary districts are school districts consisting only of elementary schools. A blank row means that the state (or the District of Columbia) does not have any elementary districts.

Source: Analysis of U.S. Bureau of the Census, 1992.

APPENDIX 1.13. COSTS OF RAISING DISTRICTS TO THE NATIONAL MEDIAN OF TOTAL REVENUES PER PUPIL FOR K–12 DISTRICTS, 1991–92, BY STATE.

State	Cost of Raising Students in Low-Spending Districts to Median ($)	Total Number of Districts	Total Number of Districts Raised to Median	Proportion of Districts Raised to Median (percent)	Total Number of Students	Total Number of Students Raised to Median	Proportion of Students Raised to Median (percent)
Alabama	$776,622,080	129	123	95%	725,695	688,135	95%
Alaska		53	0		117,359		0
Arizona	181,524,736	86	44	51	404,239	337,809	84
Arkansas	358,450,176	317	263	83	433,152	390,384	90
California	2,721,127,424	284	224	79	3,479,022	2,713,129	78
Colorado	95,086,336	175	34	19	592,763	300,261	51
Connecticut	94,467	113	1	1	436,371	2,236	1
Delaware	85,442	15	1	7	97,386	3,042	3
District of Columbia		1	0		80,618		0
Florida	3,673,472	67	1	1	1,929,239	50,836	3
Georgia	478,458,880	176	120	68	1,175,439	809,406	69
Hawaii		1	0		174,747		0
Idaho	243,253,120	103	73	71	223,734	210,278	94
Illinois	709,006,848	420	374	89	1,172,849	1,105,205	94
Indiana	86,648,960	292	81	28	951,333	259,507	27
Iowa	14,549,344	376	29	8	480,048	102,087	21
Kansas	42,291,072	304	35	12	437,034	127,244	29
Kentucky	336,790,784	172	144	84	632,906	577,125	91
Louisiana	254,091,776	66	46	70	759,465	530,327	70
Maine	26,107,456	113	30	27	183,513	71,264	39
Maryland		24	0		736,238		0
Massachusetts	273,944,960	210	129	61	741,941	454,027	61
Michigan	365,527,040	523	301	58	1,614,541	678,400	42
Minnesota	40,139,424	346	33	10	745,075	93,771	13
Mississippi	663,611,008	149	145	97	499,227	493,207	99
Missouri	920,162,560	451	395	88	810,250	701,986	87

Montana	5,014,862	16	8	50	5,619	4,943	88
Nebraska	16,144,096	277	19	7	260,533	59,290	23
Nevada	264,354,048	16	6	38	211,662	193,104	91
New Hampshire	31,033,920	68	23	34	142,065	70,209	49
New Jersey		209	0		812,757		0
New Mexico	218,695,552	88	32	36	308,667	267,737	87
New York		653	0		2,576,912		0
North Carolina	229,474,560	132	58	44	1,082,886	608,896	56
North Dakota	46,952,192	200	40	20	114,566	75,459	66
Ohio	834,161,664	609	466	77	1,769,015	1,116,405	63
Oklahoma	599,470,592	436	273	63	564,651	514,188	91
Oregon	44,769,856	155	42	27	435,448	160,397	37
Pennsylvania	19,432,128	498	34	7	1,662,596	94,625	6
Rhode Island	9,455,936	33	4	12	139,222	21,968	16
South Carolina	203,074,304	91	55	60	625,839	419,006	67
South Dakota	64,900,992	165	53	32	127,660	92,509	72
Tennessee	953,230,848	123	115	93	816,581	782,332	96
Texas	1,341,841,408	972	252	26	3,447,453	2,480,826	72
Utah	750,928,640	40	29	73	456,545	439,041	96
Vermont	500,150	38	2	5	34,813	2,329	7
Virginia	374,904,576	131	88	67	1,016,628	616,026	61
Washington	103,616,768	247	67	27	860,341	335,605	39
West Virginia	10,747,872	55	11	20	320,249	90,030	28
Wisconsin	3,503,980	369	6	2	784,866	9,811	1
Wyoming		47	0		100,263		0
United States	14,717,456,309	10,634	4,309	41	38,312,021	19,154,402	50

Source: Analysis of U.S. Bureau of the Census, 1992.

APPENDIX 1.14. COSTS OF RAISING DISTRICTS TO THE NATIONAL MEDIAN OF TOTAL REVENUES PER PUPIL FOR HIGH SCHOOL DISTRICTS, 1991–92, BY STATE.

State	Cost of Raising Students in Low-Spending Districts to Median ($)	Total Number of Districts	Total Number of Districts Raised to Median	Proportion of Districts Raised to Median (percent)	Total Number of Students	Total Number of Students Raised to Median	Proportion of Students Raised to Median (percent)
Alabama							
Alaska							
Arizona	$16,484,832	16	8	50%	57,725	35,520	62%
Arkansas	364,300,160	102	73	72	401,527	331,349	83
California							
Colorado							
Connecticut		7			6,058		
Delaware		1			600		
District of Columbia							
Florida							
Georgia							
Hawaii							
Idaho							
Illinois	28,833,744	109	34	31	193,797	38,355	20
Indiana		3			531		
Iowa							
Kansas							
Kentucky							
Louisiana							
Maine		5			1,938		
Maryland							
Massachusetts	2,801,404	6	2	33	8,231	4,531	55
Michigan							
Minnesota		11			2,690		
Mississippi	3,205,569	4	4	100	1,759	1,759	100
Montana	1,216,594	162	6	4	42,608	2,488	6
Missouri							

State						
Nebraska	21			4,196		
Nevada	5			2,512		
New Hampshire	49			74,157		
New Jersey						
New Mexico	3			14,289		
New York	4			329		
North Carolina						
North Dakota						
Ohio						
Oklahoma						
Oregon	21	24	1,967,324	20,515	10,226	50
Pennsylvania						
Rhode Island						
South Carolina						
South Dakota						
Tennessee						
Texas						
Utah						
Vermont	20	3	1,860,572	14,800	3,720	25
Virginia		15				
Washington						
West Virginia	10			8,485		
Wisconsin						
Wyoming						
United States	559	135	420,670,199	856,747	427,948	50

Note: High school districts are districts, usually small, consisting of only a high school or a few high schools. A blank row means that the state (or the District of Columbia) does not have any high school districts.

Source: Analysis of U.S. Bureau of the Census, 1992.

APPENDIX 1.15. COSTS OF RAISING DISTRICTS TO THE NATIONAL MEDIAN OF TOTAL REVENUES PER PUPIL FOR ELEMENTARY DISTRICTS, 1991–92, BY STATE.

State	Cost of Raising Students in Low-Spending Districts to Median ($)	Total Number of Districts	Total Number of Districts Raised to Median	Proportion of Districts Raised to Median (percent)	Total Number of Students	Total Number of Students Raised to Median	Proportion of Students Raised to Median (percent)
Alabama							
Alaska							
Arizona	$34,684,032	110	15	14%	191,965	87,921	46%
Arkansas		1	0		141		0
California	487,092,736	601	330	55	1,075,054	811,051	75
Colorado		1	0		44		0
Connecticut		45	0		21,580		0
Delaware							
District of Columbia							
Florida							
Georgia		7	0		2,250		0
Hawaii							
Idaho		8	0		798		0
Illinois	158,905,152	411	226	55	462,253	229,602	50
Indiana		1	0		273		3
Iowa	158,304	46	1	2	10,784	289	
Kansas							
Kentucky	135,488	4	1	25	1,192	333	28
Louisiana							
Maine	149,667	109	2	2	25,923	886	3
Maryland							
Massachusetts	1,573,321	99	5	5	62,915	3,446	5
Michigan	65,394	35	5	14	5,164	162	3
Minnesota	451,763	57	2	4	13,044	895	7
Mississippi							
Missouri	1,537,511	88	13	15	11,859	3,389	29
Montana	6,561,040	344	59	17	106,930	39,600	37

Nebraska	1,690,797	436	80	13,087	18	2,614	20
Nevada		1	0	148			0
New Hampshire	279,792	85	3	26,044	4	1,203	5
New Jersey		296	0	202,081			0
New Mexico							
New York		44	0	24,300			0
North Carolina		54	0	3,256			0
North Dakota		1	0	4			0
Ohio							
Oklahoma	3,072,398	133	23	19,991	17	5,616	28
Oregon	2,199,256	114	20	41,412	18	12,521	30
Pennsylvania		2	0	668			0
Rhode Island		4	0	2,142			0
South Carolina							
South Dakota		9	1	1,177			9
Tennessee	137,630	12	12	14,071	11	109	100
Texas	9,505,788	78	0	16,918	100	14,071	0
Utah							
Vermont		183	0	43,656			0
Virginia		2	0	1,320			0
Washington	23,385	49	2	8,986	4	744	8
West Virginia							
Wisconsin	18,308	46	1	20,193	2	177	1
Wyoming		2	0	617			0
United States	708,241,761	3,518	801	2,432,240	23	1,214,629	50

Note: Elementary districts are school districts consisting only of elementary schools. A blank row means that the state (or the District of Columbia) does not have any elementary districts.

Source: Analysis of U.S. Bureau of the Census, 1992.

APPENDIX 5.1. THE FINANCING OF GRANT-MAINTAINED SCHOOLS AND THEIR RELATIONSHIP TO THE LOCAL MANAGEMENT OF SCHOOLS (LMS) SCHEME.

As stated in the beginning of Chapter Five, England has two versions of government-funded schools: locally managed schools, which are technically part of the local education authority, and grant-maintained (GM) schools, which are independent legal entities but receive their funding from the government, teach the national curriculum, and administer the national tests to their students. GM schools were originally in a local education authority (LEA), or district, but through a vote of the school council and parents decided to opt out of the LEA for a more dramatic and complete form of independence. In a 1996 white paper (Department for Education and Employment, 1996b), GM schools were touted as "the most advanced form of self-government for state schools." The document added that the central government "remains committed to expanding and developing the GM sector." GM schools were advocated by the national government because it was a strong proponent of radical—if not total—school management autonomy.

Because of their legal status as separate entities, GM schools are more independent than U.S. charter schools, even though, just like charter schools, GM schools are part of the government system of schools. GM schools also have more responsibility for running their own schools than LEA schools do, even under the LMS system. For example, GM schools are the legal employers of all of their staff, whereas the LEA remains the legal employer in LMS schools, even though LMS school councils have personnel budget, hiring, and firing authority. (In a few LMS schools—primarily religious schools—the LEA pays the operating costs, including salaries, but the school's governing body, like GM schools, is the employer.) GM schools also have full authority over capital works and structural repairs and can enter into contracts, whereas LEAs continue to retain authority over capital works for LMS schools, often requiring schools to obtain multiple bids for repairs and sometimes demanding that schools use only "approved" contractors. GM schools also receive a greater portion of their budget—indeed, 100 percent of their operating budget. GM schools, therefore, are responsible for managing all of their resources, rather than just a percentage—albeit a high percentage—as LMS schools do (Levacic, 1995).

Consistent with their higher degree of autonomy, GM schools receive their resources through a special agency and set of funding regulations that has been evolving since 1988. Although initially GM schools simply received their funds through the LMS funding scheme in the LEA from which they opted out, in 1994 a separate entity, called the Funding Agency for Schools (FAS), was created to serve as the funding agent for GM schools. Today, the FAS distributes not only annual operating funds (called the annual maintenance grant, or AMG) to GM schools but also special-purpose operating grants (such as funds for a national literacy initiative), and monies for capital construction. However, the amount of the AMG is still linked to the LEA in which the GM school is located. Understanding that connection is crucial to understanding how GM schools are funded.

The funding requirements for GM schools have changed over time and have been the subject of considerable discussion, analysis, and regulation. Initially, LEAs were required to fund GM schools just as they funded their LMS schools. But over time, several issues emerged that led to a more complex funding structure. First, the issue of equity of funding emerged as it became apparent that per-pupil funding levels for similarly situated GM schools across the country could be quite different, depending on the education spending levels of each LEA (which varied in terms of whether LEAs spent below, at, or above their education standard spending assessment, or SSA), the split between primary and secondary school funding, and the specific pupil weights used in the LEA funding formula. Second, there were claims that LEAs began to find ways to funnel more money into LMS schools than similarly situated GM schools. As a result, more structure was developed for determining the basic operating grant for GM schools. To begin, the AMG for all GM primary schools and for GM secondary schools in LEAs for which less than 30 percent of secondary students are in GM schools is made up of three elements:

1. A basic operating grant determined through the GM funding formula structure. Basically, this is the money the school would have received if it had stayed within the LEA as an LMS school, the full aggregate schools budget (ASB).
2. An additional amount that generally reflects the revenues retained in both the potential schools budget (PSB) and the general schools budget (GSB) by the LEA for centrally managed LEA school services provided only to LEA schools. However, some services that the LEA continues to provide to GM as well as LMS schools (such as student statementing, educational welfare workers, and psychologists) are excluded from this add-on.
3. The cost of free school meals provided by GM schools is based on the LEA's funding of free school meals and redistributed through the AMG by FAS.

LEAs in which more than 30 percent of secondary students are in GM schools fund secondary GM schools via a system called the Common Funding Formula (CFF), which is developed by the Department for Education and Employment in consultation with FAS and GM schools. Although called a common funding formula, the CFF would be more accurately termed a common funding methodology. The CFF structures a method each LEA must follow in funding GM schools, but the monetary amounts (CFF formulas) that result can still differ substantially across LEAs. The CFF actually encompasses two different procedures, and GM schools receive the amount that is the greater of the two. The first procedure links GM funding to the LEA's education SSA, the standard spending assessment determined by the central government's fiscal equalization formula. The second procedure links GM funding to the regular LEA funding formula, the LMS funding scheme. The former is usually used in LEAs that spend below their SSA and the latter for LEAs that spend above their SSA.

The overall objective of the CFF is to ensure that GM secondary schools have budget levels that are, at a maximum, at the LEA secondary schools' budget for LEAs spending above the SSA and, at a minimum, at the LEA SSA for LEAs spending below the SSA. Therefore, in both cases, from a national perspective, GM secondary schools are not penalized financially for their independent status from their LEA. This policy is consistent with the national government's commitment to promoting GM schools as the preferred governance structure for schools (Department for Education and Employment, 1996a).

The first and most prominent procedure of the CFF works in the following way. It begins with the LEA's SSA. Recall that the SSA has five categories based on student ages: (1) under five, (2) five to eleven (primary school, grades 1–6), (3) eleven to fifteen (secondary school, grades 7–11), (4) sixteen to nineteen (sixth form, grades 12 and 13), and (5) other (youth, community, and adult education). First, the amount for students in categories 1 and 5 is excluded. Second, the amount for LEA responsibilities that are provided to all schools (LMS and GM) is subtracted; these are largely the mandatory exceptions. The amount remaining is the proportion of the SSA provided for both primary and secondary school students. The primary student amount is then subtracted, which leaves the total amount for secondary school students—both key stages for categories 3 and 4.

The CFF formula structure is then applied to this remaining total. This structure limits the number of factors that can be used to formula-fund secondary schools. It includes four major factors: (1) pupil numbers at three stages of the national curriculum (stages 3 and 4 and age sixteen and beyond; four LEAs receive funding for key stage 2 students who are in GM middle schools that are deemed secondary and therefore receive funding under the CFF), (2) a measure of additional education need, (3) a fixed-cost element or a base allocation for all schools, and (4) the cost of providing free school meals for eligible students. Appendix 5.2 provides details on the major student-related CFF factors as well as the fixed-cost factor in the twenty-three LEAs that are required to use the CFF for their GM schools. In addition, Appendix 5.2 provides the base allocation (the key stage 3 per-pupil amount) for each LEA.

All key stage weights are relative to the cost of providing educational services for key stage 3 students. For example, Barnet's CFF distributes 24 percent more for key stage 4 students than it does for key stage 3 students (roughly £386 more: 0.24 times £1,609). Note that the base allocation for each LEA varies, as do the various key stage weights (other than the key stage 3 weight, which is a constant 1.0 across all LEAs). Weights for key stage 5 vary the most between GM secondary schools in LEAs under the CFF, ranging from 1.25 to 1.94, with an average of 1.53. Key stage 4 weights range from 1.00 to 1.62 and average a little over 1.20.

Eligibility for special educational need and additional special educational need vary in the CFF, depending on the LEA. For instance, in Bromley, Cambridgeshire, and Hertfordshire, the special educational need weight is applied to all students who are entitled to free school meals. In contrast, the number of pupils with special educational need but no statements, as determined by a special audit, are weighted for special educational need in Enfield. In addition, students eligible for free school meals are weighted by the *additional* special educational need factor in Enfield. In other words, in Enfield, nonstatemented GM students qualifying for special educational needs are weighted by a factor of 0.1372 *and* students eligible for free school meals are weighted by 0.1816. Thus not only do the weights for special educational need vary across LEAs, but the students to whom the weight should be applied also vary by LEA. In contrast, all weights for free school meals are applied to pupils eligible for free school meals. This is true for GM secondary schools in all LEAs under the CFF.

Several other small factors may also be used to fund GM secondary schools under the CFF: small schools, split sites, floor area, pupil turnover, London area, and staff training. These generally affect only a small portion of the overall funding level. Like the weighting for special education, many of these weights are not consistently applied to the same object. For example, for GM schools in some LEAs, the CFF allocates floor area funding using acres and in other LEAs using square feet or square meters. The weights themselves also vary by LEA under the CFF, ranging from 0.90 in Ealing to 12.70 in Derby for floor area weights. The London weighting and staff training weights are consistently applied to the same objects across LEAs. The London weight is applied on a per-pupil basis to GM schools in eligible LEAs, and staff training occurs in only one LEA (Sutton), so it is consistently applied by default.

Because the CFF is really a common methodology, with all formula parameter levels set independently for each LEA, the result is a different amount of money for each student in GM schools, even though they are funded according to the same methodology. Further, although the overall CFF requirements ensure that each LEA addresses GM funding within a similar context and an equitable framework, GM funding is still linked to LEA education finance—the SSA, the degree of local preference for education (as reflected in spending above the education SSA by shifting funds from other government services or raising local council tax revenues), and the CFF parameter decisions that are made. The final result is that money per pupil can still differ among similarly situated GM schools, although the differences are somewhat more "rational" than capricious because they are justified within the same methodology.

The CFF represents a simplified way of funding schools—at least over many complicated LEA distribution formulas. The FAS has been working to continue to streamline the CFF, which also appeared to be the policy trend for many LEAs' distribution formulas to schools. Wandsworth's school funding formula provides a good comparison to the CFF methodology. It is straightforward and has very few factors. In addition, Wandsworth uses lump-sum amounts rather than complicated formulas for several of its factors. The desire to simplify school finance—for GM schools or LEAs—is a trend in England, as it is in the United States.

Recently, both the Funding Agency for Schools (1996) and the Department for Education and Employment (1996a) began to explore the possibilities of a national funding formula (NFF) for GM schools. The department argued that the NFF would simplify the CFF formulas by removing the linkage between GM secondary school funding and LEA education finance policies. In addition, the FAS contended—with some considerable logic—that an NFF is consistent with the national curriculum, the national Code of Professional Practice for special-needs students, the national pay scale for teachers, and national inspections similar to performance-based school accreditation in the United States. However, a recent white paper (Department for Education and Employment, 1996a) remained neutral on the issue of a national funding formula and simply noted that national funding posed "many challenges" and that the department wished merely to open the debate. In the meantime, the white paper intimated that the CFF would continue to be modified so that greater budgetary standardization could be accomplished across GM schools in different LEAS.

The concerns for an NFF in the context of unequal funding for GM schools across LEAs can be applied just as logically to LEAs and LMS funding. Given the national elements in the English education system together with the move to drive the money to the school site, a legitimate question is whether funding differences (other than those for special pupil or school needs or education prices) can be justified or whether a national funding formula would be more appropriate for the whole of England. The fact that GM primary and secondary schools are funded differently from each other highlights the differences in spending between all primary and secondary schools across England. In addition, the CFF formula, although initially created to ameliorate this issue, has not functioned in that way.

This accentuates the differences in secondary school spending across LEAs—or at least a high degree of variation in the justifications (factors) for spending. Thus while the national government in England funds education based on a centrally determined SSA that is applied to all LEAs, LEAs fund schools based on their own local circumstances and preferences, and these apparently vary substantially across the country. England therefore has an educational finance system where the various actors (in this case, LEA and GM schools) are keenly aware of their relationship to each other, particularly in terms of differences in school financing. School finance equity is clearly a concern that has been heightened by the creation of GM schools and school-based financing in England.

Of course, concerns over school finance equity—whether between GM or LMS schools—are constrained by political and economic issues. Any move to an NFF would either require new money to bring all GM or all LMS schools up to some common high level, if not the highest level of per-pupil funding, or the current funds would need to be redistributed from higher- to lower-funded schools. A national funding formula would also eliminate all LEA decision making on school finance, thus curtailing, if not eliminating, local financial control. The tension between an adequate, equitable national school financing system and the liberty associated with local control severely constrains the ability of England to move to such a national system—just as virtually the same issues constrain U.S. states from equalizing their education finance systems.

APPENDIX 5.2. COMMON FUNDING FORMULA (CFF) FACTORS FOR GRANT-MAINTAINED SCHOOLS FOR TWENTY-THREE QUALIFYING LOCAL EDUCATION AUTHORITIES (LEAs) IN ENGLAND FOR 1996–97.

CFF Area	Base Allocation (£)	Key Stage 3	Key Stage 4	Key Stage 5[a]	Special Educa- tional Need	Additional Special Educa- tional Need	Free School Meals
Bamet	£1,609.06	1.00	1.24	1.64	0.03	0.05	0.14
Brent	2,232.78	1.00	1.10	1.30	0.08		0.14
Bromley	1,705.75	1.00	1.22	1.94	0.31		0.17
Calderdale	1,810.23	1.00	1.22	1.25	4.81		0.11
Cambridgeshire	1,668.21	1.00	1.27	1.66	0.20		0.17
Croydon	2,006.30	1.00	1.06	1.53	0.26		0.08
Cumbira	1,641.19	1.00	1.20	1.57	0.35		0.12
Derbyshire	1,587.57	1.00	1.20	1.42	0.16	0.31	0.19
Ealing	1,862.27	1.00	1.19	1.25	0.04		0.14
Enfield	1,792.79	1.00	1.28	1.64	0.14	0.18	0.15
Essex	1,836.41	1.00	1.22	1.57	8.62	0.07	0.18
Gloucestershire	1,522.76	1.00	1.28	1.68	0.12		0.21
Hertfordshire	1,775.15	1.00	1.28	1.39	0.24		0.12
Hillingdon	1,971.12	1.00	1.17	1.50	0.15		0.11
Kent	1,853.46	1.00	1.14	1.50	0.09		0.15
Kingston	1,913.28	1.00	1.00	1.46	0.19	0.19	0.16
Lambeth	2,547.38	1.00	1.12	1.30	0.07		0.14
Lincolnshire	1,750.95	1.00	1.00	1.48			0.09
Surrey	1,707.03	1.00	1.13	1.59	0.12	0.09	0.15
Sutton	1,809.89	1.00	1.07	1.52	0.64	4.58	0.18
Walsall	1,600.74	1.00	1.29	1.41	0.28		0.17
Wandsworth	1,867.39	1.00	1.62	1.87	0.03		0.14
Wiltshire	1,597.56	1.00	1.32	1.77	0.82	0.25	0.24

Note: Figures are rounded to the second decimal place.

[a]Stage 5 is for age sixteen and above.

Sources: 1996 Education Regulations for Grant-Maintained Schools; interviews with Funding Agency for Schools staff.

APPENDIX 7.1. SCHOOL RESOURCES COMPARED TO COSTS IN AN EASTERN, URBAN MIDDLE SCHOOL WITH 1,050 STUDENTS.

Core Funding (Ideal class size: 25 students)

1 principal
32 teachers (26 elementary, 5 secondary, 1 language)

Additional Resources in Traditional Schools		Additional Resources for Modern Red Schoolhouse High-Performance NAS School Design	
2 assistant principals:	$130,000		
Regular education specialists (2 art, 1 librarian, 2 music, 2 home economics, 2 shop):	$585,000	2 schoolwide instructional facilitators (transform 2 assistant principal slots to this function):	$130,000
Categorical program specialists (10 teachers for the learning disabled, 13 instructional aides):	$845,000	Teachers with multi-functional roles (add 10 teachers to reduce class size to 25):	$650,000
Pupil support specialists (3 guidance counselors):	$195,000	2 art and 2 music teachers:	$260,000
Professional development:	$80,000	Ongoing professional development:	$110,000
		Design-specific resources Materials: Technology:	$10,000 $250,000
Total above the core:	$1,835,000	Total design costs:	$1,410,000
		Leftover funds:	$425,000

Average staff cost: $65,000
Average aide cost: $15,000

APPENDIX 7.2. SCHOOL RESOURCES COMPARED TO COSTS
IN AN EASTERN, URBAN ELEMENTARY SCHOOL
WITH 1,100 STUDENTS.

Core Funding (Ideal class size: 25 students)

1 principal
39 teachers

Additional Resources in Traditional Schools		*Additional Resources for Roots and Wings High-Performance NAS School Design*	
1 assistant principal:	$65,000	2 schoolwide instructional facilitators (transform 1 assistant principal slot to this function and add another facilitator):	$130,000
Regular education specialists (1 librarian, plus 10 total art, music, math, reading, social studies):	$715,000		
Categorical program specialists (2 teachers for the learning disabled, 12 instructional aides):	$310,000	Teachers with multi-functional roles (add 5 teachers to reduce class size to 25):	$325,000
Pupil support specialists (2 guidance counselors):	$130,000	Professional development:	$50,000
Professional development:	$80,000	Design-specific resources	
		8 tutors:	$520,000
		Full-time family liaison:	$65,000
		Materials:	$50,000
Total above the core:	$1,300,000	Total design costs:	$1,140,000
		Leftover funds:	$160,000
Left: 1 nurse 1 teacher for the severely disabled		Plus: 1 nurse 1 teacher for the severely disabled	

Average staff cost: $65,000
Average aide cost: $15,000

APPENDIX 7.3. SCHOOL RESOURCES COMPARED TO COSTS IN AN EASTERN, URBAN ELEMENTARY SCHOOL WITH 540 STUDENTS (83 PERCENT LOW-INCOME, NO TITLE I RESOURCES).

Core Funding (Ideal class size: 25 students)

1 principal
17 teachers (32 students per classroom)

Additional Resources in Traditional Schools		*Additional Resources for Roots and Wings High-Performance NAS School Design*	
No assistant principal		1 schoolwide instructional facilitator:	$65,000
Regular education specialists (1 music, 1 computer, 1 physical education, 1 reading, 1 math computer lab, 1 librarian):	$390,000	Design-specific resources 4 tutors: Half-time family liaison: Materials:	$260,000 $32,500 $50,000
Categorical program specialists (2 teachers for the learning disabled):	$130,000	Professional development:	$25,000
Pupil support specialists (1 guidance counselor):	$65,000		
Desegregation funds:	$60,000		
Total above the core:	$645,000	Total design costs:	$407,500
		Leftover funds:	$237,500
Left: 1 nurse 2 teachers for the severely disabled		Plus: 1 nurse 2 teachers for the severely disabled	

Average staff cost: $65,000

APPENDIX 7.4. SCHOOL RESOURCES COMPARED TO COSTS IN A NEW ENGLAND ELEMENTARY SCHOOL WITH 500 STUDENTS.

Core Funding (Ideal class size: 25 students) 1 principal 25 teachers (20 students per classroom)	

Current Resources for a Non-Title I School		*Additional Resources for Expeditionary Learning–Outward Bound High-Performance NAS School Design*	
1 assistant principal:	$50,000	1 schoolwide instructional facilitator (transform the assistant principal slot to this function):	$50,000
Regular education specialists (½ each of music, art, physical education, and librarian, 1 reading specialist):	$150,000	¼ district ELOB facilitator:	$12,500
Categorical program specialists (4 instructional aides):	$50,000	Teachers with multifunc-tional roles (school already exceeds typical number):	$0
Pupil support specialists (1 guidance counselor):	$50,000		
Instructional materials:	$10,000	Professional development: Stipends for summer institutes:	$55,000 $15,000
		Design-specific resources Transportation for expeditions: Materials (ropes course): Internet access:	 $5,000 $13,000 $10,000
Total above the core:	$310,000	Total design costs:	$160,500
		Leftover funds:	$149,500

Average staff cost: $50,000
Average aide cost: $12,500

APPENDIX 7.5. SCHOOL RESOURCES COMPARED TO COSTS IN A MIDWESTERN ELEMENTARY SCHOOL WITH 600 STUDENTS (50 PERCENT LIMITED ENGLISH PROFICIENCY, 30 LANGUAGES, 20 PERCENT IN POVERTY).

Core Funding (Ideal class size: 25 students)

1 principal
25 teachers (24 students per classroom)

Additional Resources in Current School		*Additional Resources for Roots and Wings High-Performance NAS School Design*	
1 assistant principal:	$50,000		
		1 schoolwide instructional facilitator:	$50,000
Regular education specialists (1 music, 1 art, 1 physical education, 1 librarian, 4 instructional aides, 1 librarian assistant):	$275,000	Design-specific resources 5 tutors: Full-time family liaison: Materials:	$250,000 $50,000 $35,000
Categorical program specialists (⅔ Title I, 1 reading, 1 gifted, 4 teachers for the learning disabled, 2 English as a second language, 8 aides):	$553,000	Professional development:	$30,000
Pupil support specialists (⅔ social worker, 1½ speech):	$108,000		
Total above the core:	$986,000	Total design costs (could be funded from the categorical program dollars):	$415,000
		Leftover funds:	$571,000
Left: 1 nurse		Plus: 1 nurse	

Average staff cost: $50,000
Average aide cost: $15,000

APPENDIX 7.6. SCHOOL RESOURCES COMPARED TO COSTS IN A PLAINS STATE ELEMENTARY SCHOOL (K–2) WITH 265 STUDENTS (70 PERCENT IN POVERTY).

Core Funding (Ideal class size: 25 students)

1 principal
13 teachers (20 students per classroom)

Note: Title I funds are used both to reduce class size and to provide full-day kindergarten for four kindergarten sections

Additional Resources in Current School		*Additional Resources for High-Cost Version of Expeditionary Learning– Outward Bound (ELOB)*	
Regular education specialists (40% each of music, art, physical education, 1 librarian):	$110,000	1 instructional facilitator team:	$50,000
		¼ district ELOB facilitator:	$12,500
Categorical program specialists (other than the above for lower class sizes and full-day kindergarten) (1 Title I, 1 at-risk strategist, 1.7 learning disabled, 1 teacher aide):	$200,000	Teachers with multifunctional roles (school already exceeds typical number):	$0
		Professional development:	$55,000
		Stipends for summer institutes:	$15,000
Pupil support specialists (1 guidance counselor):	$50,000	Design-specific resources Transportation for expeditions:	$5,000
		Materials (ropes course):	$13,000
		Internet access:	$10,000
Total above the core:	$360,000	Total design costs:	$160,500
		Leftover funds:	$199,500
Left: ½ nurse		Plus: ½ nurse	

Average staff cost: $50,000
Average aide cost: $15,000

APPENDIX 7.7. SCHOOL RESOURCES COMPARED TO COSTS IN A PLAINS STATE ELEMENTARY (3–6) PRESCOTT-LINKED SCHOOL WITH 320 STUDENTS (70 PERCENT IN POVERTY).

Core Funding (Ideal class size: 25 students)

1 principal
16 teachers (20 students per classroom)

Note: Title I funds are used both to reduce class size and to provide full-day kindergarten for four kindergarten sections

Additional Resources in Current School		*Additional Resources for High-Cost Version of Expeditionary Learning–Outward Bound (ELOB)*	
Regular education specialists (⅗ each of music, art, physical education, 1½ librarian):	$165,000	1 instructional facilitator team:	$50,000
		¼ district ELOB facilitator:	$12,500
Categorical program specialists (4½ teachers for the learning disabled, 1 behavior disorder specialist, 2 aides):	$305,000	Teachers with multifunctional roles (school already exceeds typical number):	$0
Pupil support specialists (1 guidance counselor, 1 student attendance strategist):	$100,000	Professional development: Stipends for summer institutes:	$55,000 $15,000
		Design-specific resources Transportation for expeditions: Materials (ropes course): Internet access:	$5,000 $13,000 $10,000
Total above the core:	$570,000	Total design costs:	$160,500
		Leftover funds:	$409,500
Left: ½ nurse		Plus: ½ nurse	

Average staff cost: $50,000
Average aide cost: $15,000

APPENDIX 7.8. COSTS OF RAISING DISTRICTS TO THE NATIONAL OR STATE MEDIAN (WHICHEVER IS HIGHER) OF STATE GENERAL PLUS LOCAL REVENUES PER PUPIL FOR K–12 DISTRICTS, 1991–92, BY STATE.

State	National Median ($)	State Median ($)	Cost of Raising Students in Low-Spending Districts to Median ($)
Alabama	$4,166	$2,133	$1,399,271,680
Alaska	4,166	7,240	254,703,200
Arizona	4,166	4,520	87,831,464
Arkansas	4,166	3,730	222,683,360
California	4,166	3,285	3,528,073,984
Colorado	4,166	5,560	438,592,096
Connecticut	4,166	5,988	158,521,760
Delaware	4,166	4,547	9,782,138
District of Columbia	4,166	7,441	0
Florida	4,166	3,901	425,418,912
Georgia	4,166	3,948	244,136,864
Hawaii	4,166	4,183	0
Idaho	4,166	3,256	263,585,200
Illinois	4,166	3,691	532,504,224
Indiana	4,166	4,794	201,499,872
Iowa	4,166	5,426	194,463,648
Kansas	4,166	6,142	533,143,648
Kentucky	4,166	3,797	238,722,288
Louisiana	4,166	4,081	164,165,024
Maine	4,166	4,977	59,017,860
Maryland	4,166	4,607	229,752,592
Massachusetts	4,166	4,433	297,150,240
Michigan	4,166	4,671	258,212,896
Minnesota	4,166	4,932	177,258,288
Mississippi	4,166	2,932	558,921,088
Missouri	4,166	3,031	797,050,752
Montana	4,166	4,189	2,711,546
Nebraska	4,166	6,406	331,913,376
Nevada	4,166	4,815	266,703,264
New Hampshire	4,166	4,984	41,944,140
New Jersey	4,166	6,164	435,409,792
New Mexico	4,166	4,742	307,943,968
New York	4,166	6,824	2,412,177,408
North Carolina	4,166	3,898	397,485,440
North Dakota	4,166	5,132	102,747,808
Ohio	4,166	4,160	380,269,888
Oklahoma	4,166	4,048	297,075,776
Oregon	4,166	4,999	132,189,200
Pennsylvania	4,166	4,959	264,759,984
Rhode Island	4,166	5,313	41,200,948
South Carolina	4,166	2,868	682,721,216

APPENDIX 7.8. (continued)

State	National Median ($)	State Median ($)	Cost of Raising Students in Low-Spending Districts to Median ($)
South Dakota	4,166	4,812	100,183,296
Tennessee	4,166	2,424	1,015,458,496
Texas	4,166	4,261	2,208,787,712
Utah	4,166	2,521	836,827,392
Vermont	4,166	5,635	10,404,464
Virginia	4,166	3,873	322,720,384
Washington	4,166	4,391	208,084,624
West Virginia	4,166	4,117	38,710,060
Wisconsin	4,166	5,669	395,037,600
Wyoming	4,166	7,391	131,610,784
United States			22,639,541,644

Source: Analysis of U.S. Bureau of the Census, 1992.

APPENDIX 7.9. COSTS OF RAISING DISTRICTS TO THE NATIONAL OR STATE MEDIAN (WHICHEVER IS HIGHER) OF STATE GENERAL PLUS LOCAL REVENUES PER PUPIL FOR HIGH SCHOOL DISTRICTS, 1991–92, BY STATE.

State	National Median ($)	State Median ($)	Cost of Raising Students in Low-Spending Districts to Median ($)
Alabama			
Alaska			
Arizona	$5,077	$5,322	$12,667,268
Arkansas			
California	5,077	4,148	467,702,912
Colorado			
Connecticut	5,077	8,502	1,560,202
Delaware	5,077	5,493	0
District of Columbia			
Florida			
Georgia			
Hawaii			
Idaho			
Illinois	5,077	6,095	77,523,592
Indiana			

APPENDIX 7.9. (continued)

State	National Median ($)	State Median ($)	Cost of Raising Students in Low-Spending Districts to Median ($)
Iowa	5,077	8,959	515,977
Kansas			
Kentucky			
Louisiana			
Maine	5,077	6,086	248,221
Maryland			
Massachusetts	5,077	4,868	6,541,593
Michigan			
Minnesota	5,077	6,484	1,123,324
Mississippi	5,077	3,277	3,511,599
Missouri			
Montana	5,077	9,369	107,199,696
Nebraska	5,077	8,634	4,537,209
Nevada			
New Hampshire	5,077	8,033	1,070,617
New Jersey	5,077	8,877	70,767,136
New Mexico			
New York		8,662	3,340,572
North Carolina			
North Dakota	5,077	8,929	462,004
Ohio			
Oklahoma			
Oregon	5,077	6,274	16,560,449
Pennsylvania			
Rhode Island			
South Carolina			
South Dakota			
Tennessee			
Texas			
Utah			
Vermont	5,077	6,607	9,491,865
Virginia			
Washington			
West Virginia			
Wisconsin	5,077	6,763	2,389,659
Wyoming			
United States			787,213,893

Note: High school districts are districts, usually small, consisting of only a high school or a few high schools. A blank row means that the state (or the District of Columbia) does not have any high school districts.

Source: Analysis of U.S. Bureau of the Census, 1992.

APPENDIX 7.10. COSTS OF RAISING DISTRICTS TO THE NATIONAL OR STATE MEDIAN (WHICHEVER IS HIGHER) OF STATE GENERAL PLUS LOCAL REVENUES PER PUPIL FOR ELEMENTARY SCHOOL DISTRICTS, 1991–92, BY STATE.

State	National Median ($)	State Median ($)	Cost of Raising Students in Low-Spending Districts to Median ($)
Alabama			
Alaska			
Arizona	$3,573	$6,047	$360,943,840
Arkansas	3,573	3,539	4,753
California	3,573	3,246	634,808,960
Colorado	3,573	13,843	0
Connecticut	3,573	9,208	20,673,620
Delaware			
District of Columbia			
Florida			
Georgia	3,573	5,111	919,526
Hawaii			
Idaho	3,573	4,832	768,407
Illinois	3,573	3,671	103,291,704
Indiana	3,573	7,519	0
Iowa	3,573	6,538	10,936,738
Kansas			
Kentucky	3,573	3,955	371,078
Louisiana			
Maine	3,573	6,577	15,973,008
Maryland			
Massachusetts	3,573	6,444	51,398,736
Michigan	3,573	5,596	3,202,060
Minnesota	3,573	5,069	8,095,293
Mississippi			
Missouri	3,573	4,201	7,452,007
Montana	3,573	4,931	81,660,328
Nebraska	3,573	5,128	9,213,776
Nevada	3,573	9,088	0
New Hampshire	3,573	7,686	26,243,720
New Jersey	3,573	6,797	172,153,504
New Mexico			
New York	3,573	11,578	101,003,616
North Carolina			
North Dakota	3,573	6,024	2,945,630
Ohio	3,573	22,106	0
Oklahoma	3,573	4,565	8,877,560
Oregon	3,573	4,746	22,729,430
Pennsylvania	3,573	9,406	372,051
Rhode Island	3,573	5,851	762,486

APPENDIX 7.10. (continued)

State	National Median ($)	State Median ($)	Cost of Raising Students in Low-spending Districts to Median ($)
South Carolina			
South Dakota	3,573	9,894	5,265,271
Tennessee	3,573	2,578	12,391,215
Texas	3,573	6,676	35,707,864
Utah			
Vermont	3,573	8,846	39,756,244
Virginia	3,573	5,115	90,713
Washington	3,573	4,942	5,178,390
West Virginia			
Wisconsin	3,573	5,692	9,681,486
Wyoming	3,573	8,261	47,271
United States			1,752,920,285

Note: Elementary districts are school districts consisting only of elementary schools. A blank row means that the state (or the District of Columbia) does not have any elementary districts.

Source: Analysis of U.S. Bureau of the Census, 1992.

REFERENCES

Achilles, C. (1996). Students achieve more in smaller classes. *Educational Leadership, 53*(5), 76–77.

Achilles, C., Nye, B., and Zaharias, J. (1995). *Policy use of research results: Tennessee's Project Challenge.* Paper presented at the annual meeting of the American Educational Research Association, San Francisco.

Achilles, C., Nye, B., Zaharias, J., and Fulton, B. (1993). *The Lasting Benefits Study (LBS) in grades 4 and 5 (1990–1991): A legacy from Tennessee's four-year (K–3) class size study (1985–1989), Project STAR.* Paper presented at the meeting of the North Carolina Association for Research in Education, Greensboro.

Adams, J., Jr. (1994). The local impact of school finance reform in Kentucky: Familiar patterns and new programs, but is this reform? *Educational Evaluation and Policy Analysis, 16*(4), 375–390.

Alexander, K., Augenblick, J., Driscoll, W., Guthrie, J., and Levin, R. (1995). *Proposals for the elimination of wealth-based disparities in public education.* Columbus, OH: Department of Public Instruction.

Allington, R. L., and Johnston, P. (1989). Coordination, collaboration, and consistency: The redesign of compensatory and special education interventions. In R. E. Slavin, N. L. Karweit, and N. A. Madden (Eds.), *Effective programs for students at risk* (pp. 320–354). Needham Heights, MA: Allyn & Bacon.

Barro, S. (1992). *What does the education dollar buy? Relationships of staffing, staff characteristics and staff salaries to state per-pupil spending.* Madison: University of Wisconsin, Wisconsin Center for Education Research, Consortium for Policy Research in Education, Finance Center.

Barro, S. (1994). *Federal policy options for improving the education of low-income students: Vol. 3. Countering inequity in school finance.* Santa Monica, CA: RAND Corp.

Barro, S. (1996). *How countries pay for schools: An international comparison of systems for financing primary and secondary education.* Madison: University of Wisconsin, Wisconsin Center for Education Research, Consortium for Policy Research in Education.

Barzelay, M. (1992). *Breaking through bureaucracy: A new way for managing in government.* Berkeley: University of California Press.

Beck, L., and Murphy, J. (1996). *The four imperatives of a successful school.* Thousand Oaks, CA: Corwin Press.

Berne, R., and Stiefel, L. (1984). *The measurement of equity in school finance.* Baltimore: Johns Hopkins University Press.

Bierlein, L. A., and Bateman, M. (1996). Opposition forces and education reform: Will charter schools succeed? In T. De Mitchell and R. Fossey (Eds.), *The failure of law-based school reform: Vain hopes and false promises* (pp. 109–209). Lancaster, PA: Technomic Press.

Bierlein, L. A., and Fulton, M. F. (1996). *Emerging issues in charter school financing: Policy brief.* Denver: Education Commission of the States.

Blachford, P., and Mortimore, P. (1994). The issue of class size for young children in schools: What can we learn from research? *Oxford Review of Education, 20*(4), 411–428.

Bodilly, S. (1996a). *Lessons from New American Schools Development Corporation's demonstration phase.* Santa Monica, CA: RAND Corp.

Bodilly, S. (1996b). *Phase 3 of New American Schools (NAS): A progress report on Year 1.* Presentation to NAS Leadership Conference IV, Washington, DC.

Bracey, G. (1996). Debunking the myths about money for schools. *Educational Leadership, 53*(3), 65–69.

Braddock, J. H., II, and McPartland, J. M. (1993). Education of early adolescents. In L. Darling-Hammond (Ed.), *Review of research in education* (pp. 135–170). Washington, DC: American Educational Research Association.

Bruer, J. T. (1992). *Schools for thought.* Cambridge: MIT Press.

Bryk, A., Easton, J. Q., Kerbow, D. W., Rollow, S. G., and Sebring, P. B. (1997). *Charting Chicago school reform: Democratic localism as a lever for change.* Boulder, CO: Westview Press.

Bryk, A., Lee, V. E., and Holland, P. (1993). *Catholic schools and the common good.* Cambridge, MA: Harvard University Press.

Caldwell, B., and Hill, P. (1996). *Funding models for locally-managed schools: The case of schools of the future in Victoria.* Melbourne, Australia: University of Melbourne, Faculty of Education.

Caldwell, B., Hill, P., Odden, A. R., Hind, I., and Marshall, G. (1996). *The School Global Budget in Victoria: Best practice in matching funding to student learning needs.* Victoria, Australia: Education Committee, School Global Budget Research Project.

Caldwell, B., and Spinks, J. (1992). *Leading the self-managing school.* London: Falmer Press.

Chambers, J. G. (1995). Public school teacher cost differences across the United States: Introduction to a teacher cost index (TCI). In *Developments in school finance* [On-line]. Available: http://www.ed.gov/NCES/pubs/96344cha.html.

Clotfelter, C. T., and Ladd, H. F. (1996). Recognizing and rewarding success in public schools. In H. F. Ladd (Ed.), *Holding schools accountable* (pp. 23–63). Washington, DC: Brookings Institution.

Cohen, M. C. (1997). Issues in school-level analysis of education expenditure data. *Journal of Education Finance, 22*(3), 255–279.

Comer, J. P. (1993–1994). *A brief history and summary of the School Development Program: Summary of School Development Program (SDP) effects.* New Haven, CT: Yale University Child Study Center.

Comer, J. P., Haynes, N. M., Joyner, E. T., and Ben-Avie, M. (1996). *Rallying the whole village: The Comer process for reforming education.* New York: Teachers College Press.

Conley, S., and Odden, A. R. (1995). Linking teacher compensation to teacher career development: A strategic examination. *Educational Evaluation and Policy Analysis, 17*(2), 253–269.

Cooper, B. (1993). *School site cost allocations: Testing a microfinancial model in 23 districts in ten states.* Paper presented at the annual meeting of the American Education Finance Association. Albuquerque, NM.

Cooperative Research Project. (1994). *One year later.* Melbourne, Australia: Directorate of School Education.

Cooperative Research Project. (1995). *Taking stock.* Melbourne, Australia: Directorate of School Education.

Cooperative Research Project. (1996). *A three-year report card: Leading Victoria's schools of the future.* Melbourne, Australia: Directorate of School Education.

Corcoran, T. B. (1995). *Helping teachers teach well: Transforming professional development.* New Brunswick, NJ: Consortium for Policy Research in Education Policy Briefs.

Corcoran, T. B., and Goertz, M. E. (1995). Instructional capacity and high-performance schools. *Educational Researcher, 24*(9), 27–31.

Cyert, R. (1988). *The economic theory of organization and the firm.* New York: New York University Press.

Cyert, R., and March, J. G. (1963). *A behavioral theory of the firm.* Upper Saddle River, NJ: Prentice Hall.

Darling-Hammond, L. (1996). Restructuring schools for high performance. In S. H. Fuhrman and J. A. O'Day (Eds.), *Rewards and reform: Creating educational incentives that work* (pp. 144–192). San Francisco: Jossey-Bass.

Darling-Hammond, L., and McLaughlin, M. (1995). Policies that support professional development in an era of reform. *Phi Delta Kappan, 76*(8), 597–604.

Department for Education and Employment. (1996a). *National funding for GM schools.* London: Author.

Department for Education and Employment. (1996b). *Self-government for schools.* London: Author.

Department of School Education. (1994). *Local management of schools* (Circular No. 2/94). London: Author.

Edison Project. (1994). *An invitation to public school partnership.* New York: Author.

Edison Project (1996a). *Boston Renaissance Charter School end-of-year report: Follow-up data on student achievement and customer satisfaction.* New York, NY: Author.

Edison Project (1996b). *Dodge-Edison Partnership School end-of-year report: Follow-up data on student achievement and customer satisfaction.* New York, NY: Author.

Edison Project (1996c). *Dr. Martin Luther King, Jr., Academy end-of-year report: Follow-up data on student achievement and customer satisfaction.* New York, NY: Author.

Edison Project (1996d). *Washington Elementary School end-of-year report: Data on student achievement and customer satisfaction.* New York, NY: Author.

Education Commission of the States. (1997). *State policymakers' guide to networks.* Denver: Author.

Education Committee. (1995). *The School Global Budget in Victoria: Matching resources to learning needs in schools of the future: Interim report.* Melbourne, Australia: Department of School Education.

Elley, W. B. (1992). *How in the world do students read?* International Association for the Evaluation of Educational Achievement.

Elmore, R. F. (1996). *Staff development and instructional improvement in Community District 2, New York City.* Cambridge, MA: Harvard University, Graduate School of Education, Consortium for Policy Research in Education.

Elmore, R. F., Abelmann, C., and Fuhrman, S. H. (1996). The new accountability in state education policy. In H. F. Ladd (Ed.), *Performance-based strategies for improving schools* (pp. 65–98). Washington, DC: Brookings Institution.

Farland, G. (1997). Collection of fiscal and staffing data at the school-site level. *Journal of Education Finance, 22*(3), 280–290.

Fashola, O. S., and Slavin, R. E. (1997). Promising programs for elementary and middle schools: Evidence of effectiveness and replicability. *Journal of Education for Students Placed at Risk, 2*(3), 251–307.

Finn, C. E., Bierlein, L. A., and Manno, B. V. (1996). Finding the right fit. *Brookings Review, 14*(3), 18–21.

Finnan, C., St. John, E., McCarthy, J., and Slovacek, S. (1996). *Accelerated schools in action.* Thousand Oaks, CA: Corwin Press.

Firestone, W. A. (1994). Redesigning teacher salary systems for education reform. *American Educational Research Journal, 31*(3), 549–574.

Firestone, W. A., Goertz, M. E., Nagle, B., and Smelkinson, M. F. (1994). Where did the $800 million go? The first year of New Jersey's Quality Education Act. *Educational Evaluation and Policy Analysis, 16*(4), 359–374.

Fuhrman, S. H. (Ed.). (1993). *Designing coherent education policy: Improving the system.* San Francisco: Jossey-Bass.

Fuhrman, S. H., and Elmore, R. F. (1992). *Takeover and deregulation: Working models of new state and local regulatory relationships.* New Brunswick, NJ: Rutgers University, Consortium for Policy Research in Education.

Funding Agency for Schools. (1996). *Response to the DFEE's discussion paper "National funding for GM schools."* York, England: Author.

Gandal, M. (1996). *Making standards matter.* Washington, DC: American Federation of Teachers.

General Accounting Office. (1997). *School finance: State efforts to reduce funding gaps between poor and wealthy districts.* Washington, DC: Author.

George, P. S., and Shewey, K. (1994). *New evidence for the middle school.* Columbus, OH: National Middle School Association.

Goertz, M. E., Floden, R., and O'Day, J. A. (1995). *Evaluating education reform: Systemic reform: Vol. 1. Findings and conclusions.* New Brunswick, NJ: Rutgers University, Consortium for Policy Research in Education.

Gold, S. (1995). *The outlook for school revenue in the next five years* (Research Report No. 34). Philadelphia: University of Pennsylvania, Graduate School of Education, Consortium for Policy Research in Education.

Gold, S., Smith, D. M., and Lawton, S. B. (1995). *Public school finance programs in the United States and Canada, 1993–94.* Albany: State University of New York, Center for the Study of the States.

Guskey, T. R., and Peterson, K. D. (1996). The road to classroom change. *Educational Leadership, 53*(1), 10–14.

Hale, R. (1996). *SSAs: A guide for school governors.* London: Rita Hale and Associates, Ltd.

Hannaway, J. (1996). Management decentralization and performance-based incentives: Theoretical consideration for schools. In E. A. Hanushek and D. W. Jorgenson (Eds.), *Improving America's schools: The role of incentives* (pp. 97–109). Washington, DC: National Academy Press.

Hanushek, E. A., and Jorgenson, D. W. (Eds.). (1996). *Improving America's schools: The role of incentives.* Washington, DC: National Academy Press.

Hanushek, E. A., and Associates. (1994). *Making schools work: Improving performance and controlling costs.* Washington, DC: Brookings Institution.

Hartman, W. T. (1994). District spending disparities revisited. *Journal of Education Finance, 20*(1), 88–106.

Haynes, D. D. (1995). One teacher's experience with National Board assessment. *Educational Leadership, 52*(6), 58–60.

Heneman, H., III. (1997). *Assessment of the motivational reactions of teachers to a school-based performance award program.* Madison: University of Wisconsin, Wisconsin Center for Education Research, Consortium for Policy Research in Education.

Herman, R., and Stringfield, S. (1997). *Ten promising programs for educating all children: Evidence of impact.* Arlington, VA: Educational Research Service.

Hertert, L., Busch, C. A., and Odden, A. R. (1994). School financing inequities among the states: The problem from a national perspective. *Journal of Education Finance, 19*(3), 231–255.

Hess, F. (1995). *Restructuring urban schools: A Chicago perspective.* New York: Teachers College Press.

Hill, P. T., Pierce, L. C., and Guthrie, J. W. (1997). *Reinventing public education.* Chicago: University of Chicago Press.

Hinrichs, W. L., and Laine, R. D. (1996). *Adequacy: Building quality and efficiency into the cost of education.* Springfield: Illinois Board of Education.

Hirsch, E. D. (1996). *The schools we need and why we don't have them.* New York: Doubleday.

Hirschhorn, D. (1993). A longitudinal study of students completing four years of UCSMP mathematics. *Journal of Research in Mathematics Education, 24*(2), 136–158.

Joyce, B., and Calhoun, E. (Eds.). (1996). *Learning experiences in school renewal: An exploration of five successful programs.* Eugene, OR: ERIC Clearinghouse on Educational Management.

Katzenbach, J. R., and Smith, D. K. (1993). *The wisdom of teams: Creating the high-performance organization.* Boston: Harvard Business School Press.

Kelley, C. (1997). Teacher compensation and organization. *Educational Evaluation and Policy Analysis, 19*(1), 15–28.

Kelley, C., and Odden, A. R. (1995). *New ideas for reinventing teacher compensation.* Madison: University of Wisconsin, Wisconsin Center for Education Research, Consortium for Policy Research in Education.

Kelley, C., and Protsik, J. (1997). Risk and reward: Perspectives on the implementation of Kentucky's school-based performance award program. *Educational Administration Quarterly, 33*(4), 474–505.

King, M. B., Louis, K. S., Marks, H. M., and Peterson, K. D. (1996). Participatory decision making. In F. M. Newmann and Associates, *Authentic achievement: Restructuring schools for intellectual quality* (pp. 245–263). San Francisco: Jossey-Bass.

Lankford, H., and Wyckoff, J. H. (1995). Where has the money gone? An analysis of school spending in New York. *Educational Evaluation and Policy Analysis, 17*(2), 195–218.

Lawler, E. E., III. (1986). *High-involvement management: Participative strategies for improving organizational performance.* San Francisco: Jossey-Bass.

Lawler, E. E., III. (1992). *The ultimate advantage: Creating the high-involvement organization.* San Francisco: Jossey-Bass.

Lawler, E. E., III. (1996). *From the ground up: Six principles for building the new logic organization.* San Francisco: Jossey-Bass.

Lee, V., and Smith, J. B. (1993). Effects of school restructuring on the achievement and engagement of middle grade students. *Sociology of Education, 66,* 164–187.

Levacic, R. (1995). *Local management of schools: Analysis and practice.* Buckingham, England: Open University Press.

Levin, H. (1996). Economics of school reform for at-risk students. In E. A. Hanushek and D. W. Jorgenson (Eds.), *Improving America's schools: The role of incentives* (pp. 225–240). Washington, DC: National Academy Press.

Levin, H. (1997). Raising school productivity: An X-efficiency approach. *Economics of Education Review, 16*(3), 303–311.

Little, J. W. (1993). Teachers' professional development in a climate of educational reform. *Educational Analysis and Policy Analysis, 15*(2), 129–152.

Louis, K. S., Kruse, S. D., and Marks, H. M. (1996a). Schoolwide professional community. In F. M. Newmann and Associates, *Authentic achievement: Restructuring schools for intellectual quality* (pp. 179–203). San Francisco: Jossey-Bass.

Louis, K. S., Kruse, S., and Marks, H. M. (1996b). Teachers' professional community in restructuring schools. *American Educational Research Journal, 33*(4), 757–798.

Malen, B., Ogawa, R. T., and Kranz, J. (1990). What do we know about school-based management? A case study of the literature—a call for research. In W. H. Clune and J. F. Witte (Eds.), *Choice and control in American education: Vol. 2. The practice of decentralization and school restructuring* (pp. 289–342). Bristol, PA: Falmer Press.

Massell, D., Kirst, M., and Hoppe, M. (1997). *Persistence and change.* Philadelphia: Pennsylvania University, Graduate School of Education, Consortium for Policy Research in Education.

McMahon, W. W. (1994). Intrastate cost adjustment. In *Selected Papers in School Finance* [Online]. Available: http://www.ed.gov/NCES/pubs/96068ica.html.

Miles, K. H. (1995). Freeing resources for improving schools: A case study of teacher allocation in Boston public schools. *Educational Evaluation and Policy Analysis, 17*(4), 476–493.

Miles, K. H., and Darling-Hammond, L. (1997). *Rethinking school resources in high performing schools.* Madison: University of Wisconsin, Wisconsin Center for Education Research, Consortium for Policy Research in Education.

Ministerial Council on Education, Employment, Training and Youth Affairs. (1996). *National report on schooling in Australia: Statistical annex.* Melbourne: Curriculum Corporation.

Mohrman, A. M., Jr., Mohrman, S. A., and Odden, A. R. (1996). Aligning teacher compensation with systemic school reform: Skill-based pay and group-based performance rewards. *Educational Evaluation and Policy Analysis, 18*(1), 51–71.

Mohrman, S. A. (1994a). High-involvement management in the private sector. In S. A. Mohrman, P. Wohlstetter, and Associates, *School-based management: Organizing for high performance* (pp. 25–52). San Francisco: Jossey-Bass.

Mohrman, S. A. (1994b). Making the transition to high-performance management. In S. A. Mohrman, P. Wohlstetter, and Associates, *School-based management: Organizing for high performance* (pp. 187–214). San Francisco: Jossey-Bass.

Mohrman, S. A., Lawler, E. E., III, and Mohrman, A. M., Jr. (1992). Applying employee involvement in schools. *Education Evaluation and Policy Analysis, 14*(4), 347–360.

Mohrman, S. A., Wohlstetter, P., and Associates. (1994). *School-based management: Organizing for high performance.* San Francisco: Jossey-Bass.

Molnar, A. (1995). School funding: The right issue, the wrong logic. *Educational Leadership, 53*(3), 58–59.

Monk, D. H., Roellke, C. F., and Brent, B. O. (1996). *What education dollars buy: An examination of resource allocation patterns in New York State public school systems.* Madison, WI: University of Wisconsin, Wisconsin Center for Education Research, Consortium for Policy Research in Education.

Mosteller, F., Light, R., and Sachs, J. (1996). Sustained inquiry in education: Lessons from skill grouping and class size. *Harvard Educational Review, 66*(4), 797–842.

Murnane, R., and Levy, F. (1996). *Teaching the new basic skills.* New York: Free Press.

Murphy, J., and Beck, L. (1995). *School-based management as school reform.* Thousand Oaks, CA: Corwin Press.

Murphy, J., and Louis, K. S. (1994). Transformational change and the evolving role of the principal: Early empirical evidence. In J. Murphy and K. S. Louis (Eds.), *Reshaping the principalship.* Thousand Oaks, CA: Corwin Press.

Murphy, J., and Picus, L. O. (1996). Special program encroachment on school district general funds in California: Implications for Serrano equalization. *Journal of Education Finance, 21*(3), 366–386.

Musik, M. D. (1996). Setting education standards high enough. *Network News and Views, 15*(9), 14–20.

Nakib, Y. (1995). Beyond district-level expenditures: Schooling resource allocation and use in Florida. In L. O. Picus and J. L. Wattenbarger (Eds.), *Where does the money go? Resource allocation in elementary and secondary schools* (pp. 85–105). Thousand Oaks, CA: Corwin Press.

National Center for Education Statistics. (1993). *Digest of education statistics.* Washington, DC: U.S. Department of Education.

National Center for Education Statistics. (1994). *Schools and staffing survey, 1993–94.* Washington, DC: U.S. Department of Education.

National Center for Education Statistics. (1996a). *Digest of education statistics, 1996.* Washington, DC.: U.S. Department of Education.

National Center for Education Statistics. (1996b). *Projection of education statistics to 2006.* Washington, DC.: U.S. Department of Education.

National Center for Education Statistics. (1996c). *Trends in academic achievement, 1996.* Washington, DC.: U.S. Department of Education.

National Center for Education Statistics. (1996d). *How widespread is site-based decision making in the public schools?* (Issue Brief IB–8–96). Washington, DC: U.S. Department of Education.

National Center for Education Statistics (1997a). *Pursuing excellence: A study of U.S. fourth-grade mathematics and science achievement in international context.* Washington, DC: U.S. Government Printing Office.

National Center for Education Statistics. (1997b). *Time spent teaching core academic subjects in elementary schools.* Washington, DC: U.S. Department of Education.

National Commission on Teaching and America's Future. (1996). *What matters most: Teaching for America's future.* New York: Teachers College Press.

National Council of Teachers of Mathematics. (1989). *Curriculum and evaluation standards for school mathematics.* Reston, VA: Author.

National Education Association. (1996). *1995–96 estimates of school statistics.* Washington, DC: Author.

New American Schools. (1995). *An introduction.* Arlington, VA: Author.

New American Schools. (1996). *Working towards excellence: Early indicators from schools implementing New American Schools designs.* Arlington, VA: Author.

Newmann, F., King, M. B., and Rigdon, M. (1997). Accountability and school performance: Implications from restructuring schools. *Harvard Educational Review, 67*(1), 41–74.

Newmann, F., Secada, W., and Wehlage, G. (1995). *A guide to authentic instruction and assessment: Vision, standards, and scoring.* Madison: Wisconsin Center for Education Research.

Newmann, F., and Wehlage, G. (1995). *Successful school restructuring.* Madison: Wisconsin Center for Education Research, University of Wisconsin.

Newmann, F. M., and Associates. (1996). *Authentic achievement: Restructuring schools for intellectual quality.* San Francisco: Jossey-Bass.

Odden, A. R. (Ed.). (1991). *Education policy implementation.* Albany: State University of New York Press.

Odden, A. R. (1994a). Decentralized management and school finance. *Theory into Practice, 33*(2), 104–111.

Odden, A. R. (1994b). *Including school finance in systemic reform strategies: A comment.* Philadelphia: University of Pennsylvania, Consortium for Policy Research in Education.

Odden, A. R. (1996). Incentives, school organization, and teacher compensation. In S. H. Fuhrman and J. A. O'Day (Eds.), *Rewards and reform: Creating educational incentives that work* (pp. 226–256). San Francisco: Jossey-Bass.

Odden, A. R. (1997a). *Getting better by design series, Vol. 2: How to create and manage a decentralized education system.* Arlington, VA: New American Schools.

Odden, A. R. (1997b). *Getting better by design series, Vol. 3: How to rethink school budgets to support school transformation.* Arlington, VA: New American Schools.

Odden, A. R. (1997c). Raising performance levels without increasing funding. *School Business Affairs, 63*(6) 4–12.

Odden, A. R., and Conley, S. (1992). Restructuring teacher compensation systems. In A. R. Odden (Ed.), *Rethinking school finance: An agenda for the 1990s* (pp. 41–96). San Francisco: Jossey-Bass.

Odden, A. R., Heneman, H., Wakelyn, D., and Protsik, J. (1996). *School-based performance award case.* Madison: University of Wisconsin, Wisconsin Center for Education Research, Consortium for Policy Research in Education.

Odden, A. R., and Kelley, C. (1997). *Paying teachers for what they know and do: New and smarter compensation strategies to improve schools.* Thousand Oaks, CA: Corwin Press.

Odden, A. R., and Kotowski, N. (1992). Financing public school choice: Policy issues and options. In A. R. Odden (Ed.), *Rethinking school finance: An agenda for the 1990s* (pp. 225–259). San Francisco: Jossey-Bass.

Odden, A. R., and Massy, W. (1993). *Education funding for schools and universities: Improving productivity and equity.* Madison: University of Wisconsin, Wisconsin Center for Education Research, Consortium for Policy Research in Education, Finance Center.

Odden, A., Monk, D., Nakib, Y., and Picus, L. (1995). The story of the educational dollar: No Academy Awards and no fiscal smoking guns. *Phi Delta Kappan, 77*(2), 161–168.

Odden, A. R., and Odden, E. (1995). *Educational leadership for America's schools.* New York: McGraw-Hill.

Odden, A. R., and Odden, E. (1996a). Applying the high-involvement framework to local management of schools in Victoria, Australia. *Educational Research and Evaluation, 2*(2), 150–184.

Odden, A. R., and Odden, E. (1996b). *The Victoria, Australia, approach to school-site management.* Madison: University of Wisconsin, Wisconsin Center for Education Research, Consortium for Policy Research in Education.

Odden, A. R., and Picus, L. O. (1992). *School finance: A policy perspective.* New York: McGraw-Hill.

Odden, A. R., Wohlstetter, P., and Odden, E. (1995). Key issues in effective school-based management. *School Business Affairs, 61*(5), 4–16.

Odden, E., and Wohlstetter, P. (1995). Strategies for making school-based management work. *Educational Leadership, 52*(5), 32–36.

Olson, L. (1997, June 4). Power of the purse. *Education Week*, 23–28.

Organization for Economic Cooperation and Development. (1995). *Education at a glance: OECD indicators.* Paris: Author.

Picus, L. O. (1993a). *The allocation and use of educational resources: District-level analysis from the Schools and Staffing Survey.* Madison: University of Wisconsin, Wisconsin Center for Education Research, Consortium for Policy Research in Education, Finance Center.

Picus, L. O. (1993b). *The allocation and use of educational resources: School-level analysis from the Schools and Staffing Survey.* Madison: University of Wisconsin, Wisconsin Center for Education Research, Consortium for Policy Research in Education, Finance Center.

Picus, L. O. (1994). The local impact of school finance reform in four Texas school districts. *Educational Evaluation and Policy Analysis, 16*(4), 391–404.

Picus, L. O., and Bhimani, M. (1993). *Determinants of pupil-teacher ratios at school sites: Evidence from the Schools and Staffing Survey.* Madison: University of Wisconsin, Wisconsin Center for Education Research, Consortium for Policy Research in Education, Finance Center.

Picus, L. O., Tetreault, D. R., and Murphy, J. (1996). *What money buys: Understanding the allocation and use of educational resources in California.* Madison: University of Wisconsin, Wisconsin Center for Education Research, Consortium for Policy Research in Education.

Pikulski, J. J. (1994). Preventing reading failure: A review of five effective programs. *Reading Teacher, 43*, 64–84.

Raimondo, H. J. (1994). *How much for administration? Expenditure priorities across New Jersey school districts, FY90–91.* New Brunswick, NJ: Rutgers University, Eagleton Institute of Politics.

Robertson, P. J., Wohlstetter, P., and Mohrman, S. A. (1995). Generating curriculum and instructional changes through school-based management. *Educational Administration Quarterly, 31*(3), 375–404.

Rosenholtz, S. J. (1989). *Teachers' workplace: The social organization of schools.* Reading, MA: Addison Wesley Longman.

Rothstein, R., and Miles, K. H. (1995). *Where's the money gone?* Washington, DC: Economic Policy Institute.

Schwartz, M., and Moskowitz, J. (1988). *Fiscal equity in the United States.* Washington, DC: Decision Resources Corp.

Secada, W. G., Gamoran, A., and Weinstein, M. G. (1996). Pathways to equity. In F. M. Newmann and Associates, *Authentic achievement: Restructuring schools for intellectual quality* (pp. 228–244). San Francisco: Jossey-Bass.

Shapiro, B. C. (1995). The NBPTS sets standards for accomplished teaching. *Educational Leadership, 52*(6), 55–57.

Sizer, T. (1996). *Horace's hope.* Boston: Houghton Mifflin.

Slavin, R. E., Madden, N. A., Dolan, L. J., and Wasik, B. A. (1996). *Every child, every school: Success for all.* Thousand Oaks, CA: Corwin Press.

Slavin, R. E., Madden, N. A., Dolan, L. J., Wasik, B. A., Ross, S., Smith, L., and Dianda, M. (1996). Success for all: A summary of research. *Journal of Education for Students Placed at Risk, 1*(1), 41–76.

Smith, M. S., and O'Day, J. A. (1991). Systemic reform. In S. H. Fuhrman and B. Malen (Eds.), *The politics of curriculum and testing* (pp. 233–267). Bristol, PA: Falmer Press.

Smylie, M. A., Lazarus, V., and Brownlee-Conyers, J. (1996). Instructional outcomes of school-based participative decision-making. *Educational Evaluation and Policy Analysis, 18*(3), 181–198.

Speakman, S., Cooper, B., Holsomback, H., May, J., and Sampieri, R. (1995). *The 3 Rs of education finance reform: Rethinking, retooling, and reevaluating school-site analysis.* Madison: University of Wisconsin, Wisconsin Center for Education Research, Consortium for Policy Research in Education.

Stringfield, S., Ross, S., and Smith, L. (1996). *Bold plans for school restructuring: The New American School designs.* Hillsdale, NJ: Erlbaum.

Summers, A. A., and Johnson, A. W. (1996). The effects of school-based management plans. In E. A. Hanushek and D. W. Jorgenson (Eds.), *Improving America's schools: The role of incentives* (pp. 75–96). Washington, DC: National Academy Press.

Talbert, J., and McLaughlin, M. (1994). Teacher professionalism in local school contexts. *American Journal of Education, 102*(2), 123–153.

Thomas, H., and Martin, J. (1996). *Managing resources for school improvement: Creating a cost-effective school.* London: Routledge.

Thompson, Q., and Lakin, J. (1997). *Local management of schools and school site-based financing: The experience in England and Wales since 1988.* Paper prepared for the University of Wisconsin, Wisconsin Center for Education Research, Consortium for Policy Research in Education.

U.S. Bureau of the Census. (1992). *The data collection agent for the National Center for Education Statistics, common core of data (F–33).* Washington, DC: Author.

Usiskin, Z. (1986). The UCSMP: Translating grade 7–12 mathematics recommendations into reality. *Educational Leadership, 44*(4), 30–35.

Verstegen, D. (1996). Concepts and measures of fiscal inequality: A new approach and effects for five states. *Journal of Education Finance, 22*(2), 145–160.

Wasik, B. A., and Slavin, R. E. (1993). Preventing early reading failure with one-to-one tutoring: A review of five programs. *Reading Research Quarterly, 28*(2), 180–200.

Wehlage, G. G., Osthoff, E., and Porter, A. C. (1996). Support from external agencies. In F. M. Newmann and Associates, *Authentic achievement: Restructuring schools for intellectual quality* (pp. 264–285). San Francisco: Jossey-Bass.

Wells, A. S. (1996). *Charter schools.* Presentation to the National Academy of Sciences and the National Research Council Committee on Education Finance, Equity, Adequacy and Productivity, Washington, DC.

Wohlstetter, P. (1995). Getting school-based management right: What works and what doesn't. *Phi Delta Kappan, 77*(1), 22–26.

Wohlstetter, P., and Briggs, K. L. (1994). The principal's role in school-based management. *Principal, 74*(2), 14–17.

Wohlstetter, P., Briggs, K. L., and Van Kirk, A. (1997). School-based management: What it is and does it make a difference. In D. L. Levinson, A. R. Sadovnik, and P. W. Cookson, Jr. (Eds.), *Education and sociology: An encyclopedia.* New York: Garland.

Wohlstetter, P., and Mohrman, S. A. (1993). *School-based management: Strategies for success.* Philadelphia: University of Pennsylvania, Graduate School of Education, Consortium for Policy Research in Education.

Wohlstetter, P., and Mohrman, S. A. (1996). *Assessment of school-based management.* Washington, DC: U.S. Department of Education, Office of Educational Research and Improvement.

Wohlstetter, P., Mohrman, S. A., and Robertson, P. J. (1996). Successful school-based management: Lessons for restructuring urban schools. In D. Ravitch and J. Viteritti (Eds.), *New schools for a new century: The redesign of urban education.* New Haven, CT: Yale University Press.

Wohlstetter, P., and Odden, A. R. (1992). Rethinking school-based management policy and research. *Educational Administration Quarterly, 28*(4), 529–549.

Wohlstetter, P., Smyer, R., and Mohrman, S. A. (1994). New boundaries for school-based management: The high-involvement model. *Educational Evaluation and Policy Analysis, 16*(3), 268–286.

Wohlstetter, P., Van Kirk, A., Robertson, P. J., and Mohrman, S. A. (1997). *Successful school-based management: A report with cases.* Alexandria, VA: Association for Supervision and Curriculum Development.

Wohlstetter, P., Wenning, R., and Briggs, K. L. (1995). Charter schools in the United States: The question of autonomy. *Educational Policy, 9*(4), 331– 358.

Wyckoff, J. H. (1992). The intrastate equality of public primary and secondary education resources in the U.S., 1980–1987. *Economics of Education Review, 11*(1), 19–30.

INDEX